BRANCH LINE BRITAIN

Printed in China by Toppan Leefung for David & Charles
Brunel House   Newton Abbot   Devon

Commissioning Editor Mic Cady
Art Editor Alison Myer
Production Controller Kelly Smith

F+W Media publishes high-quality books on a wide range
of subjects.
For more great book ideas visit:www.fwmedia.co.uk

Produced for David & Charles by
OutHouse Publishing
Shalbourne, Marlborough, Wiltshire SN8 3QJ

Designer and Picture Researcher Julian Holland
Editor Sue Gordon
Design Assistant Nigel White
Cartographer Ethan Danielson

Half-title page: *Leadhills station in the days of the Highland Railway.*

Title page: *The trackbed of the long-closed Dornoch branch in northern Scotland can still be seen as a low embankment across the fields and marshland beside Loch Fleet.*

BRANCH LINE BRITAIN

Paul Atterbury

D&C
David and Charles

CONTENTS

Introduction	6
About This Book	8
The West Country	10
St Erth to St Ives	12
Liskeard to Looe	16
On Holiday	18
Lynton & Barnstaple Railway	20
West Somerset Railway	22
Swanage Railway	26
Seaton Electric Tramway	28
Branch Line Stations	30
Boscarne Junction to Wenfordbridge	32
Yelverton to Princetown	34
Tiverton Junction to Hemyock	36
The Milk Train	38
Axminster to Lyme Regis	40
Maiden Newton to Bridport	44
Enthusiasts	48
Southern England	50
Brockenhurst to Lymington Pier	52
The Isle of Sheppey	56
Kent & East Sussex Railway	58
Down on the Farm	60
Romney, Hythe & Dymchurch Light Railway	62
Dunton Green to Westerham	64
The Isle of Grain	68
Paddock Wood to Hawkhurst	70
Working on the Railway	72

Chippenham to Calne	74
Camping Coaches	76
Newbury to Lambourn	78
The Isle of Wight	80
East Anglia	86
Ipswich to Felixstowe	88
Marks Tey to Sudbury	90
North Norfolk Railway	94
Toy Trains	96
St Margarets to Buntingford	98
Saxmundham to Aldeburgh	100
Railway Gardens	104
Kelvedon to Tollesbury	106
Mellis to Eye	108
Branch Line Railcars	110
Central England	112
Twyford to Henley-on-Thames	114
Stourbridge	118
Off to Town for the Day	120
Cholsey & Wallingford Railway	122
Foxfield Railway	124
Wantage Tramway	126
Kemble to Tetbury	128

▼ *Onlookers greet the arrival of the first train at Hythe station, on the Fawley branch, in Hampshire, on 25 July 1925.*

Making Tracks	132	
Stonehouse to Nailsworth	136	
Leek & Manifold Railway	140	
Woodhall Junction to Horncastle	144	

Wales	**148**
Llandudno Junction to Blaenau Ffestiniog	150
Railway Films	154
Snowdon Mountain Railway	156
Talyllyn Railway	158
Railway Hotels	162
Pencader to Newcastle Emlyn	164
Pyle to Porthcawl	168
Whitland to Cardigan	170
Gaerwen to Amlwch	174

Northern England	**178**
Oxenholme to Windermere	180
Middlesbrough to Whitby	184
School Days	188
Keighley & Worth Valley Railway	190
Lakeside & Haverthwaite Railway	192
Haltwhistle to Alston	194

Ravenglass & Eskdale Railway	196
When Coal was King	200
Alne to Easingwold	202
Skipton to Grassington	206
Abbey Town to Silloth	210
Eryholme to Richmond	214
Industrial Railways	216

Scotland	**218**
Fort William to Mallaig	220
Branch Line Locomotives	224
Bo'ness & Kinneil Railway	226
Leadhills & Wanlockhead Railway	228
Castle Douglas to Kirkcudbright	230
Roxburgh to Jedburgh	234
Old Railway Carriages	236
Killin Junction to Loch Tay	238
Ballinluig to Aberfeldy	240
Dingwall to Strathpeffer	242
Railwayana	244
The Mound to Dornoch	246
Humorous Postcards	250

Index	**252**
Railway Websites & Acknowledgements	**256**

▼ *Abingdon station, the terminus of the line from Radley, near Oxford, was one of the grander branch line termini.*

INTRODUCTION

In this book, a branch line is a railway that links a local terminus with a junction on a main line, operated by trains that shuttle to and fro. There are three types of branch line described here. The first are those that survive in the national network, with services run by one of the independent operating companies. Second are those lines now reopened as preserved steam railways, and operated largely by volunteers. Timetables can be found on the websites listed on page 256. The third group are long-closed lines, traces of which survive in the landscape. Some are now established as footpaths and cycleways, some are semi-official footpaths, some are hidden away on private land. Others have completely vanished.

Hunting for lost lines can be an entertaining activity. An Ordnance Survey map is required, as these mark the visible traces of lost railways. They can often be explored from nearby roads and tracks, and from footpaths. A keen eye for the lie of the land will spot many clues: it is often easy to identify an old embankment or cutting in the countryside, whether it is grassy or edged with trees, simply because there are no straight lines in the natural landscape. Sometimes bridges and other structures survive in the fields and woods. Other evidence includes characteristic

▲ Unexpected remains of long-lost railways are sometimes waiting to be found, hidden in bushes or partly buried beside the old trackbed. Typical is this pile of old concrete platform supports and signalling equipment from a branch line closed in the early 1960s.

CHEERIO!—I'M OFF FOR MY HOLIDAY!

railway concrete fencing, gateposts and old buildings. Practice soon makes perfect. Remember that many lost lines are now on private land, and so permission to explore should always be sought from the landowner.

The book is illustrated with photographs of the remains of lost lines, along with numerous pictures of the railways in their active days – many taken by enthusiasts over the last fifty years. Old postcards show the places served by the branch lines and recall the way of life associated with branch line Britain. Some routes feature tickets and luggage labels issued by the original operating companies.

▼ *In 1968 children all over Britain still travelled to and from school by train, and in some cases it was this school traffic that helped to keep the line open. Here, in the summer of that year, a group of children leave the two-coach diesel multiple unit at Lambley, returning home from a day at school at Haltwhistle, on the Alston branch.*

ABOUT THIS BOOK

Key to map of routes

The West Country

1	St Erth to St Ives	12–15
2	Liskeard to Looe	16–17
3	Lynton & Barnstaple Railway	20–21
4	West Somerset Railway	22–25
5	Swanage Railway	26–27
6	Seaton Electric Tramway	28–29
7	Boscarne Junction to Wenfordbridge	32–33
8	Yelverton to Princetown	34–35
9	Tiverton Junction to Hemyock	36–37
10	Axminster to Lyme Regis	40–41
11	Maiden Newton to Bridport	44–45

Southern England

12	Brockenhurst to Lymington Pier	52–55
13	The Isle of Sheppey	56–57
14	Kent & East Sussex Railway	58–59
15	Romney, Hythe & Dymchurch Light Railway	62–63
16	Dunton Green to Westerham	64–67
17	The Isle of Grain	68–69
18	Paddock Wood to Hawkhurst	70–71
19	Chippenham to Calne	74–75
20	Newbury to Lambourn	78–79

East Anglia

21	Ipswich to Felixstowe	88–89
22	Marks Tey to Sudbury	90–93
23	North Norfolk Railway	94–95
24	St Margarets to Buntingford	98–99
25	Saxmundham to Aldeburgh	100–103
26	Kelvedon to Tollesbury	106–107
27	Mellis to Eye	108–109

Central England

28	Twyford to Henley-on-Thames	114–117
29	Stourbridge	118–119
30	Cholsey & Wallingford Railway	122–123
31	Foxfield Railway	124–125
32	Wantage Tramway	126–127
33	Kemble to Tetbury	128–131
34	Stonehouse to Nailsworth	136–139
35	Leek & Manifold Railway	140–143
36	Woodhall Junction to Horncastle	144–145

Wales

37	Llandudno Junction to Blaenau Ffestiniog	150–153
38	Snowdon Mountain Railway	156–157
39	Talyllyn Railway	158–161
40	Pencader to Newcastle Emlyn	164–167
41	Pyle to Porthcawl	168–169
42	Whitland to Cardigan	170–171
43	Gaerwen to Amlwch	174–177

Northern England

44	Oxenholme to Windermere	180–183
45	Middlesbrough to Whitby	184–187
46	Keighley & Worth Valley Railway	190–191
47	Lakeside & Haverthwaite Railway	192–193
48	Haltwhistle to Alston	194–195
49	Ravenglass & Eskdale Railway	196–199
50	Alne to Easingwold	202–205
51	Skipton to Grassington	206–209
52	Abbey Town to Silloth	210–213
53	Eryholme to Richmond	214–215

Scotland

54	Fort William to Mallaig	220–223
55	Bo'ness & Kinneil Railway	226–227
56	Leadhills & Wanlockhead Railway	228–229
57	Castle Douglas to Kirkcudbright	230–233
58	Roxburgh to Jedburgh	234–235
59	Killin Junction to Loch Tay	238–239
60	Ballinluig to Aberfeldy	240–241
61	Dingwall to Strathpeffer	242–243
62	The Mound to Dornoch	246–249

Symbols used in this book

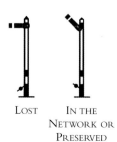

LOST   IN THE NETWORK OR PRESERVED

A signal is used to denote the current status of the branch lines. The horizontal signal on the left indicates a lost line or a line now used only for freight. The signal in the up position indicates that the branch is in the national network or that at least a section of it is now operated as a preserved line.

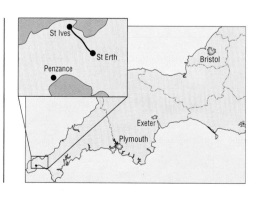

The maps

The individual maps show the location of the branch line and its full route, from the junction on the main line to the terminus. The whole branch line is shown, regardless of whether it is now lost, partially open – as in the case of some preserved lines – or in the national network.

SCOTLAND

62

61
• Inverness

54

60

59

55

Glasgow •   Edinburgh •

58

56

52
Carlisle •

Newcastle
-upon-Tyne •

48

49   44

47

53   45

51   50

46
• Leeds

ENGLAND

43   Llandudno
37

Lincoln •   36

38

35
31

23

39

Norwich •

29   Birmingham •

27   25

WALES

Cambridge •

40

24

22   21

42

26

34

Swansea •

33   32   30   28

London •   17

41   Cardiff •

Oxford •

16   13

Bristol •   19   20   Reading •

18

3   4

5   12

Southampton •   14   15   Dover

9

6   10   11

Exeter •

7   2   8

1

Plymouth

9

THE CORNISH COAST

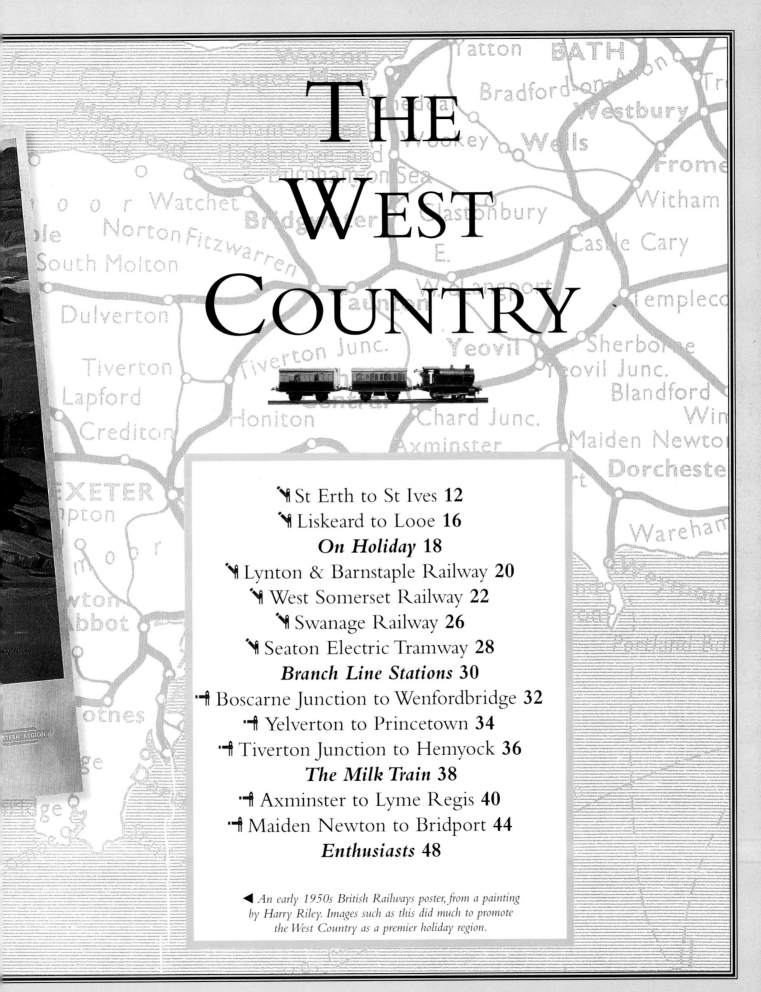

THE WEST COUNTRY

St Erth to St Ives **12**
Liskeard to Looe **16**
On Holiday **18**
Lynton & Barnstaple Railway **20**
West Somerset Railway **22**
Swanage Railway **26**
Seaton Electric Tramway **28**
Branch Line Stations **30**
Boscarne Junction to Wenfordbridge **32**
Yelverton to Princetown **34**
Tiverton Junction to Hemyock **36**
The Milk Train **38**
Axminster to Lyme Regis **40**
Maiden Newton to Bridport **44**
Enthusiasts **48**

◄ *An early 1950s British Railways poster, from a painting
by Harry Riley. Images such as this did much to promote
the West Country as a premier holiday region.*

St Erth to St Ives

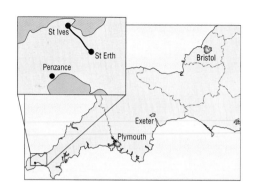

244

C.R.

TO

Lelant

When it opened in 1877, the branch to St Ives was the last stretch of Brunel's broad gauge line to be built in Britain. While this represented the end of one era, it heralded another: the development of an obscure little fishing village into a popular resort – a significant part of the Great Western's plan to bring tourism to the West Country. With its lively harbour and almost surrounded by beaches, St Ives was always something special, and soon visitors in their thousands were taking the branch line train from St Erth. Artists and writers were quick to respond to its charms, notably the painters associated with the nearby Newlyn school. Among the many who spent childhood holidays here was Virginia Woolf, whose novel *To the Lighthouse* was inspired by St Ives.

Today, there is a regular service on the 4½-mile branch in both directions from Monday to Saturday, with some journeys starting or finishing in Penzance. But there is a Sunday service only in summer, although St Ives is busy all year round now. In the past it was different: the famous Cornish Riviera Express, the pride of the GWR's West Country services, departed from Paddington daily at 10.30am, with through carriages for St Ives. Branch line trains connected with other main line expresses and, naturally, there was a full Sunday service. This pattern was maintained by British Railways well into the 1960s.

St. Ives.

As I was going to St Ives
I met a man with Seven Wives;
Each wife had Seven Sacks,
Each Sack had Seven Cats,
Each Cat had Seven Kits --
Kits, Cats, Sacks, and Wives.
How many were there
going to St Ives ?

◀ *For most people, it is the old riddle, illustrated on this Edwardian postcard, that makes the name of St Ives familiar. The answer is not as simple as it might seem, however well we know our seven times table.*

▼ *Much of the St Ives line runs right above the shore, and the views across the bay to The Towans and Godrevy Point are wonderful at any time of year. The blue Atlantic waves roll on to the golden sands, to make this a classic branch line journey.*

► *The railway made St Ives a resort, and it brought hotels – most famously the GWR's own hotel, the Tregenna Castle. Set high above the town, this castellated building has splendid views. Had the German invasion of Britain been successful in 1940, it would have another tale to tell: Ribbentrop had marked it down for his country house, with Hitler's approval.*

▼ *It is summer in the 1950s, and a GWR tank locomotive hauls a long train full of holidaymakers towards their journey's end in St Ives. The spectacle of sun, sea and sand and the magnificent views across the bay make the long, careful planning of the holiday in an era of austerity, and the hours of travelling, all seem worthwhile.*

The classic seaside journey

The St Ives branch is a remarkable survivor in an age when branch lines are an endangered species. Despite its short length, it is a glorious journey, and a classic among branch lines because of its proximity to the sea.

The start is subdued, for St Erth station is set among housing estates and industry. However, things rapidly improve as the train curves away to run parallel to the saltings and mudflats of the tidal Hayle estuary. There is a pause at Lelant, where a park-and-ride system operates in the summer, and then the rest of the journey is dominated by the great sweep of the Atlantic across St Ives Bay. The train hugs the coast, offering a succession of wonderful views out across the sandy beaches and the bay. After another brief stop at Carbis Bay, St Ives comes into view and soon the train reaches the little platform that now makes do as a station, right on the outskirts of the town. Originally bigger, and nearer the town, the station was for much of its life a hive of activity, with a continual traffic of both passenger and freight services. Car parks have now overtaken a large proportion of the station site but, despite the dominance of the car, the train is still by far the best way to travel to St Ives.

▼ *From the late 1800s there were two routes to Cornwall from London, a reflection of the great rivalry between railway companies. The prime operator was the Great Western, whose services included the Cornish Riviera Express and overnight sleepers. The rival London & South Western Railway, later part of the Southern Railway, operated its service from Waterloo. The routes met at Exeter. This curious situation lasted into the 1960s.*

▶ *As generations of artists have discovered, St Ives is all about light, colour and picturesque scenes – elements that, as the Great Western found out, have a broad appeal to holidaymakers of all ages. This 1930s poster, after a painting by Herbert Truman, captures these qualities, while underlining the way the GWR took great care of its image and its reputation for efficiency and modernity.*

▼ *In high summer, the beach was always packed and the station was always busy. This 1950s view shows the full extent of the original station at St Ives, now reduced to a single line and a single platform. There were many lines and sidings, required for handling and storage of the long passenger trains that arrived on scheduled services and excursions from many parts of Britain.*

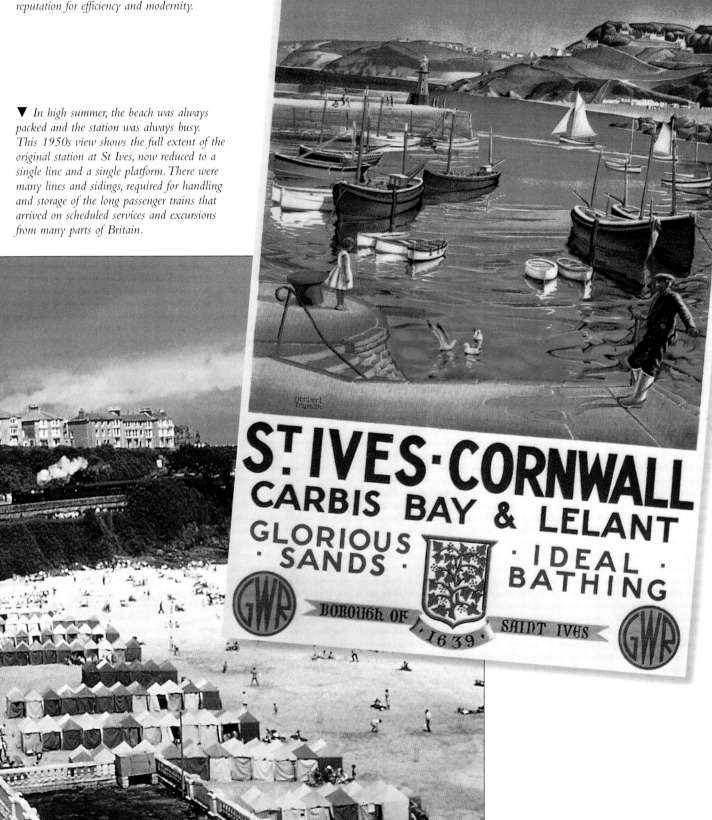

LISKEARD TO LOOE

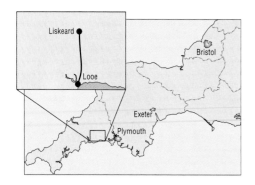

G.W.R.

Looe

▼ *Beyond Sandplace, where boats in the sand trade used to load at the head of the estuary, the track runs along the river shore. This section of the journey is a complete contrast to the earlier passage through woods and fields. The views are wonderful, as is the birdlife on the estuary at low tide. Modern railcars, like this one, make excellent viewing platforms.*

With railways to St Ives and Looe, Cornwall can justly claim two of the best surviving branch lines in Britain. While tourism has kept the St Ives branch open, the mainstay of the Looe line has been the clay industry. Quarries and clay were what built the line early in the nineteenth century, and it is the clay from Moorswater that keeps it going. Its origins were in two mineral lines, the Liskeard & Looe Railway, opened in about 1828, and the Liskeard & Caradon Railway, opened in 1844; both had connections with the much earlier Liskeard & Looe Canal. Until 1901, when the present link with the main line at Liskeard station was completed, the railways had little interest in carrying passengers. However, this new link encouraged the development of both the port at Looe and tourism, and since then the journey to Looe by train has been a popular experience.

The real branch line experience
At Liskeard, the train for Looe leaves from what is in effect a separate station, an old timber building set to one side. From here it plunges 200 feet, curving under the great viaduct that carries the main line. At Coombe it joins the old Moorswater line, where it has to reverse. Those in the know turn to face the other way, so the best of the route is still ahead. The journey is a series of delights, passing through woods and flower-filled fields, closely following the river and its tidal estuary. Birds, boats and the occasional remains of the old canal add to the appeal. It is a remote and leisurely journey, a constant reminder of the nearly extinct pleasures of true branch line travel. Looe station is outside the town, but the ride makes up for this minor inconvenience.

▶ *Looe is divided by the river into two parts, East Looe and West Looe, linked by the road bridge. The railway is on the east side, just visible in the distance on this Edwardian postcard. Also apparent are the two quays, busy with fishing boats and coastal trading vessels, some of which would have engaged in the clay trade. Fred, writing on the front of the card, told his friend Ernest in Bradford, that he 'had a peep at this spot on Saturday'.*

21814   Looe, View from West Looe.

◀ *Until the 1960s Looe was a busy place, with some freight as well as passenger trains. The line used to extend beyond the station to the East Quay, to serve the harbour. In this 1950s photograph the locomotive has pulled the train clear of the station in order to run round it for the return journey. There is none of this today, and the distant station buildings have been replaced by a minimal shelter and a single track.*

▶ *A journey on the Looe branch is rich in old-fashioned railway experiences. Here the guard has got out of the train to change the points at Coombe Junction, where the train reverses. The train itself may be modern, but the old branch line atmosphere lives on.*

ON HOLIDAY

The running of excursion trains dates back to the earliest days of the railway. It was not long before monster trains of up to forty-six carriages were carrying 1,700 people on a day's outing. This practice continued through the nineteenth century, greatly encouraged by the popularity of such events as exhibitions and race meetings. However, while the day trip, particularly to the seaside and at Easter and on bank holidays, was a big phenomenon in the Victorian era, the habit of going off on holiday by train did not become fully established until the early 1900s.

Many railway companies, seeing the potential for extra traffic, played significant roles in developing and promoting coastal and inland resorts all over Britain. Resorts in the West Country, the Lake District, North Yorkshire, East Anglia, Wales and Scotland owed much to the railway companies, which not only exploited the resorts themselves but also encouraged activities such as cycling, walking and golf. The emphasis, however, was always on the seaside, and by 1914 about 200 towns and villages around the coast were served by railways and could, as a result, be called resorts. Going on holiday by train remained universally popular until the 1950s.

▲ *After the 1923 Grouping, the 'Big Four' railway companies became renowned for their sophisticated, well-designed and image-conscious holiday promotions, such as this GWR holiday brochure of the 1920s.*

◀ *Sport, for participants and spectators, became increasingly popular in late Victorian Britain, and the railways actively encouraged support for horse racing, golf, football and other sports. These amateur cricketers, probably on holiday, will almost certainly have travelled by train.*

▼ *In the holiday season railways ran numerous excursion specials, often using rolling stock kept for this purpose. Many resort stations were enlarged to cope with this extra traffic.*

On the Sands.

▼ No seaside holiday was complete until a saucy postcard had been sent back home. This 1930s classic by Donald McGill was posted in Bournemouth, with an equally classic message: 'Comfortable ride down. Very nice digs. Lovely weather. Everything OK.'

"View of the Sea from the Promenade!"

▲ For a child, a traditional part of any seaside holiday was, and in some places still is, a ride along the beach on a donkey. This smart little girl, clearly a young lady, is riding side-saddle. Looking a bit uneasy, she is certainly not smiling for the Edwardian photographer – unlike the donkey's elderly, and rather over-dressed, attendant.

▼ Seaside holidays in pre-World War I Britain were about sea, sun and fun. This jolly family is having a good time, perhaps at a resort on the Yorkshire coast. At traditional resorts such as Scarborough, bathing machines remained in use throughout this period.

Lynton & Barnstaple Railway

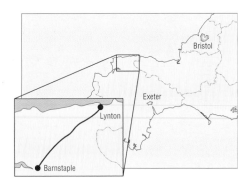

Few local railways attract as much interest as the Lynton & Barnstaple. In any case, narrow gauge lines were something of a rarity in England, particularly ones whose primary inspiration was the carriage of passengers rather than freight. The railway's long and meandering 2ft gauge line was opened in May 1898, and from the start it made a significant contribution to the tourist development of Lynton, Lynmouth and the remote coastline of north Devon. Smart, well run and with great local support, the Lynton & Barnstaple soon made its mark, despite the fact that its trains took up to an hour and a half to complete the 19-mile journey. Travellers benefited from the direct connection with the main line at Barnstaple Town station. In 1923 the line became part of the Southern Railway, and its locomotives were repainted in SR green. By this time, however, the railway was already suffering from road competition, and by the end of the decade freight traffic had almost gone and motor coaches were making serious inroads into the passenger carrying. By the early 1930s, closure was an ever-present threat, but when it came, with little warning, on 30 September 1935 there was local outrage.

However, an ambitious preservation society was formed in 1979 and has been working on plans to reopen the line. Being small and lightly engineered, much of the trackbed quickly disappeared back into the landscape. But bridges and other structures survive, notably the great Chelfham viaduct, as well as some stations converted to private houses. In 2004 the first steam trains operated from Woody Bay since 1935.

▼ In September 1933 one of the line's distinctive Manning Wardle tank locomotives stands at the head of its train while the few passengers take their seats for the leisurely journey from Lynton to Barnstaple. A local resident, possibly the writer Henry Williamson, who was a great supporter of the line, chats with the driver.

◀ This 1920s postcard shows Blackmoor Gate station, midway between Lynton and Barnstaple. The popularity of the line was reflected in the number of postcards produced in this period, showing the stations, the trains and the line in the north Devon landscape. The stations were built to a pattern, echoing the Arts and Crafts styling in fashion when the line was built. Today, Blackmoor Gate station is a pub.

▼ The Lynton & Barnstaple is coming back to life. Woody Bay station has been fully restored and trains are running on a section of relaid track. In April 2004 the locomotive 'Emmet' poses at the platform at Woody Bay.

Major, Darker & Lorraine (Photo).

Lynton and Barnstaple Railway. Blackmoor Gate Station.

▲ One day the Lynton & Barnstaple Railway may reopen the whole length of its original route, but at the moment much of the trackbed is hidden in the landscape, waiting to be discovered by intrepid explorers with good maps. Confrontations with local residents are not uncommon. Much of the route is, in any case, on private land.

WEST SOMERSET RAILWAY

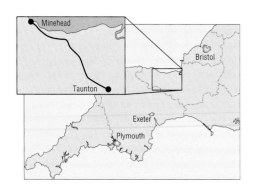

The West Somerset Railway, now one of Britain's premier preserved lines, has had a long history. First authorized in 1857, the original West Somerset Railway was opened in 1862 as a broad gauge line from Norton Fitzwarren, near Taunton, to Watchet. Plans to extend the route to Minehead were launched in 1865 but were not fulfilled until 1874. Minerals and freight were the line's primary inspiration, along with the desire to open up a part of north Somerset and its coastline that had hitherto been inaccessible to railway passengers. Prior to the coming of the railway, the region had depended largely on Minehead's sheltered harbour, which had enjoyed a thousand years of use.

Operated from the start by the Bristol & Exeter Company, the line was converted to standard gauge in 1882 and eventually came under GWR control. By then the emphasis had switched to tourism, as more and more holidaymakers discovered the particular appeal of Watchet, Blue Anchor, Dunster and Minehead itself: firm beaches, extensive at low tide and suitable for family games of cricket, rugged red- and alabaster-veined cliffs pierced with caves, and wide panoramas. At the same time, the qualities of the Quantock Hills, through which the route passed between Watchet and Taunton, were also appreciated by a public who were increasingly drawn to rambling and exploring the countryside. It was this region that at the end of the eighteenth century had attracted and inspired the poet Samuel Taylor Coleridge to write his *Rime of the Ancient Mariner*. His friend William Wordsworth came to live here too, before moving to the Lake District.

▼ *With its combination of local, long-distance and holiday services, Minehead was a busy station in the 1950s. Long platforms catered for the holiday specials, and there was still a considerable amount of freight traffic. Well placed for the town centre, the beaches and the holiday camp, the station was a natural focal point for the town. Luckily, thanks to the relatively late closure date and rapid moves towards preservation, the old station has largely survived and still has the atmosphere of a seaside terminus.*

▼ All the Butlin holiday camps were close to railway stations, and Minehead, although it was a late addition to the stable and did not open until 1962, was no exception. Billy Butlin's motto was 'our true intent is all for your delight'; the dancers in the Olde Tyme ballroom in the mid-1960s seem to be living up to this perfectly.

▲ This photograph, showing the arrival of the parliamentary candidate Dudley Ward at Watchet station on 24 January 1906, makes it abundantly clear that the railway was at that time the centre of social, business and domestic life. People of all ages, predominantly well dressed, throng to hear what he has to say.

BUTLIN'S MINEHEAD
The Olde Tyme Ballroom

▲ *The lady station master at Stogumber is the oldest serving volunteer on the West Somerset Railway.*

▼ *As its route is longer than most preserved lines, the West Somerset Railway is well able to re-create the old atmosphere of the rural GWR. Here, in 1999, a Mogul locomotive hauls a train at speed through the north Somerset landscape, complete with milk tanker. Until the 1960s, sights such as this were common on many West Country lines.*

From closure to preservation

The holiday business grew rapidly in the twentieth century, bringing through trains from London and Birmingham, mainline connections from the Midlands, South Wales, the North and Scotland, as well as plenty of holiday specials. In the 1920s there were six direct trains a day in the summer to Minehead from Paddington. The opening of the Butlin's Holiday Camp in 1962 gave a further boost to traffic, but by the mid-1960s the future of the line looked uncertain, mainly because of the seasonal nature of that same holiday traffic. Closure came in January 1971, a relatively late date, which made the line a prime candidate for preservation.

Five years later, the West Somerset Railway brought the line back to life, along with its original title, and began operating steam trains between Minehead and Blue Anchor. Steadily extended over the years to Bishop's Lydeard, just outside Taunton, the railway now has nine stations and, at 20 miles, is the longest preserved line in Britain. Thanks to its length, and the sense of reality that this gives to the journey, the line is able to re-create particularly successfully the atmosphere of a busy rural railway during the last decades of the steam age. The style is predominantly GWR, but there are plenty of echoes of British Railways as it was in the 1950s.

◀ *Blue Anchor, with its beaches, cliffs and caravan parks, was a resort effectively created by the railway. Until the trains arrived in the 1870s, it was a very remote spot indeed. This card was posted from Minehead to Bridgwater in 1955, showing that people did not travel far for their holiday at that time. The message is typical: 'Having a fine time. Weather perfect up to date.'*

COAST ROAD FROM WATCHET

BLUE ANCHOR BAY

G.W.R.

Blue Anchor

SWANAGE RAILWAY

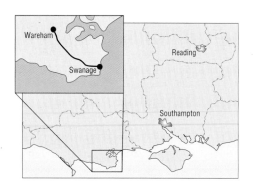

Expanding tourist traffic in the late Victorian period was the inspiration for the opening of the branch from Wareham to Swanage on 20 May 1885. The London & South Western was an ambitious railway, ever keen to consolidate its hold on south-west England in the face of constant competition from the Great Western. Opening up the Isle of Purbeck and the glorious Dorset coastline proved to be a sensible move, bringing thousands of new visitors to Swanage, Studland, Corfe Castle and the more secret delights of the Purbeck hinterland. With through trains running from London and other places, the Swanage route was in some ways never a typical branch line. For example, in 1924, by which date it was part of the Southern Railway, there were seven trains a day from Waterloo, as well as a busy timetable of local and freight services.

All this came to an end in January 1972 with the closure of the line, except for a short section retained for the Furzebrook oil trains. But plans to reopen the line as a preserved railway were quickly in place, and soon steam trains were once again to be seen in Swanage station. The route now reaches Norden, just north of Corfe. The plan is to run trains into Wareham, to meet the main line again. Today, the Swanage Railway re-creates a branch line from the heyday of the Southern Railway.

▲ *A 1920s postcard, after a painting by AR Quinton, reflects the popularity of Swanage during this era. With its fine beach, glorious landscape and plethora of hotels, as well as easy access by train, it thrived as a resort both in and out of season.*

▶ *This late Victorian photograph shows Swanage station soon after the line opened in 1885. Although the building is substantial, the single track, elderly locomotive and assortment of carriages have a classic branch line flavour.*

▶ At Worgret Junction, west of Wareham, the Swanage branch swings south from the main line. In the 1950s this local push-pull train pauses at the signal box while the driver takes the single-line token. Such trains, designed to be driven from either end, were the mainstay of branch lines from the 1920s to the early 1960s.

▼ Another 1920s Quinton postcard shows the powerful ruins of Corfe Castle, a picturesque and popular place between Wareham and Swanage. The railway, just visible on a viaduct on the far right, circled the town, offering superb views of the ruined castle.

▼ Corfe Castle and a steam train in the Purbeck landscape: a classic view, resurrected by the Swanage Railway. Here, photographed in the late 1990s, a Bulleid Light Pacific locomotive, the kind that used to haul through trains from London along the line in the days of British Railways, makes its way towards Swanage.

SOUTHERN RAILWAY. 787
FROM WATERLOO TO
CORFE CASTLE

SEATON ELECTRIC TRAMWAY

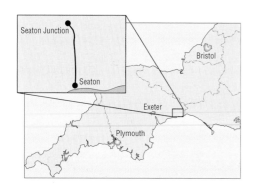

SOUTHERN RAILWAY.

FROM WATERLOO TO

SEATON

Certain towns and seaside resorts in south-west England have a particular resonance in railway terms, namely Padstow, Bude, Ilfracombe, Exeter, Exmouth, Torrington, Plymouth, Sidmouth and Seaton. The common factor is that for years all were served by the famous Atlantic Coast Express, a daily departure from London Waterloo with carriages for all these destinations. At Seaton Junction, as at the other stops, the relevant carriages would be slipped from the train and then delivered to their destination by a local engine, allowing the passengers to finish their tea and enjoy the ever-improving views.

Mid-twentieth-century memories are one thing, but Seaton's railway history is much older. The Seaton & Beer Railway, incorporated in 1863, opened its 4½-mile branch to Colyton, where it met the L&SWR's main line in 1868. Initially it was a freight line, but the emphasis switched to tourism after the take-over by the L&SWR in 1879. Over sixty years of prosperity followed, as the line kept pace with the ever-increasing popularity of Devon's coastal and inland resorts. In the early 1960s, however, came rapid decline, and the branch closed in March 1966. Then, just three years later, in 1969, the Eastbourne Tramway closed and relocated to Devon, re-emerging as the Seaton Tramway. With its 2ft 9in gauge and one-third scale tramcars running between Seaton and Colyton, this line is one of the West Country's railway highlights.

▼ *Seaton's terminus station, almost on the seafront, always had plenty of seaside atmosphere. Here, in 1949, with the holiday traffic just getting into its stride again after the war years, a local train waits at the platform. The smart art deco lamps in Southern Railway concrete reflect Seaton's success as a fashionable resort in the 1920s and 1930s.*

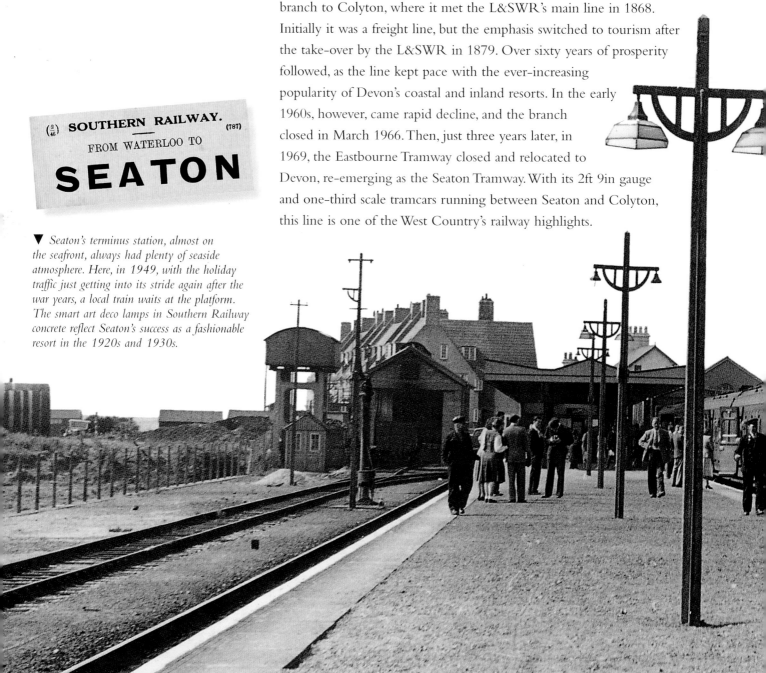

▶ Seaton's popularity as a resort was based partly on its setting, framed by cliffs, and partly on the broad sweep of beach beyond the esplanade, where the best hotels made the most of the sea views. When this postcard was sent in 1934, paddle steamers from Weymouth called regularly at several Dorset and Devon resorts, including Seaton.

▼ The Seaton branch today has a new life as the Seaton Electric Tramway. The one-third scale tramcars, based on famous examples from various old British networks, run regularly between Seaton and Colyton. A highlight of the journey is the road crossing at Colyford.

THE BEACH LOOKING EAST. SEATON.

BRANCH LINE STATIONS

Many branch lines served rural areas with sparse populations and so they were built cheaply, with only limited passenger facilities. The terminus station at the end of the branch was often fairly substantial, but many intermediate stations, which in fact were little more than halts serving small communities, were very basic. Many railway companies developed their own styles of local stations, for example, the Great Western's pre-fabricated corrugated-iron pagodas, or Southern Railway's open-fronted concrete shelters. Some buildings were more substantial, echoing vernacular traditions in local materials, but the majority were temporary-looking timber structures that still achieved a rustic charm. Often halts were made from reused structures, such as redundant carriage or goods wagon bodies.

◀ *This delightful 1905 postcard shows the private halt at Miteside, on the Ravenglass & Eskdale Railway in Cumbria, where an old boat served as a waiting room.*

▲ *Drayton Green, near Ealing, West London, in the 1950s: a typical, minimally equipped, unstaffed halt with a characteristic Great Western pagoda-style shelter.*

▼ *The Southern Railway's range of prefabricated concrete railway buildings and structures, from footbridges to fence posts, continued to be made into the British Railways era and so can still be found all over southern England. Chetnole station, on the Weymouth to Bristol line, survives unchanged.*

Eskdale   Miteside Station

The Wrench Series No. 5506

Chetnole

◀ For many rural railways and branch lines the basic halt was just a platform and some kind of open-fronted shelter, often made of wood, with a name board and sometimes a light. This example is Sesswick halt, between Wrexham and Ellesmere on the Welsh borders. It appears to be in the middle of nowhere, the platform is overgrown and the shelter is about to be swallowed by the encroaching plants. Despite appearances, trains did call here.

▶ The most minimal halt of all was no more than a platform at ground level, with a name board and a lamp. This is Wortlington Golf Links halt on the Mildenhall branch in Suffolk. In October 1954 an elderly passenger, helped by the guard, struggles to mount the short steps attached to the carriage.

▼ Vernacular styling at its most appealing is seen here, on the Abbotsbury branch in Dorset, where the stone-built stations were fitted with generous platform canopies. Photographed after closure, the line returns to nature, but the famous platform flower beds still flourish.

BOSCARNE JC TO WENFORDBRIDGE

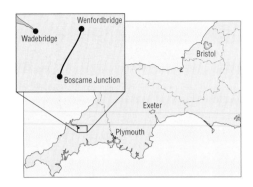

A very local enterprise, and one of the earliest railways in Britain, the Bodmin & Wadebridge was primarily a low-cost mineral line. Opened in 1834, it ran from Wadebridge to Wenfordbridge, with a branch to Bodmin. Despite other local railway developments, it remained isolated from the national network for some fifty years. In 1888 a connection was made with the GWR, when a line opened between Boscarne Junction and Bodmin Road (now Parkway), and in 1895 the railway was linked to the L&SWR's network when their north Cornwall line reached Wadebridge. In 1899 the L&SWR extended the Bodmin to Wadebridge section, now used by passengers and freight, to Padstow. This remained unchanged until the 1960s, when most of the network around Bodmin closed.

Only the section from Bodmin Road to Boscarne Junction and Wenfordbridge survived, kept open for the clay traffic. Much of this had always been a freight line, initially carrying sea sand to farms inland and later china clay from the deposits at Wenfordbridge. This continued until the line closed in 1983, never having carried passengers. The closure was contentious, throwing heavy lorries on to narrow roads, and there have been plans to reopen it. The debate has been made forceful by the creation of a cycle path, the Camel Trail, on the entire line, from Padstow to Bodmin and up to Wenfordbridge. It is a long ride; the section along the Camel estuary from Padstow to Wadebridge is exciting and busy, while the less used path through the woods from Boscarne Junction to Wenfordbridge is a quiet delight.

▼ *For a long period towards the end of its life, the Wenfordbridge line was the last home of a very individual type of locomotive, the Beattie Well Tank of 1874. Here, in the 1960s, one of the veterans approaches Wenfordbridge with a train of empty clay wagons.*

► *When the track between Boscarne Junction and Wenfordbridge was lifted after closure in 1983, a proper surface was laid for cyclists and walkers. For some reason, the track was left in place at the level crossings, as seen here at Hellandbridge, where the railway emerged between two cottages. The tracks remind us of the line's history and hint at the possibility of its reopening.*

◄ *In this 1960s photograph a short train hauled by a Beattie Well Tank creeps over the same crossing, but from the other direction.*

▼ *A pioneering cycle path, and still one of the best in England, the Camel Trail is wonderfully diverse. Its route takes in glorious coastal and estuarine scenery, small towns and farmland, as well as the secret way from Boscarne through the woods up to Wenfordbridge.*

YELVERTON TO PRINCETOWN

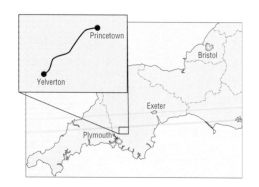

Today the idea of a railway into the remote heart of Dartmoor seems both curious and unlikely, yet such an idea was planted and took root right at the start of railway history. The first part of a horse-drawn railway from Plymouth to Princetown was authorized in 1819, and four years later 23 miles of track opened between Sutton Pool and King Tor. The name of the railway's promoter, politician and diplomat Sir Thomas Tyrwhitt, lives on in the Tyrwhitt Trail, the footpath and cycleway that follows the route. His plan was to transport stone from local quarries down to Plymouth, bringing back manure and materials to develop the moor. It was largely defunct by the 1860s, but a 10-mile section between Yelverton, on the main Tavistock to Plymouth line, and Princetown was revived by the GWR as the Princetown Railway. This was opened on 11 August 1883. Although instigated and operated by the GWR, it remained nominally independent until 1922.

Closure came in the 1960s, along with most of the main line to Plymouth via Okehampton and Tavistock. However, thanks to the wild nature of the landscape, much of the branch line's trackbed remained. Now, part of it makes a glorious walk across the moors. There is not much to see around Yelverton, but from Dousland the route is spectacular, passing Burrator Reservoir and then climbing into increasingly empty moorland to reach the desolation of King Tor before dropping down to Princetown.

▼ *Freight was important throughout the life of the Princetown branch, and mixed passenger and freight trains ran regularly. Here, in the 1950s, the freight wagons are shunted while the single coach waits in the platform. Today only the houses on the left remain.*

▲ Much of the trackbed remains today as an exciting footpath and cycleway winding its way across Dartmoor through a wonderfully remote landscape. The circuitous route, particularly the great loop around King Tor, is a legacy of the first railway, built in the early 1820s.

▶ King Tor Platform was one of England's most inaccessible stations, a legacy of the 1820s Dartmoor railway. A particular passion among some enthusiasts was visiting obscure stations. Here, in the 1950s, two well-dressed and well-heeled rail buffs cross King Tor off their list, without an anorak to be seen.

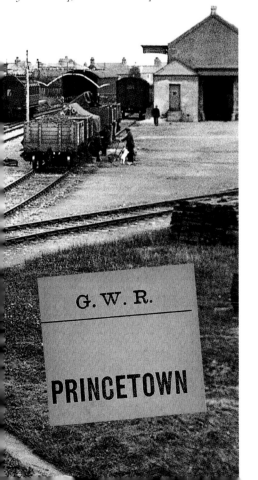

G.W.R.

PRINCETOWN

▲ It is near the end of the line's life in the early 1960s, and the mixed train sets off from Burrator, leaving a single passenger on the wooden platform. Today the line has gone, but the views across the reservoir and around its wooded shores are as good as ever.

TIVERTON JUNCTION TO HEMYOCK

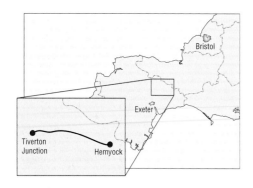

The Culm Valley Light Railway is a typical example of a small railway built on local enthusiasm and optimism – misplaced optimism, as it turned out, for the traffic in fact never arrived. After a prolonged struggle against financial difficulties, compounded by significantly underestimated construction costs, the Culm Valley line opened on 29 May 1876. Four years later it was sold to the GWR. For eighty-three years trains continued to meander up and down the line from Tiverton Junction to Hemyock, vaguely adhering to a leisurely timetable that allowed up to an hour for the 7-mile journey. Trains were often composed of both passenger and freight vehicles, and so sometimes passengers had to be patient while shunting activities were carried out. The mainstay of the line was milk traffic, and this continued until 1975, several years after passenger services had ceased in September 1963.

For much of the route from Tiverton Junction the line follows the river Culm, with stations at Uffculme and Culmstock and some minor halts built by the GWR to try to encourage traffic. It was a delightful journey through a gentle landscape, into which the railway seemed to fit naturally.

▼ *This classic 1950s view across the river Culm shows the end of the line at Hemyock, with the single-carriage train waiting by the water tower. The rural setting, while typical of the line, is slightly misleading here, for the station was set on the edge of the town, and just out of view to the right of the picture were substantial industrial buildings, including the milk depot that kept the line in business.*

▲ *A wintry scene near Tiverton Junction shortly before the end of passenger traffic in 1963. This section of the line has largely disappeared, buried beneath road developments, industry and housing.*

THE SQUARE & COMMERCIAL ROAD, UFFCULME.

▲ *In this Edwardian view of Uffculme, the Commercial Road is hardly busy. A group of girls, carefully posed on the green by the photographer, is the only sign of life in this Devon village. The postcard was published by the proprietor of the post office, on the left. His sales cannot have been dramatic.*

▶ *The Hemyock branch followed a rural route along the river valley, with few engineering features. As a result, much of the route has been absorbed back into the landscape. The line can be followed on minor roads, and its track along the valley is often visible from the road. The major stations have gone, although the platform from Whitehall halt survives in a private garden. One of the few remaining engineering features is this bowstring bridge, near Uffculme.*

THE MILK TRAIN

The carriage of milk by train started in the 1830s but it remained a local activity until the emergence of large national wholesale and distribution companies, such as Express Dairies, founded in 1864. This was followed by the development of railhead milk depots, the first of which was opened in Wiltshire in 1871. Long-distance milk traffic became the norm towards the end of the nineteenth century, initially on passenger trains and then from the 1890s on special milk trains. All milk was transported in the familiar cans, or churns, owned by the dairy companies. Milk tank wagons were not introduced until 1927. Supplying the big cities with daily supplies of milk became the priority, reflecting concerns about improving the diet of the urban poor. By 1914 the railways were carrying 93 million gallons of milk into London each year; by the 1920s, over 260 million gallons. In 1942 the Milk Marketing Board took over and long-distance deliveries diminished. The last regular milk trains ran in 1980, and rail surrendered to road.

▲ *The many scheduled special trains that transported milk in bulk were often assembled from tankers collected from a number of smaller depots. Here, at Leyburn, Wensleydale, in 1954 an LNER shunting locomotive attaches a few milk tankers to a waiting passenger train.*

GREAT WESTERN RAILWAY.
(5041 k)
MILK
FROM

TO

BOW (L.M.S.)
VIA KENSINGTON

Date........... No. of Tank........... Train...........
5,000 BM. 884 4/47.

▼ *Milk traffic at Highbridge, Somerset, in 1928. The lorry has collected the churns from from the farms and they will now be loaded into the ventilated box vans. Cans, or churns, were of a standard conical shape, holding 17 gallons and weighing 2cwt when full. Later, smaller and more manageable cans were introduced.*

▶ *Milk was not supplied for domestic use in glass bottles until well into the twentieth century, when bottling plants were established at rail-based distribution depots. In the pre-bottle age, milk was sold in bulk, with customers fetching it in their own containers. This man is carefully making his way back to his house with his personal supply of milk.*

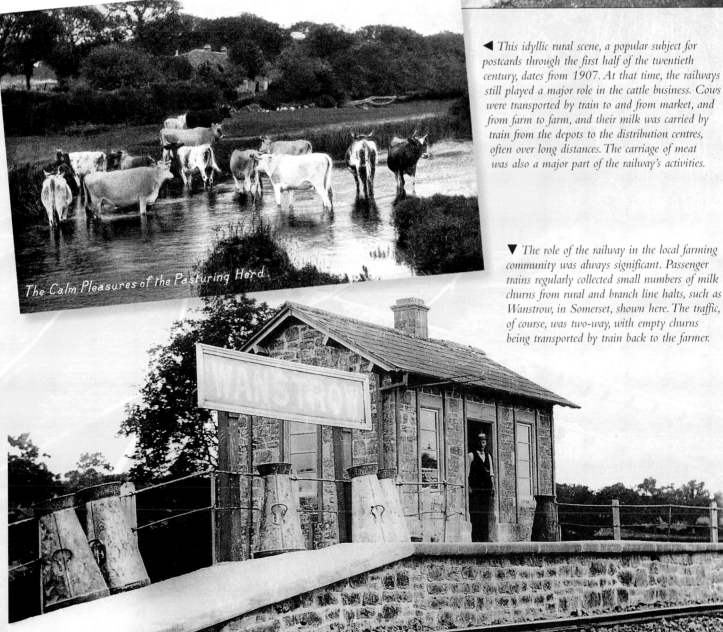

The Calm Pleasures of the Pasturing Herd

◀ *This idyllic rural scene, a popular subject for postcards through the first half of the twentieth century, dates from 1907. At that time, the railways still played a major role in the cattle business. Cows were transported by train to and from market, and from farm to farm, and their milk was carried by train from the depots to the distribution centres, often over long distances. The carriage of meat was also a major part of the railway's activities.*

▼ *The role of the railway in the local farming community was always significant. Passenger trains regularly collected small numbers of milk churns from rural and branch line halts, such as Wanstrow, in Somerset, shown here. The traffic, of course, was two-way, with empty churns being transported by train back to the farmer.*

AXMINSTER TO LYME REGIS

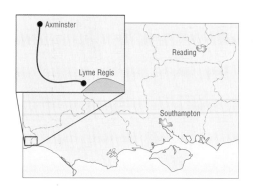

When it opened in August 1903, the Lyme Regis branch line had already enjoyed a chequered history. Plans for a railway to Lyme were first drawn up in the 1840s, the first of many schemes to be developed during the Victorian era. In September 1874 the first sod for the line was ceremoniously cut, but that was as far as it got. Eventually, the passing of the Light Railways Act in 1896, which encouraged the building of many rural railways, inspired the formation of the Axminster & Lyme Regis Railway, and in 1897 work started on the construction of the line. There were problems with engineering and finance, but the line finally opened to great local celebrations, despite the fact that the station was half a mile from the town and 250ft above sea level. The line was operated from the start by the London & South Western Railway Company, which took over complete control in 1907.

Successful and popular during the Edwardian era and between the wars, the railway saw a boom in both passenger traffic and freight, and helped to put Lyme on the map as a tourist resort. In 1914 a magazine described the resort as 'highly esteemed by visitors desiring holidays of a quieter kind, and those who reckon scenic, climatic and natural attractions as of greater value than bandstands and the like…'. At its peak, the service included twelve trains a day each way, some of which were through trains to and from London.

Decline began in the 1950s, as a result of increasing competition from road transport. British Railways improved the track and introduced diesel railcars, but to no avail. By the early 1960s some trains were carrying an average of only two passengers. Closure, hastened by the Beeching Report, became inevitable. The last train ran on 29 November 1965.

▼ *The route from Axminster to Lyme included one intermediate stop at Combpyne, a station very much in the middle of nowhere. This 1950s colour photograph shows a typical single-coach train on its way to Lyme, hauled by an Adams radial tank locomotive, the mainstay of the line for thirty years. In the background is the camping coach that was stabled at Combpyne over many years, offering notably quiet holidays. The one local attraction was the landslip at Downland Cliffs.*

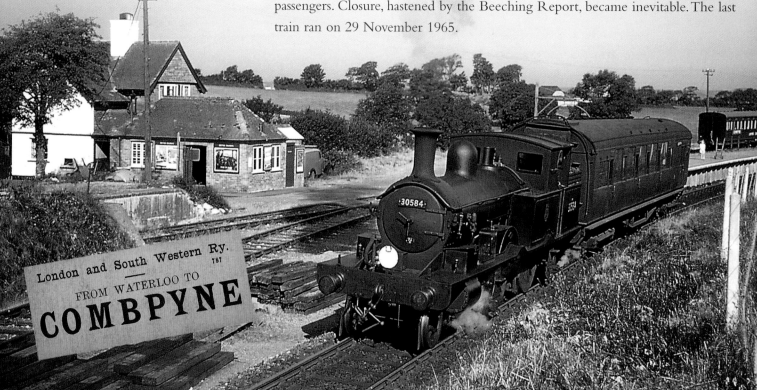

London and South Western Ry. 757
FROM WATERLOO TO
COMBPYNE

◄ *This Edwardian postcard shows quite a substantial train making its way through the woods near Combpyne. This part of the route was particularly attractive, with many lineside flowers. On the card these look like rhododendrons but, as it is hand-coloured, this may be artistic licence.*

▼ *An unusual combination of celebrities come together on this card, made to promote Lyme Regis before World War I. The Duke of Monmouth is not everyone's hero, and Jane Austen was not as popular at that time as she is now. Mary Anning, an early student of prehistory and a great fossil hunter, was the true Lyme heroine.*

▼ *Many long-lost branch lines are now little more than a walk through the woods, the only clue to their previous life sometimes being old lineside concrete fencing posts hidden in the bushes. Often these lost lines look their best in winter and early spring, with the soft sunlight filtering through the trees, and the autumn leaves still under foot.*

CELEBRITIES OF

LYME REGIS.

Duke of Monmouth, 1685.

Jane Austen, Novelist.

Mary Anning, Geologist.

▶ *The hilly route made demands on the line's builders but these were mostly overcome without massive expenditure. At Cannington, however, a ten-arch viaduct presented a major challenge. One of the first to be constructed from concrete, and the second highest of its kind in Britain, the viaduct caused engineering and financial problems that delayed the railway's opening. One arch subsided and had to be additionally supported. Today, long after the line's closure, the viaduct still strides across the valley, a permanent memorial to the trains that once ran to Lyme Regis.*

◀ *Popular since the late eighteenth century, and made famous by Jane Austen, Lyme Regis was known as a relatively undeveloped and quiet resort, famous for its fossils, its fishing and its exceptional setting. The railway did little to change this, for the resort continued to offer the kind of holiday that had little appeal to mass tourism. This advertisement of the 1930s, while listing many conventionally desirable holiday features, still manages to suggest that Lyme was somehow different.*

Lovely
Lyme Regis

SAFE
BATHING
BOATING
FISHING
SUPERB
SCENERY

SEA SUN SANDS

WRITE FOR GUIDE (P.O. 1/- PLEASE) FROM
INFORMATION BUREAU, LYME REGIS. PHONE 609

▶ *It is a sunny day in the 1950s and a typical single-coach train has arrived at Lyme Regis, hauled by one of the line's characteristic Adams 4-4-2 radial tank engines. These venerable survivors of the Victorian era were designed by William Adams while he was the locomotive superintendent of the London & South Western Railway. Even in the 1950s they were popular with railway enthusiasts, as indicated by the boy in the foreground taking a photograph. Meanwhile the solitary passenger prepares to hand her ticket to the station master.*

The route from Axminster to Lyme Regis

Winding its way through the landscape on a steeply graded track, the Lyme Regis branch in its early days was hard on both locomotives and drivers, and the short journey rarely took less than 25 minutes. However, there were few complaints as the scenery along the route was exciting and varied, with plenty of good views across the Dorset hills and valleys. In any case, the railway opened up an area hitherto relatively inaccessible. In many ways a classic branch line, in its latter years the route attracted many passengers who simply wanted to experience the kind of journey that was soon to be extinct.

A couple of years after closure the track was lifted, and the railway began to disappear back into the landscape. Various schemes to reopen the line have been announced, but to no avail, even though Lyme Regis is one of those small towns that would benefit enormously from a complete ban on cars in its crowded centre.

What remains today

Today it is quite hard to explore the remains of the line. Much is now private and inaccessible, and considerable sections have disappeared. The remains of the bay platform can still be seen at Axminster, a station whose recent restoration has given it a Victorian look. It also boasts one of the best station cafés in southern Britain. The location of Combpyne station can also be traced, as well as the route through the woods. Some of the bridges survive, spanning overgrown cuttings, but Lyme Regis station has vanished without trace. The best, and most accessible feature, is the great viaduct at Cannington.

MAIDEN NEWTON TO BRIDPORT

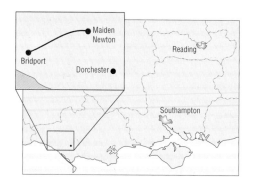

A number of branch lines in the south-west were built by small, independent companies set up by local merchants and businessmen keen to expand trade by linking their towns and villages to the national railway network. Typical was the Bridport Railway, whose 9-mile line to Maiden Newton opened amid great local celebration on 11 November 1857. Initially a broad gauge line to suit its GWR surroundings, it was later rebuilt to standard gauge. Independence was short-lived, for within a year or so the line was leased to the Great Western. In 1901 the GWR took complete control, and continued to operate it until the British Railways era.

In 1884 the line was extended to Bridport harbour, a busy local trading and fishing port. This reflected the ambitions of the GWR, which was keen to develop a harbour and port that could rival Weymouth. Thinking also of the developing tourist trade, the company renamed the harbour West Bay and hoped that the hotels would soon arrive, inspired by the beautiful coast and the new railway link. In the event, not much happened, and West Bay remained much the same as before, a small but busy local port. However, the carriage of beach gravel became a mainstay of the line and remained so until the closure of the West Bay extension in 1962.

▲ The route of the West Bay extension along the valley of the Brit from Bridport town, visible in the distance, to the harbour, just off the picture to the left, can clearly be seen. Here, in the 1920s, a locomotive shunts on the siding while carriages and a gravel train wait in the platform.

▼ In the 1960s a single diesel railcar pauses at Toller. Two ladies, probably back from a shopping trip to Maiden Newton – and clearly not the focus of the photographer's interest – leave the train. Today, the platform survives, as does the road bridge just beyond the station, but all around are new houses.

GREAT WESTERN RAILWAY. (135 a)

TOLLER
TO
SHEFFIELD L.N.E.

No. of Packages   CARRIAGE PAID

Route via

Always popular with local users, the Bridport branch enjoyed a busy service. Indeed, in the early days of the West Bay extension a special bathing train left Bridport at seven each morning. In the early 1960s there were twenty trains each way on weekdays. Steam gave way to diesel and services carried on. The line survived the Beeching plan and by the early 1970s had escaped a number of closure schemes, its Houdini-like behaviour giving rise to plenty of local support and optimism. However, it was all in vain, and full closure came in May 1975 – one of Britain's last branch line closures. Had the line lived on for another couple of years, it would surely have survived.

What there is to see today

Today there are plenty of remains to be seen. West Bay station survives, but both Bridport's stations have gone. A solitary crossing gate just outside the town is the town's railway memorial. The steeply graded route followed valleys through the hills up to Maiden Newton and can easily be identified from nearby minor roads. Cuttings, embankments and bridges survive, along with platforms at Powerstock and Toller, the only intermediate stations. Powerstock station always looked like a private house, and that is now exactly what it is. At Maiden Newton station there are still trains, on the Weymouth to Bristol route. This was the service that used to connect with the Bridport branch, whose trains waited in the bay platform. For those wanting to travel from Bridport in any other direction, notably to London, the journey was tortuous and involved a number of changes. This makes it even more remarkable that this essentially local railway kept going for so long.

▼ *With closure in 1975 still relatively recent, much of the Bridport branch survives in the landscape. Parts of the route are walkable, others are private, but the route can easily be traced through the valleys and up over the Dorset hills. There are some unexpected survivals to be seen, such as this former platelayer's hut beside the trackbed.*

▼ In the late 1980s West Bay station was a sorry sight, derelict and tumbledown, and the platform was used as a store for old boats and marine bits and pieces. Since then this pretty stone building, built in the typical vernacular style of rural Dorset stations, has been fully restored and given a new lease of life as a café. Track has been relaid beside the platform, a signal has been erected, and the trackbed towards Bridport has been turned into a public footpath.

▼ (Inset) In 1908 a four-coach train, hauled by the type of GWR tank locomotive long associated with the branch, hurries along the line towards Bridport's East Street station, having left West Bay a few minutes earlier. A road has buried this part of the route.

G.W.R. WEST BAY BRANCH.

ENTHUSIASTS

From the earliest days of railways, trains were regarded as objects of curiosity and fascination, with the locomotive the focus of popular interest. Largely for practical operating reasons, locomotives have usually carried names or numbers. Initially these were applied in a random manner, by the many independent railway companies. With the formation of the 'Big Four' railway companies in 1923, however, numbering was rationalized, and so the trainspotter was born. Since then the sight of small, and not so small,

boys standing on platforms and recording train numbers and names has been a feature of the railways in Britain.

While a major station or terminus was the preferred spotting location for many, others enjoyed the more limited, but more leisurely, qualities of the rural railway or branch line, where unusual, elderly or rare locomotives and vehicles might be seen.

With the advent of British Railways came the introduction of a national numbering system. This led directly to the publication of trainspotters' handbooks, most famously the Ian Allan *ABC* series, shown above. For a trainspotter, nothing could eclipse the excitement and sense of triumph that followed the recording of the last missing locomotive from a particular class or group.

◄ *For many children a railway is irresistible and hours can happily be spent watching trains. Indeed, for many children this is the start of something that turns into a lifelong enthusiasm, or even passion. Such an apprenticeship is common among railway historians. This small boy, photographed in the 1970s as he watches the passage of an ordinary diesel railcar on the Severn Beach branch at Ashley Hill, near Bristol, may now be such a person.*

◄ Some young enthusiasts grow up to become wholly dedicated to the pursuit of railway history and the railway experience. This remarkable photograph shows a group of the country's foremost railway photographers in action at Camden, north London, probably in the 1950s. Many of the photographs that these men took are now in important railway collections, including that of the National Railway Museum in York. From left to right: CCB Herbert, CRL Coles, M Pinder, ED Bruton, W Bell, and MW Earley.

▶ While trainspotting was often a solitary activity, railway enthusiasm was widespread, resulting in the setting up of railway clubs all over Britain, with members of all ages. School railway clubs enabled many pupils to share their interests and to undertake activities that otherwise would have been inaccessible. This photograph, taken in the 1950s, shows a school group on a visit to a shed or depot, making the most of this 0-6-0 goods locomotive

◄ As the rural railway, and the steam locomotive, came increasingly under threat, so railway clubs and similar organizations began to charter special rail tours dedicated to the exploration of threatened routes, preferably in historic vehicles. As a noted publisher of railway books, David & Charles arranged a number of such tours for their staff and other enthusiasts. This shows one such an outing, organized in May 1974 for the Booksellers Association.

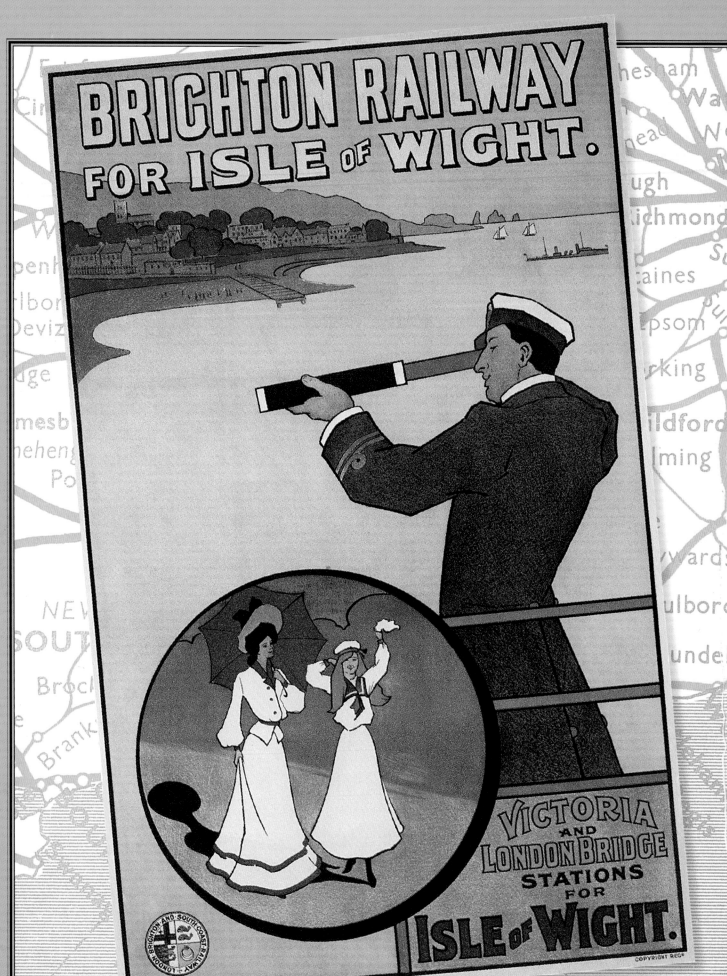

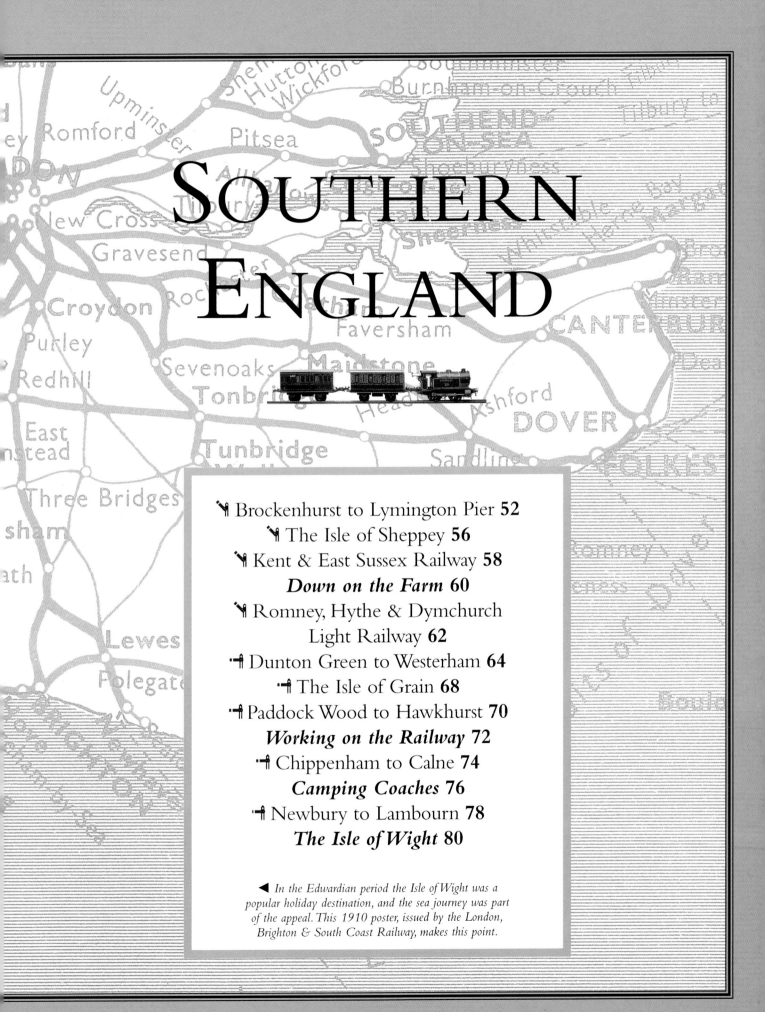

SOUTHERN ENGLAND

Brockenhurst to Lymington Pier **52**
The Isle of Sheppey **56**
Kent & East Sussex Railway **58**
Down on the Farm **60**
Romney, Hythe & Dymchurch
Light Railway **62**
Dunton Green to Westerham **64**
The Isle of Grain **68**
Paddock Wood to Hawkhurst **70**
Working on the Railway **72**
Chippenham to Calne **74**
Camping Coaches **76**
Newbury to Lambourn **78**
The Isle of Wight **80**

◀ *In the Edwardian period the Isle of Wight was a popular holiday destination, and the sea journey was part of the appeal. This 1910 poster, issued by the London, Brighton & South Coast Railway, makes this point.*

BROCKENHURST TO LYMINGTON PIER

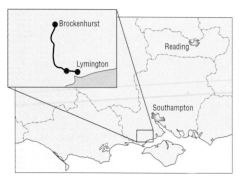

Three railway stations today serve the Isle of Wight ferries: Portsmouth Harbour, Southampton and Lymington, of which the best-known and the busiest is Portsmouth Harbour. Least familiar to most people is Lymington where, as at Portsmouth Harbour, the trains are carried out on a pier over the water to meet the ferry boats.

The 4-mile line from Brockenhurst to Lymington was opened in May 1858 by the independent Lymington Railway, as a rival to the by then well-established route to the Isle of Wight via Portsmouth. At that point the railway did not extend beyond Lymington and passengers faced a long walk to the harbour. Not surprisingly, traffic did not live up to expectations, and Portsmouth, always busier and more convenient, remained the favourite departure point for the island. In 1878 the company sold out to its rival, the huge London & South Western Railway. Investment soon followed, and the line was then extended to the harbour. The Pier station opened in 1884. Since then, the Lymington branch has continued to operate through the eras of the Southern Railway and British Railways. It survived the Beeching axe, was electrified in 1967 and is now in the care of South West Trains.

▶ *For years the Lymington to Yarmouth service was operated by paddle steamers, one of which can be seen in this 1920s view of the Pier station. At this time Lymington harbour was still relatively empty and undeveloped.*

$\binom{10}{45}$ **SOUTHERN RAILWAY.** (787)

—

FROM WATERLOO TO

LYMINGTON TOWN

▼ *In the 1950s, the paddle steamers were still in service. In an image full of period railway and maritime detail, the regular shuttle service from Brockenhurst approaches the Pier station, where the passengers will transfer to the steamer for a wintry crossing to the Isle of Wight.*

The route to the isle

For over a century the Lymington branch has offered passengers a relaxed and enjoyable route to the Isle of Wight, via Yarmouth, with the added bonus of an attractive journey through the New Forest to Brockenhurst. Although operated by relatively modern electric stock with no individuality, the route is still a good branch line experience.

At Brockenhurst passengers cross from the main line to the bay platform where the branch line shuttle waits. For a while the route of the branch runs parallel to the main line, then it swings away to the south to begin a journey across the open heathland and through the woods of the New Forest. The views are initially excellent, offering wide sweeping panoramas, and then the woods increase as the line follows the river to Lymington Town. Those not in a hurry will get out here to explore the attractions of Lymington and its harbour.

The final stretch of the train ride, across the Lymington river on a raised causeway and on to the Pier station, is a classic maritime journey, a rare survivor from the Victorian period, when branch lines met steamers all over Britain. There are exciting views, and the harbour is busier than ever, filled with pleasure boats of all kinds moored close to the raised track. At the terminus, the Isle of Wight ferry waits, just a short walk away. It may no longer be a paddle steamer, but the atmosphere is still the same, as is the experience of the journey. This is usually best enjoyed on the deck of the ferry, as it weaves its way out of the harbour through the crowded moorings to begin its crossing of the Solent.

▼ *In 1967, in the very last days of steam haulage on the branch, an ex-LMS Ivatt 2-6-2 tank locomotive pauses at the end of the pier. When the fireman has changed the points, the engine will run round its carriages to be ready to haul them back to Brockenhurst. This operation, which had to take place before every journey along the branch, is a reminder of the complexity of steam haulage, something often overlooked by modern enthusiasts who never knew the real thing. The setting, with views across the estuary towards the Isle of Wight, is magnificent.*

▲ *In the mid-1990s a modern electric train waits at the Pier station, adjacent to the ferry. The view is modern, but the whole process of taking a train directly to a ship is delightfully Victorian and the atmosphere of Lymington Pier station has changed little over the years.*

▼ *Although primarily a passenger line, the Lymington branch did carry freight. In this Edwardian postcard of the harbour and pier line in LSWR days, a locomotive hauls a long train of fully loaded wagons back towards Lymington Town.*

Lymington

THE ISLE OF SHEPPEY

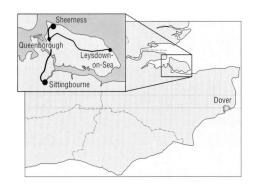

The presence of the important naval base at Sheerness, established since the time of Charles II, was the principal reason for the construction of the branch line from Sittingbourne. Built by an independent company in 1860, it was quickly taken over by the London, Chatham & Dover Railway, which equally quickly expanded it, adding extensions to Sheerness town, a developing resort, and to Queenborough Pier, for steamer services to Holland (largely abandoned after 1914). It also added through trains from London. Tourism was also the inspiration for the Sheppey Light Railway, a 9-mile line from Queenborough to Leysdown-on-Sea, at the far eastern point of the island. Cheaply built by a young engineer who later became better known as Colonel Stephens, it opened in 1901. Holiday traffic, which never really lived up to expectations, holiday camps and the RAF airfield at Eastchurch kept this line going until 1950.

It is the river Swale that makes Sheppey an island. To cross this busy navigation, used by many types of vessel, the railway had to build a lifting bridge. In the 1960s this complex and by then archaic and decrepit structure was replaced by a more modern bridge, whose four concrete lifting towers still dominate the low-lying landscape. Shared by road and rail, this bridge is the highpoint of the 7-mile journey to Sheerness on the electric shuttle service from Sittingbourne. The navy left Sheerness years ago, but the dockyard lives on and so the line is enlivened by the regular sight of large, diesel-hauled freight trains either serving the steel works or carrying imported cars.

▼ *The branch was electrified in 1959 but in that year was still used by steam trains. Here, at Sheerness, the locomotive prepares to run round its train. At this time, the station still had London, Chatham & Dover features, such as the lamps. The enamel station name boards are being changed, with the pre-war Southern Railway ones giving way to British Railways' unified totem style.*

Right by the Sea!
MINSTER BEACH HOLIDAY CAMP

not a big Camp but its friendly atmosphere ensures a

HAPPY HOLIDAY FOR **ALL** THE FAMILY

The Pier, Sheerness

Ward's Hill, Minster-on-Sea,
Isle of Sheppey, Kent

▲ *In the Edwardian era Sheerness was, briefly, a fairly smart resort. This early card shows elegant people taking the air while steamers call at the pier pavilion. The pier boasted its own little tramway, along which a naval cadet is proudly marching.*

◄ *Sadly, by the time this leaflet was produced, the Sheppey Light Railway and Minster station had closed – just before the great holiday camp boom of the 1950s.*

SOUTHERN
BRITISH RAILWAYS
CLOSING OF THE SHEPPEY LIGHT RAILWAY

On and from 4th December, 1950, all services on the above railway between the junction at Queenborough and Leysdown will be withdrawn.

THE FOLLOWING STATIONS WILL BE CLOSED:—

SHEERNESS EAST	EASTCHURCH
EAST MINSTER-ON-SEA	
HARTY ROAD HALT	MINSTER-ON-SEA
LEYSDOWN	BRAMBLEDOWN HALT

Omnibus services are operated by the Maidstone and District Motor Services Ltd between SHEERNESS and the localities now served by the above stations.

Parcels and miscellaneous traffic for cartage by the Railway Executive in the area will be dealt with at Sheerness-on-Sea Station ; freight traffic for cartage by the Railway Executive in the area will be dealt with at Sheerness: Dockyard Station. Enquiries should be addressed to the Station Master at Sheerness-on-Sea, Tel. Sheerness 2027 (Parcels, Luggage in Advance, etc.) and 2726 (Freight Traffic).

Facilities for dealing with traffic to be carried by the public exist at Queenborough and Sheerness Stations.

Further information may be obtained from the Divisional Superintendent, British Railways, Orpington–Tel. Orpington 3940 Ext 24 or 25.

▲ *The Sheppey Light Railway was closed on 12 December 1950. Closure notices such as this became increasingly common at branch line stations in the late 1950s and early 1960s.*

◄ *The Sheerness branch is unusual today in having both passenger and freight traffic. Much of the latter is for the steel terminal. In a grimy industrial environment, a class 08 diesel shunter in the colours of EWS has some running repairs while 'Bill', one of the resident locomotives, sits in the foreground.*

KENT & EAST SUSSEX RAILWAY

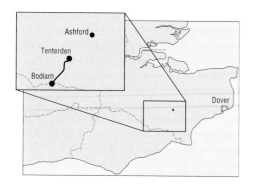

▼ *In February 2002 the Kent & East Sussex resurrects the spirit of the 1950s with a mixed passenger and freight train making its way along the track between Wittersham Road and Rolvenden. The little Victorian tank locomotive, typical of the line, is in British Railways livery. It, and its carriage, are sparklingly clean, always an anomaly when preserved railways try to re-create the past.*

The Light Railway Act of 1896 added numerous small and local lines to the national network. The first of these, authorized in that year, was the Rother Valley Light Railway, between Robertsbridge and Tenterden. It opened four years later and was soon extended as far as Headcorn, with the ultimate aim of reaching Maidstone. In 1904 the line was taken over by Colonel Stephens, and it became a key component of his collection of local railways. These he typically operated as cheaply as possible, with elderly and second-hand equipment. At this point it was renamed the Kent & East Sussex Light Railway.

The railway continued to operate its essentially local services until Colonel Stephens' death in 1931. The following year the railway went into liquidation, but it managed to remain in business until it was absorbed into British Railways in 1948. By the 1950s short, rural lines of this type were increasingly under threat from road transport, and in 1954 the K&ESLR was closed, although hop-pickers' specials continued to run until 1959 and freight until 1961.

At that point a preservation society was formed and, after a long battle involving court cases, a section of the original route was reopened in 1974.

A Wealden preserved line

Today the Kent & East Sussex Railway very successfully brings to life the atmosphere of a rural English railway during the pre-war era, with steam trains running for 10 miles along the sharply graded, tightly curved and scenic valley route linking Tenterden Town and Bodiam, where a visit can be made to its fairy-tale, moated medieval castle.

▲ In the years immediately before it closed to passengers in 1954, the line was operated by British Railways. During this time the former K&ESLR was run down and woebegone, and services were operated by a variety of elderly vehicles long past their sell-by date.

► An attractive market town with a wide main street, Tenterden has long attracted visitors. This early 1960s view has plenty of period detail, especially the cars and bus.

▼ Under British Railways the style changed little. Only the livery on the 1880s class A1X locomotive reveals the 1950s date. This typical mixed passenger and freight train is getting ready for service on the meandering line linking Headcorn and Robertsbridge.

DOWN ON THE FARM

GREAT WESTERN RAILWAY. (1135)

EGGS
WITH CARE

400 Pads, 100 lvs.—N.B. 4 41—1937-8. (8) S.

BRITISH RAILWAYS BR. 21719

PERISHABLE

The rapid expansion of the railway network into rural areas during the latter part of the nineteenth century was driven largely by the needs of agriculture. Industry and passengers were generally of secondary importance in the minds of the railway companies and those investing in them. Local railways changed the nature of farming almost beyond recognition by offering farmers access to rapid and efficient transport for the first time in the history of agriculture. The farmers could not only distribute and sell their produce more effectively, they could also buy raw materials and equipment. For a farmer, the branch railway was a lifeline, bringing in building materials, seeds, fertilizers and machinery and taking out crops and produce. By the same process the railway opened up new markets, far beyond the limits imposed by poor roads and horse-drawn traffic. As a major part of the railway's traffic was livestock, many local stations were equipped with holding pens, loading bays and other special facilities required by the agricultural business. In many cases, markets were moved so as to be closer to the stations and goods yards. Until the 1950s agriculture was the mainstay of the local railway, but from then on the shift from rail to road sounded the death knell. It is an irony that farming was both the main inspiration for the building of branch lines and the primary reason for their closure.

▼ *The seasonal nature of agriculture was well understood by the railway companies, which regularly laid on special trains and special facilities. Hop picking in Kent was one such activity with a very short season, and a huge temporary labour force was transported into the country from the cities on special trains. This card, posted in 1912, shows hop-picking families on their way back to London at the end of the season.*

"HOP-PICKING" HOMEWARD BOUND LONDONERS ON THEIR WAY TO RAILWAY STATION. 8.

◄ The railway managed the transport of perishable goods very efficiently, ensuring that delicate and seasonal produce was carried quickly to market in prime condition. Eggs, cauliflowers from Cornwall, daffodils from Lincolnshire, apples from Herefordshire and soft fruits from the garden of England were typical cargoes on the fleets of special trains. Here, in a photograph from the Edwardian era, panniers of freshly picked strawberries stand on platform trucks at Axbridge station, near Cheddar in Somerset, ready to be loaded. The wagon nearest the camera seems to be labelled Sheffield, a distant destination for West Country soft fruit.

► The transport of livestock was a vital component in the economy of the rural railway, but transport facilities were usually better than this. A single goat stands tethered to a column on the platform at Axminster, in Devon, one summer's day in 1929. It has a label on its neck, so presumably is on its way to or from market. Perhaps its owner is having a quick drink.

▼ Cattle, sheep, horses, goats, poultry and all other kinds of livestock were the local railway's bread and butter. Here, in the 1920s, sheep housed in special pens in the goods yard at Lyminge station, in Kent, are being loaded on to cattle wagons. Farmers, railway staff and onlookers are all involved in what was then a familiar scene.

LONDON MIDLAND AND SCOTTISH RAILWAY COMPANY.
P. F. 792.
R 4—1/25.

LIVE BIRDS.

ROMNEY, HYTHE & DYMCHURCH

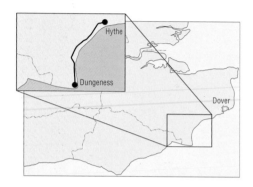

Proudly proclaiming itself 'The World's Smallest Public Railway', the Romney, Hythe & Dymchurch Light Railway was opened in 1927, at a time when miniature, park and garden railways were all the vogue. This 15in gauge line, designed initially as an amusement by two 1920s racing drivers, Captain Jack Howey and Count Zborowski, and built by the engineer and garden railway specialist Henry Greenly, has over the years become an established part of the community in this relatively inaccessible part of Kent. With a fleet of locomotives, both steam and diesel, built as small-scale replicas of mainline engines, the line has always appealed greatly to both tourists and enthusiasts. However, it is also a real railway, running scheduled year-round services and school specials. During World War II an armoured train patrolled the coast.

When it was built, the line enjoyed a number of connections with 'grown-up' Southern Railway services, at Dungeness, Lydd, New Romney and Hythe, but these have all gone, leaving the RH&D isolated. Nonetheless, it survives. The 13½-mile line has a particular appeal, unique in Britain, based partly on the trains themselves and partly on the distinctive landscape of this remote part of east Kent. Never far from the sea, the railway is the perfect way to explore the flat, wild landscape of the Romney Marsh, with its church towers, dykes and grazing sheep.

▼ *In a conscious echo of the very famous Southern Railway poster that features a small boy on the platform at Waterloo station telling an engine driver about his holiday, another small boy has an earnest conversation with another engine driver.*

▼ *At the opening of the line in 1927 large crowds turned up to watch, attracted partly by the trains and partly by the presence of the Duke of York, the future King George VI, who is seen here driving the locomotive with Henry Greenly. Everything looks very new and spic and span.*

▲ *This 1950s postcard, showing a number of the line's locomotives, the distinctive landscape and famous features such as Dungeness lighthouse, was always popular.*

▼ *At the western, Dungeness, end of the line, a large circle of track enables the trains to turn. Formerly wild and desolate, this spot is now dominated by the massive structures of the nuclear power station – a dramatic background for the toy train, which on this occasion is hauled by an American-style diesel locootive. At the Hythe end of the line there is a conventional turntable.*

DUNTON GREEN TO WESTERHAM

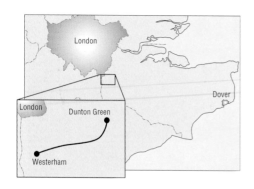

On 7 July 1881, amid great local celebrations, a short 5-mile branch line was opened to link Westerham with the South Eastern Railway main line at Dunton Green. Conceived as a longer route along the valley below the North Downs to meet another main line at Oxted, the railway in fact never progressed beyond Westerham. This small market town, the birthplace of General Wolfe, victor at Quebec, benefited greatly from the coming of the railway. Shops and businesses flourished and, more importantly, tourists arrived, often with their bicycles, to explore the Kent and Surrey borders and the Pilgrim's Way. As Westerham was only 26 miles from both Charing Cross and Cannon Street, the railway had the advantage of being one of the few rural branch lines easily and quickly accessible from central London, something that continued to attract passengers, and later railway enthusiasts, throughout the lifetime of the line. A journey time to London of under an hour also meant that the branch was used by commuters. In the 1920s there were at least fifteen trains in each direction on weekdays. Passengers on the first train from Westerham, the 07.07, would reach Charing Cross at 08.19. In its later years it was the commuters who kept the line running. While local freight was important, this was primarily a passenger line. For this reason, it was one of the first branches to have steam rail motors. These were introduced in April 1906 but were soon replaced with push-pull units, which became the standard vehicles on the line for the rest of its life. Towards the end, as on so many branch lines, these units were positively antiquated.

▼ *A classic branch line scene on a summer's day in 1959, as an ancient push-pull unit drifts into Brasted station. Only one person waits on the platform, probably a friend of the photographer, not a passenger. The traditional timber station has plenty of period details, notably the South Eastern Railway lamp and the 1930s Southern Railway target-style, enamel name plaque.*

▶ *Thanks to the railway, Westerham attracted many walkers and cyclists. This Edwardian postcard shows one of the steep hills rising into the woodlands to the south of Westerham. The cyclist shown here is enjoying the steep descent into the valley, while a horse-drawn wagon labours uphill.*

Hill Climb. Westerham. Kent.

COUNTRY AFTERNOON TICKETS

FROM LONDON AND SUBURBS

MARCH 26th to OCTOBER 29th *inclusive* 1961

SOUTHERN
BRITISH RAILWAYS

▲ *British Railways' Country Afternoon Tickets promoted outings to rural stations easily accessible from central London. The text sets the scene: 'No early morning rush. A lie-in, and then an easy run out when the day is nicely aired.' Westerham is included in this 1961 schedule, with tickets priced at 5s 3d return.*

Closure, which came quickly, in October 1961, was partly for political reasons, as the trackbed was required for the route of the proposed London orbital motorway (M25) and the Sevenoaks bypass. It was the building of these roads that prevented an active and well-supported preservation group, which revived the old name, the Westerham Valley Railway, from saving or restoring the line. After closure, the remains of the line lingered on for some years until the new roads were built, at which point most of the route was completely obliterated.

Lost to the motorway

The Westerham branch traversed the pleasant valley of the Darenth, at this point little more than a stream, running parallel to the Pilgrim's Way in the shadow of the North Downs. The route was predominantly rural, and the intermediate stops at Brasted and Chevening Halt were well away from the settlements they served. To the south lay the wooded expanses of Hosey Hill and Brasted Chart, an area whose many roads and tracks were popular with walkers and cyclists. Chartwell, home of Sir Winston Churchill, is at the heart of this hilly and secluded landscape.

Finding traces of the railway today is quite hard. Westerham station has been completely redeveloped, and the line survives only in local road names, such as The Flyer's Way. The few remains that are to be found are mostly just to the west of the junction at Dunton Green, an area away from the motorway's route. At Dunton Green itself, the bay platform from which the Westerham trains departed can still be identified amid the overgrowth.

▼ *Very little of the Westerham branch remains as most of the route is now under the M25. However, a wooded section survives to the east of Dunton Green, marked by a dense line of trees along the edge of a meadow, seen here filled with the soft greens of spring.*

▼ *(Inset) Westerham station, seen here near the end of the line's life, was the archetypal branch line terminus, with a small engine shed, signal box, goods yard, sidings, loading gauge and water tower – plus a delightful sense of leisurely inactivity. The push-pull unit simmers in the platform, having arrived on one of its many journeys from the junction at Dunton Green. No passengers seem to be arriving or departing; in fact, there is no one to be seen at all on this lazy summer's day.*

"THE FEW", WHITE HART HOTEL, BRASTED, KENT.

...RT HOTEL, BRASTED, KENT

96178

▲ In the 1940s the White Hart became one of the best-known pubs in southern England because of its popularity with fighter pilots stationed at Biggin Hill. It was famous for a blackboard, made from an old black-out panel, that was signed by many of the great names of the Battle of Britain. The pilots raced down from the airfield in cars, and probably never used the railway station. The blackboard is now in a local museum.

BRASTED

THE ISLE OF GRAIN

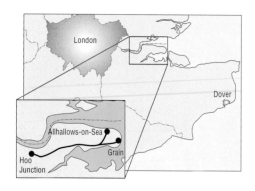

The Isle of Grain, partly separated from the rest of Kent by the Medway estuary and surrounded on its other side by the wide expanse of the river Thames, is a strange, isolated and low-lying region, one that appealed greatly to Charles Dickens. The Victorians built forts, in order to defend the Thames, and a complex network of railways. First came a long branch across Grain, running from Hoo Junction, on the South Eastern Railway's Rochester to Gravesend main line, to Port Victoria, a new steamer pier for Continental services. Opened in 1882, this was inspired by the similar pier at Queenborough, directly opposite, on Sheppey, opened in 1876 by the SER's deadly rival, the London, Chatham & Dover Railway. Port Victoria remained in public use until 1904, and then continued to be used by royalty and other dignitaries desiring the privacy the port offered. It closed completely in 1951, when a station was opened at Grain, mainly for the workers at the ever-expanding oil refinery. This survived for a while as the terminus of one of England's more remote journeys, but passenger services ceased finally in December 1961. In the meantime, the network had been enlarged by a number of small branches serving industrial and military establishments and by a short passenger line from Stoke to Allhallows-on-Sea. However, hoped-for commuter and tourist traffic turned out to be almost non-existent, mainly because Allhallows-on-Sea never got going as a resort.

Today, the line to Grain is still there, carrying freight traffic for the power station, the container port and other industrial users. However, Port Victoria vanished into the Medway mud many years ago, and there is little to see of the branch to Allhallows-on-Sea, except a few sections of the trackbed that can be seen running across the flat landscape now populated by horses and chalets.

▼ *Shortly before the end of passenger services in 1961, the local gets ready to depart from Allhallows-on-Sea. There seem to be no passengers, a common situation by that time. The size of the station reveals the optimism with which the branch was built in 1932, when it was widely believed that Allhallows had huge potential as a resort. The scattering of chalets and caravans in the background reveals the truth of the matter. Today the station, and most of the branch, has vanished, its life of 29 years being one of the shortest on record, and Allhallows has surrendered to chalets, holiday camps and suburban housing, in a flat landscape grazed by horses.*

◀ The service to Allhallows ended on 4 December 1961. Here, on the previous evening, the last train is about to depart from Allhallows, attended by more passengers and spectators than the line had ever seen. Such scenes were about to be repeated all over Britain, as the branch line age came to an end.

▲ A remote wooden station in a landscape populated by sheep, Grain was always a lonely place. By the time this photograph was taken, in about 1910, the main traffic to Port Victoria had already ended. A railwayman, two soldiers, a workman, two ladies and a dog await the approaching train.

▲ Industrial and freight-only branches are often surprisingly old-fashioned, and the line to Grain is no exception. Old-style crossing gates, semaphore signals and no hint of any modern infrastructure give such lines a particular appeal. Crossing the flat marshland, the branch approaches storage tanks, standing like an advance guard for the various industries at the end of the line, all users of the railway.

PADDOCK WOOD TO HAWKHURST

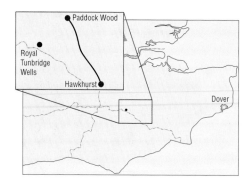

Born, like so many minor Victorian railways, out of intercompany rivalry, the Hawkhurst branch was a classic of its type. Single tracked and steam worked through its life, it ran through lovely countryside from nowhere to nowhere in particular, calling at stations that were generally a long way from the villages they claimed to serve. The branch was opened in September 1892, having been built by the South Eastern Railway mainly to keep their rival, the London, Chatham & Dover, out of their territory. For decades it slumbered on, passing in due time into the care of the Southern Railway and thence to British Railways. Towards the end of its life there was even a scheme to electrify it, in the hope of building commuter traffic, but it amounted to nothing and closure came in June 1961.

Ironically, today it would have been a valuable and busy commuter line. There was freight traffic, but more significant, and a defining characteristic of the branch, were the annual hop-pickers' specials, long trains of ancient carriages hauled by equally elderly locomotives that made their way from London Bridge to the branch line's stations via meandering routes. When the mechanization of hop picking brought these to an end in the 1950s, the line was doomed.

Although much of the trackbed is still there in the rolling Kent countryside, it is hard to see today because most of the route is rural and away from roads. The bits that can be seen are private. Bridges have gone, along with most of the stations. Some of the tall, grand station houses survive, for example at Horsmonden, and at Hawkhurst there are engine and goods sheds, and a preserved signal box.

▼ *A red-letter day in Goudhurst in September 1892 with the arrival of the first train, greeted by a large and entirely male crowd, notable for the range of heights and the variety of headgear. The South Eastern Railway's locomotive, elaborately garlanded, was already a bit long in the tooth, setting the standard for the branch throughout its life. The carriages also seem to be a mixed lot. The station was then called Hope Mill, an acknowledgement that it was a long way from Goudhurst.*

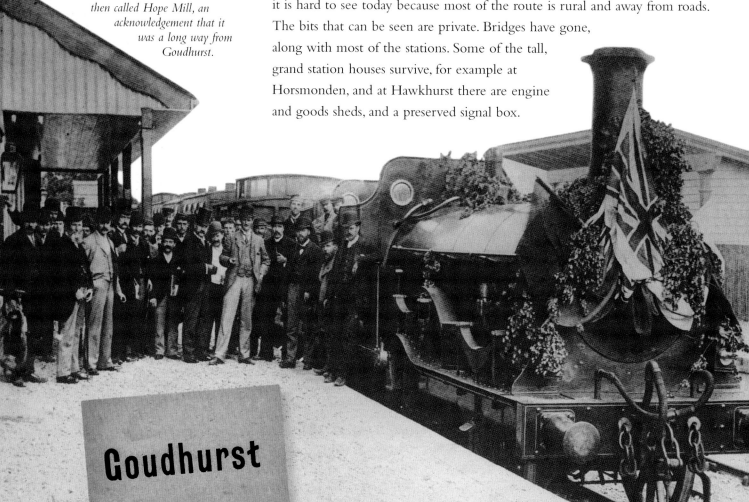

Goudhurst

▲ *Looking out of place in the rail-less environment of an industrial estate, Hawkhurst's preserved signal box is nevertheless carefully painted and named in classic Southern Railway style. This is the site of Hawkhurst's former station, which, like most on the branch, was a long way from the place it was designed to serve. Other railway survivors include the old goods shed and the old engine shed, conveniently labelled for easy identification.*

▼ *A classic branch line scene at Hawkhurst, shortly before the line's closure in 1961. It is the British Railways era, yet the station and its lamp are pure South Eastern Railway, while the station name board and the push-pull unit date from pre-war Southern days. The driver watches his passengers assemble on a grey day in the late 1950s. Most of them, including the smartly dressed lady, seem to be off to London for the day. The man looking at the camera has the air of a railway enthusiast; he and his friend, taking the photograph, are perhaps on a branch line tour.*

WORKING ON THE RAILWAY

Once a railwayman, always a railwayman: a familiar phrase, reflecting the particular, and dedicated, nature of a way of life that at its peak, in about 1918, gave employment to around 650,000 men and women in Britain. When British Railways started in 1948, the figure was 629,000. By 1994 it had dropped to 116,000, reflecting the massive closure programme and wholesale restructuring of an industry that had been famous for its stability, its traditional nature and its family atmosphere. When the railways started, staff were often recruited from the armed services and from established centres of engineering and industry, so discipline was strong. Later, many junior employees came from the land. This established a way of life with traditional values, a commitment to education, and a respect for order and individual responsibility. The railways represented solidity, stability and, above all, respectability. There were many benefits: uniforms, cheap housing, travel passes and permits, free coal, education and training, medical services and even, from an early date, pension funds. The disadvantages included long hours of work and relatively low pay. Many employees stayed in one place most of their working lives, ensuring a position at the centre of the community.

▲ *This Great Western station master, photographed in the late Victorian era, shows his pride in a job that demanded complete dedication and great practical experience.*

▼ *As was typical of the rural railwayman, this Cornish crossing-keeper would have had a high level of responsibility, working long hours and leading a solitary life in his railway cottage.*

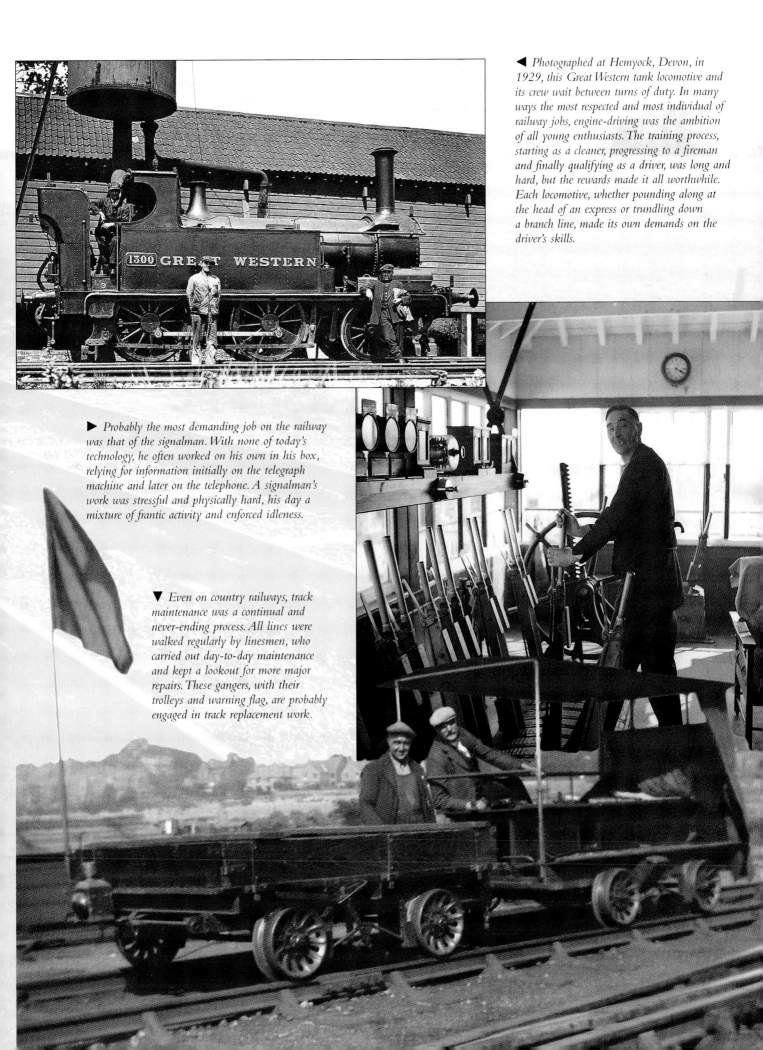

◀ Photographed at Hemyock, Devon, in 1929, this Great Western tank locomotive and its crew wait between turns of duty. In many ways the most respected and most individual of railway jobs, engine-driving was the ambition of all young enthusiasts. The training process, starting as a cleaner, progressing to a fireman and finally qualifying as a driver, was long and hard, but the rewards made it all worthwhile. Each locomotive, whether pounding along at the head of an express or trundling down a branch line, made its own demands on the driver's skills.

▶ Probably the most demanding job on the railway was that of the signalman. With none of today's technology, he often worked on his own in his box, relying for information initially on the telegraph machine and later on the telephone. A signalman's work was stressful and physically hard, his day a mixture of frantic activity and enforced idleness.

▼ Even on country railways, track maintenance was a continual and never-ending process. All lines were walked regularly by linesmen, who carried out day-to-day maintenance and kept a lookout for more major repairs. These gangers, with their trolleys and warning flag, are probably engaged in track replacement work.

CHIPPENHAM TO CALNE

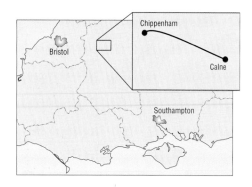

The Calne Railway opened its five and a bit miles of branch line from Chippenham in November 1863. Originally broad gauge, it was converted to standard gauge in the 1870s by the Great Western, who took over the branch completely in 1892. It was a line that had its own character, meandering prettily along the valley of the river Marden with two intermediate halts that appeared to serve nowhere in particular, Stanley Bridge and Black Dog. The latter was decidedly eccentric. It was built for the Marquis of Landsdowne, whose family estate at Bowood lies just to the south. In effect Black Dog was a private station (it did not appear in timetables until 1952) but it nevertheless boasted a waiting room, ticket office, siding and station master, a position subsequently reduced to leading porter. It seems the marquis insisted that the appointment of the station master was dependent upon his having no political views. As late as the 1960s, intending passengers at Black Dog halt were required to 'inform the guard' or 'give the necessary hand signal to the driver'. For many years the mainstay of the line was Calne's major industry, Harris & Company's manufacturing of sausage, pie and meat products. Towards the end of the line's life, sausages were regularly transported in passenger trains, a practice that continued until the branch closed in September 1964.

The line has now been given a new lease of life by the sustainable transport charity Sustrans, as part of the National Cycle Network's Severn and Thames Route. Exploration is therefore easy and pleasant for both cyclists and walkers. The surface is good, access is well marked by typical Sustrans sculptures, and there is the excitement of a fine timber bridge across the A4 outside Calne. There is not much to see in Calne itself, but the trackbed wanders delightfully through green and undulating farmland interspersed with woods. Beyond Stanley Bridge it goes straight across the low-lying fields to Chippenham.

▼ *Calne was a typical branch line terminus, with some freight sidings and a single platform covered by a generous canopy. The line was never busy, so the scene below, with nothing much going on, must have been very typical. The railings have just been painted, and a carriage waits at the far end of the platform. Today, the station site is an industrial estate.*

▶ 'Station Road, Calne' is the title of this Edwardian postcard, issued by a local publisher. Children watch as sheep are driven along the road in a somewhat desultory manner on a lazy summer's afternoon.

▼ Calne's major employer, and a prime user of the railway, was Harris & Company, meat purveyors and manufacturers of meat products. For years, Harris's pies were famous across Britain. This card, showing a very different view of Station Road from the rural scene above, makes clear the size of the factory. Today, both factory and station have gone.

CLN 2   CALNE, VIEW FROM STATION ROAD.

Copyright
A. F. Sergeant

G.W.R.

Calne

▶ The Calne branch survives today as a well-surfaced and pleasant path through the countryside, popular with both walkers and cyclists. Part of the National Cycle Network's Thames and Severn route, it is a typical Sustrans track, with sculptural route markers and a dramatic new bridge over the A4 road.

CAMPING COACHES

CAMPING COACHES

FULLY EQUIPPED FOR 8 PERSONS

SITUATED AT NUMEROUS ATTRACTIVE SEASIDE AND COUNTRY SITES. IDEAL FOR FAMILY HOLIDAYS

AVAILABLE 30th MARCH TO 19th OCTOBER. 1957 REDUCED CHARGES - EARLY AND LATE SEASON

ASK FOR ILLUSTRATED FOLDER AT STATIONS AND ENQUIRY OFFICES OR APPLY TO CHIEF COMMERCIAL MANAGER. WESTERN REGION. PADDINGTON STATION. LONDON, W.1

WESTERN **BRITISH RAILWAYS** REGION

Since the dawn of railways, old carriages and wagons have been used as store rooms, waiting rooms and, frequently, homes. However, the idea of using elderly or redundant carriages specifically for camping purposes did not emerge until 1933, when the London & North Eastern Railway put a batch of converted coaches on to sidings at various sites in eastern England. The LMS, the GWR and the SR rapidly followed suit, and by 1939 more than 430 carriages were scattered over England, Wales and Scotland, placed at popular seaside resorts or at remote inland or coastal spots, to be let by the week to families or groups of friends. Well converted, equipped and maintained, and offering a relatively cheap holiday, the coaches proved very popular.

During the war, camping coaches were withdrawn, but they reappeared in the 1950s, many with more modern facilities. The most luxurious were some Pullman cars converted in the 1960s. However, by then patterns of family holidays were changing, and some of the most popular sites vanished under the Beeching axe. The last camping coaches disappeared at the end of the 1971 season.

◄ *Camping coaches were always widely promoted by the railway companies. Posters, in characteristic colours, highlighted the levels of comfort and the splendours of the setting. This Western Region scene, somewhere in Wales, depicts a few of the qualities of a holiday in a camping coach.*

▶ *The first camping coaches had no internal corridors, which made life difficult, especially in wet weather. By the late 1930s, more spacious and convenient layouts had been developed. This shows the internal plan of a six-berth camping coach in use on the Eastern Region in the late 1950s. There were variations: Southern Region coaches, for example, had beds side by side rather than bunks.*

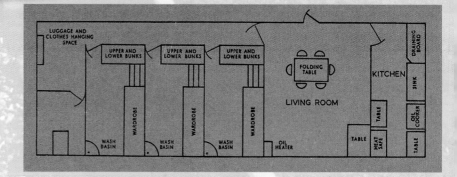

► *Issued by the LNER publicity machine in 1935, this photograph illustrates the pleasures of camping-coach life 'at a secluded spot in Essex adjoining the LNER station at Southminster'. In most camping coaches, water was either pumped by hand or brought in daily in cans. Campers generally made use of the lavatories on the station platform. In many cases, daily supplies of food were delivered by train.*

▼ *This photograph shows a living room in one of the Southern Railway's first camping coaches, taken to promote the 1936 season. The wireless, curtains, oil lamp and heater all underline the marketing department's claim that the coaches 'contain everything that a camper would require'. Headed 'Camp on Wheels', the caption goes on: 'The railway company have selected sites on the beauty spots of the South Coast to establish these luxury camps.'*

BRITISH RAILWAYS

CAMPING COACHES
for delightful inexpensive holidays
1957

LIVING ROOM
EASTERN REGION
CAMPING COACH

Camping Coaches provide

● Holidays in specially selected places in England, Scotland and Wales

● Out of doors camping holiday with the comfort of well-appointed living accommodation at reasonable cost

● A cheap and ideal holiday for the family

Apply to the addresses shown under "Location of Coaches and Rental Charges"

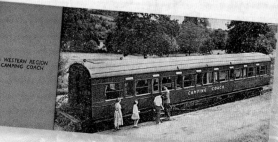

A WESTERN REGION
CAMPING COACH

► *Through the 1950s and into the 1960s, British Railways issued brochures to promote camping coaches nationwide. The standard eight-page folder included a location map, price schedule, booking form and illustrations of scenes of camping-coach life. In 1957 weekly hire fees ranged from £5 10s to £11 10s depending on the location, the number of berths and the time of year. The leaflet stipulated that a set number of the party must travel to and from the location by train.*

NEWBURY TO LAMBOURN

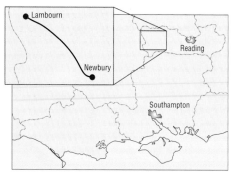

The river Lambourn, which rises high in the downs to the north-west of Newbury, flows through a valley long famous for the training of racehorses. However, the carriage of coal was of greater concern to the supporters of the Lambourn Valley Railway, whose 12-mile line finally opened in April 1898 after a gestation period stretching back to 1881. Constructed with economy in mind, the line closely followed the river along the valley. The company had its own carriages, its own fleet of three blue-painted locomotives and a selection of second-hand goods vehicles. The stations were numerous but small, and the staff tended to be jacks of all trades. Despite this, finances were always a problem, and in 1905 the whole enterprise was sold to the GWR for £50,000. Improvements were made, and in 1937 a diesel railcar was introduced, specially adapted to haul freight wagons and horseboxes. By now the carriage of racehorses was one of the mainstays of the line, and remained so until closure. Some racehorse trainers even had their own horseboxes to take horses to and from race meetings. In 1954 an additional 2-mile branch was built from Welford Park to the USAF stores depot, and this helped to keep the branch in business. However, passenger traffic, never significant, fell continuously through the 1950s and in January 1960 passenger services stopped. Shortly after, the section from Lambourn to Welford Park was closed completely. Ministry of Defence traffic continued along the rest of the route until 1972. The last trains to run on the branch were four enthusiasts' specials in November 1973.

Today, the route is easily followed along the valley from adjacent roads. A short section forms part of the Lambourn Valley Way.

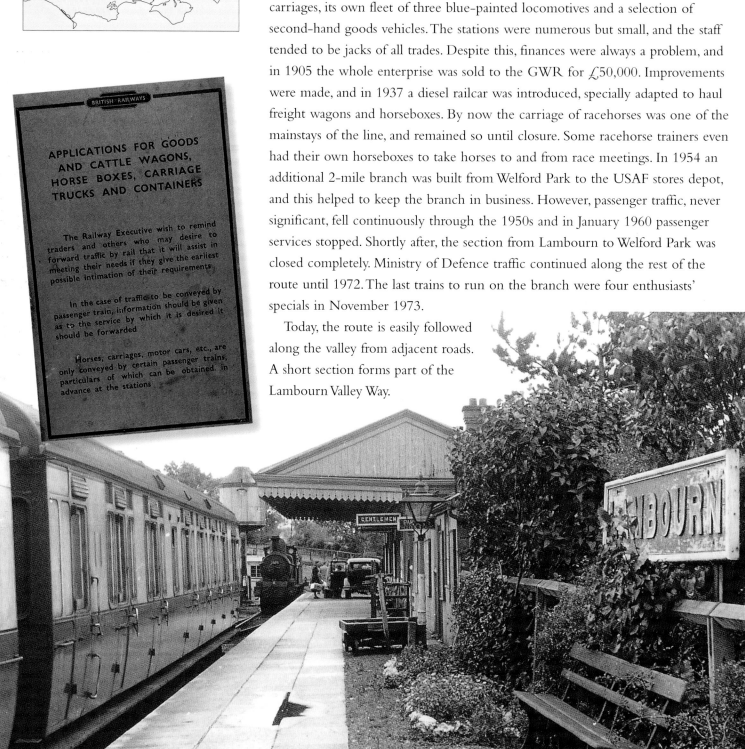

APPLICATIONS FOR GOODS AND CATTLE WAGONS, HORSE BOXES, CARRIAGE TRUCKS AND CONTAINERS

BRITISH RAILWAYS

The Railway Executive wish to remind traders and others who may desire to forward traffic by rail that it will assist in meeting their needs if they give the earliest possible intimation of their requirements

In the case of traffic to be conveyed by passenger train, information should be given as to the service by which it is desired it should be forwarded

Horses, carriages, motor cars, etc., are only conveyed by certain passenger trains, particulars of which can be obtained in advance at the stations

◀ *A GWR diesel railcar was first used on the line in 1937, specially adapted to haul horseboxes and freight wagons. These stylish vehicles lived on into the British Railways era. At Welford Park on a late September afternoon in 1950, one of these vehicles, bound for Lambourn, meets a locomotive-hauled train going the other way. The branch's only passing loop was at Welford.*

▲ *The trackbed of the Lambourn branch is largely inaccessible and private, especially the southern section through the woods. However, up on the downs near East Garston, it is walkable, as part of the Lambourn Valley Way.*

▶ *This 1953 view shows a deserted Welford Park station, with one of the low signal boxes typical of the line. The following year the branch to the USAF depot was opened and the additional traffic generated by this kept the Welford Park to Newbury section busy until cost of maintenance forced its closure in 1972.*

◀ *In late September 1952 the train from Newbury has arrived in Lambourn, and the old 0-6-0 goods locomotive has pulled forward to run round the carriages. The station sign, the bench and the water tower are all GWR. Nothing of all this remains today.*

THE ISLE OF WIGHT

The Isle of Wight's distinctive character was created by the Victorians, and the survival of this today is part of the appeal of a place that seems to encompass the best features of Britain's past. The comprehensive railway system, built between 1862 and 1900 by a series of fiercely independent local companies, was the key to its development. These merged into two railways, the Isle of Wight and the Isle of Wight Central. In 1923 the network became part of the Southern Railway, and, later, of British Railways, but nothing much changed. Until the early 1950s the entire island was criss-crossed by what were, in effect, Victorian branch lines. Sadly, closures broke the pattern and by the mid-1960s all had gone except the line from Ryde Pierhead to Shanklin. Electrified in 1967, this has been operated for many years by retired London tube trains, an eccentricity that underlines the island's particular quality.

▲ *Complete with a border of embossed shells, this postcard captures the flavour of the Isle of Wight during the nineteenth century. Having seduced Queen Victoria, Prince Albert and Lord Tennyson, the island became a popular and fashionable place to visit from the 1850s. Seaside holidays, rural retreats and souvenirs were all part of the picture, and exploration was made easy by the railway and the bicycle.*

▼ *The last railway to be opened on the island ran from Newport to Ventnor via Godshill. It was also one of the first to be closed. Here, on 26 July 1897, a surprisingly small group stands by the inaugural train, which is lavishly adorned with flags and greenery. The opening of a railway was still something to celebrate at the very end of Queen Victoria's reign.*

► Ryde's new railway pier was completed in 1880, enabling passengers to walk straight from the steamer on to one of the trains that ran to many parts of the island. Miraculously, this can still be done today, although the train goes only to Shanklin. Previously, there was a tramway service along the pier, to carry passengers from the ferry to Ryde's town station.

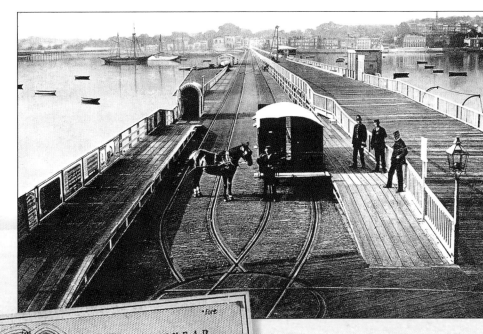

▼ The complete Isle of Wight railway system can be seen on this 1930s map. Newport was the hub of the network, and from here lines radiated west to Yarmouth and Freshwater, north to Cowes, east to Ryde, Bembridge, Sandown and Shanklin, and south to Ventnor, via two routes. This series of interconnected branch lines made island exploration very easy.

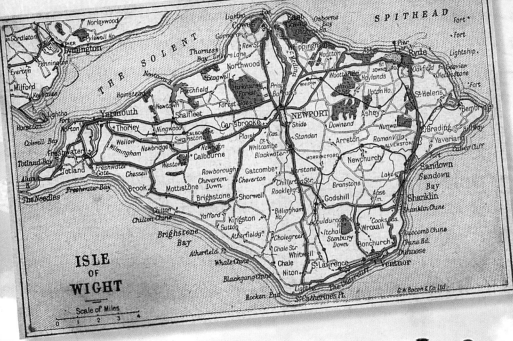

▼ A popular place for rail enthusiasts was the Medina bridge at Newport, and the scene below was captured by many photographers. This shows a train from Cowes to Ryde crossing the bridge in the 1950s, hauled by one of the island's distinctive tank locomotives. Some of these remained in service right up to the closure of the network in 1966. Cars complete the period look.

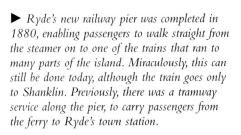

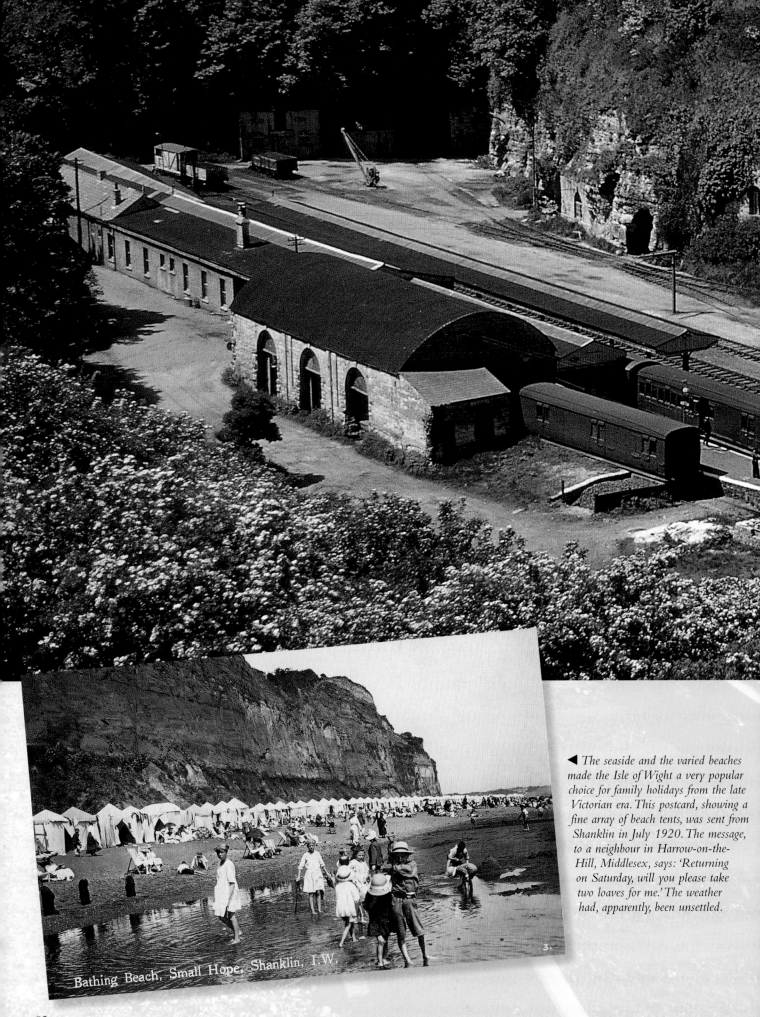

Bathing Beach, Small Hope, Shanklin, I.W.

◀ The seaside and the varied beaches made the Isle of Wight a very popular choice for family holidays from the late Victorian era. This postcard, showing a fine array of beach tents, was sent from Shanklin in July 1920. The message, to a neighbour in Harrow-on-the-Hill, Middlesex, says: 'Returning on Saturday, will you please take two loaves for me.' The weather had, apparently, been unsettled.

▲ The island's most remarkable station was Ventnor, built in 1866 on the site of a former quarry and approached directly from a long tunnel under St Boniface Down. This was a busy place, and the railway was Ventnor's lifeline over a long period. As can be seen in this 1960 photograph, the railway, even then, carried plenty of freight, notably coal and other basic commodities.

◄ Despite the expansion of private motoring in the 1950s and early 1960s, the railways were still a major part of the island's economy. This view of the front of Ventnor station shows an interesting range of cars old and new. Their owners were no doubt meeting friends and relatives newly arrived from Ryde or Cowes.

"THE ISLE OF WIGHT EXPRESS."

◄ In August 1953 a young boy called David sent this card to his Sunday School teacher, declaring in big letters: 'I am having a good holiday.' The theme, the slowness of local trains, was a popular one from the early years of the twentieth century. This scene of the railway staff playing cricket while the passengers wait was widely available, overprinted with the names of many places where the train service was considered to be erratic.

► In 1971 steam trains returned to the Isle Wight with the opening of a preserved line from Wootton to Havenstreet. Twenty years later, the line was extended to Smallbrook Junction, enabling the steam trains to connect with services on the Ryde to Shanklin main line. Using locomotives and vehicles that served on the island, the Isle of Wight Steam Railway re-creates in a particularly evocative manner the great days of the island's railway past.

▲ In December 1966, right at the end of the Isle of Wight's railway network, a classic branch line scene takes place as the driver of the Ryde to Shanklin train reaches out to take the single-line token from the signalman at Ryde St John's Road.

► Ryde's pier carries cars and trains on either side of the remains of the pier tramway. On a sunny day early in the 1990s a retired London tube train, resplendent in Network SouthEast livery, makes its way along the pier, serving the surviving route from Ryde Pierhead to Shanklin, now operated by Island Line.

CROMER
GEM OF THE NORFOLK COAST
Guide (9d.) from Advertising Association, Dept. R., Cromer, Norfolk

Train services and fares from **BRITISH RAILWAYS** stations offices and agencies

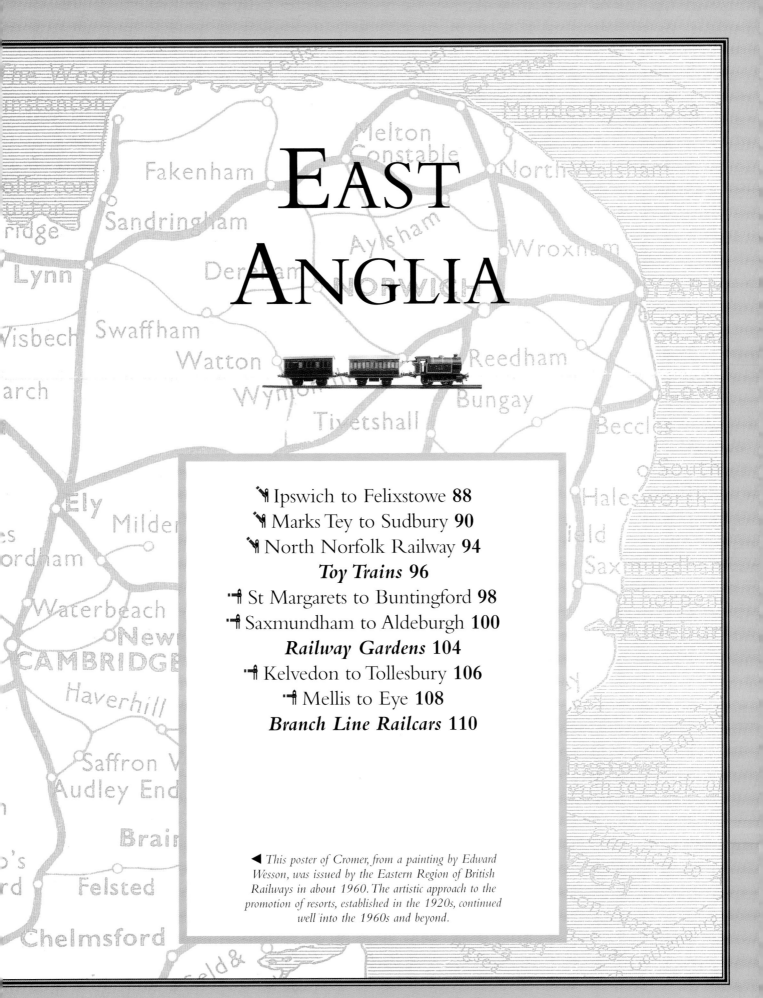

EAST ANGLIA

Ipswich to Felixstowe **88**
Marks Tey to Sudbury **90**
North Norfolk Railway **94**
Toy Trains **96**
St Margarets to Buntingford **98**
Saxmundham to Aldeburgh **100**
Railway Gardens **104**
Kelvedon to Tollesbury **106**
Mellis to Eye **108**
Branch Line Railcars **110**

◄ *This poster of Cromer, from a painting by Edward Wesson, was issued by the Eastern Region of British Railways in about 1960. The artistic approach to the promotion of resorts, established in the 1920s, continued well into the 1960s and beyond.*

IPSWICH TO FELIXSTOWE

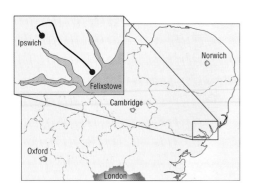

The Felixstowe Railway & Pier Company was set up in July 1875 with the aim of building a 13-mile branch line from Westerfield, near Ipswich, to the then undeveloped Felixstowe. The first passengers reached Felixstowe Beach station in June 1877, and at that point a new resort was born. A pier and hotels were built, making the most of the broad curve of the red shingle beach. The line's promoter, Colonel Tomline, renamed his business the Felixstowe Railway & Dock Company and built a large dock complex served by railway jetties. In 1887 the line was bought by the Great Eastern Railway, which maintained its dual resort and dock function. Promenades, theatrical shows, beach huts and hanging gardens continued to attract the crowds, and Felixstowe remained a popular family resort for much of the twentieth century. There were frequent through trains from London, and in 1929 the LNER included the town in the list of seaside resorts visited by the Eastern Belle Pullman.

However, things were changing. Little by little the dock complex began to dominate, a process that accelerated after World War II with the development of the container terminal. Today this massive enterprise has absorbed much of the area that was formerly devoted to tourism. The Beach station is no more but, away from the container port, plenty of the late Victorian resort atmosphere does survive. Local trains from Ipswich still carry passengers to Felixstowe. However, the bulk of the traffic on the line is container-based, making the Felixstowe branch one of the busiest in Britain. No doubt Colonel Tomline was pleased by the success of his dock complex, but the scale of operations today must be way beyond even the wildest dreams of that typical Victorian entrepreneur.

▼ *In the late 1950s a local Felixstowe-bound train hauled by an LNER tank locomotive pauses at the signal box controlling Westerfield junction, while the driver has a conversation with the signalman. From its early days the Felixstowe branch was consistently busy, so the management of traffic on the route was always a demanding job.*

◄ *By 1984, when this picture was taken, Felixstowe Beach station was long closed, and the noisy crowds that once arrived on excursion trains were a distant memory. Today's traffic is all containers. Here, one of the regular container services leaves the port complex, under the control of a class 47 diesel locomotive.*

▼ *It is hard today to imagine that Felixstowe was once a very smart resort, with some of the grandest hotels on the east coast. This 1920s postcard shows the Ordnance, a typical late Victorian hotel, tastefully set among gardens, and offering its guests comfort, relaxation and plenty of tennis.*

G. E. R.

From _____
TO
FELIXSTOWE
TOWN

ORDNANCE HOTEL, FELIXSTOWE.

WESTERFIELD JUNC.

MARKS TEY TO SUDBURY

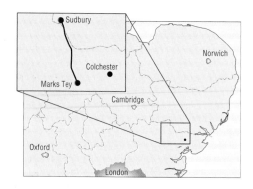

Some branches still in use today are in fact the truncated remains of former through routes, turned into branch lines by the closures of the Beeching era. A typical example is the 12-mile line from Marks Tey to Sudbury, now in many ways a classic branch line but originally part of an East Anglian network linking Colchester with Bury St Edmunds, Haverhill, Cambridge and Bishop's Stortford. The main line of this network was the Colchester, Stour Valley, Sudbury & Halstead Railway, authorized in two parts, in 1846 and 1847, and opened progressively from 1849. A link to Cambridge was completed in 1865.

These predominantly rural lines did much to open East Anglia up to both passenger and freight traffic in the mid-nineteenth century. Construction was simplified by the relatively flat nature of the landscape, requiring few major engineering features but a very large number of level crossings. Each crossing was originally accompanied by a cottage for the crossing-keeper, and many of these are still to be seen, decades after the railways they guarded have vanished.

Much of the network was taken over by the Great Eastern Railway in the 1880s, and from 1923 it all passed into the control of the LNER. Increasingly under-used and under threat from the late 1950s, the line saw its first closures in 1962 but, for reasons that now seem unclear, the short section from Marks Tey to Sudbury was kept open. So, in effect, another branch line was added to the map.

▼ *In the 1950s elderly locomotives were still to be found at work all over Britain, but particularly on minor and rural lines. Here, at Marks Tey in 1958, two Great Eastern veterans, Class J15 goods locomotives, are hard at it, having lived through World War I, the LNER era and ten years of British Railways. Very few such antiques were to survive the next ten years.*

▲ Marks Tey, on the London to Colchester line, is the start point for the Sudbury branch. This 1950s view shows the bay platform still used by trains for Sudbury. The Colchester-bound train at the platform could have come from Bury St Edmunds or Cambridge.

G. E. R.

From

TO

SUDBURY

MARKET HILL, SUDBURY.

▲ Sudbury is an ancient market town, famous for cloth and as Gainsborough's birthplace. At its heart is Market Hill, dominated by St Peter's Church, seen here in a 1908 postcard before it was ruined by cars. The message is intriguing: 'Rose & I are spending a few days here. Are you not surprised?' A secret romance?

91

G. E. R.

From

TO

CHAPPEL AND WAKES COLNE

The survival of the branch has also facilitated the setting up of the East Anglian Railway Museum, at Chappel & Wakes Colne station, and the Colne Valley Railway, a preserved railway centred on the restored Castle Hedingham station on the old Chappel to Haverhill line.

Constable country

The main attraction of the Sudbury branch is the landscape through which it passes, on the borders of Essex and Suffolk. This is the landscape of the Stour, whose blend of gentle hills and farmland broken by woods and river valleys is pure John Constable. Above it all are the huge East Anglian skies, bringing that particular sense of light and colour that defines Constable's paintings. On the right kind of day, the view from the train window offers delightful glimpses of Constable, and with it echoes of the East Anglian countryside of the pre-railway age. At the same time, it is a journey rich in railway sights, such as the well-preserved station and buildings at Chappel and the traditional level crossing, complete with cottage, at Bures. Constable died before the railway had made any significant impact on the landscape, but his frequent depictions of the locks and barges on the Stour navigation suggest an enthusiasm for the modern world. Had he lived another ten years he would probably have been impressed by the major feature of the Sudbury branch, the great viaduct at Chappel, whose thirty-two tall arches were built between 1847 and 1849 from over seven million bricks made at Bures. Engineering on this scale was unusual in East Anglia and has in any case mostly been lost. It is lucky, therefore, that the line still crosses this magnificent structure, exciting when seen from the train over 70ft above the ground, and spectacular when seen from the valley below. Peter Bruff was the engineer responsible, and he could not have asked for a better monument.

▼ *Constable is the key word for the Sudbury branch. The railway, and with it the splendid Chappel viaduct, came after the death of the great East Anglian artist, but throughout the journey there are glimpses from the train window of the countryside that he loved and painted so extensively in the early years of the nineteenth century.*

▲ *In the autumn of 1996 a modern Class 153 railcar pauses at Bures. This type of vehicle is now universal to railways all over Britain, bringing to an end the regional characteristics that gave railways their appealing individuality. Only the liveries change, depending on which operating company holds the franchise. On this day no passengers get on or off, a common event on rural lines. At peak times, however, the Sudbury branch is busy, with commuters going to London and children going to school.*

NORTH NORFOLK RAILWAY

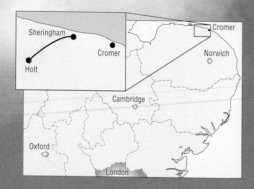

The railway history of East Anglia is a complex and sometimes impenetrable subject, featuring a large number of companies. Independently and together, they managed to spread a dense network of mostly rural lines across the map. One of these companies was the Eastern & Midlands Railway, whose lines from Melton Constable to Norwich and to Cromer via Sheringham were opened in 1887. Five years later, much of this network was brought together by the Midland & Great Northern Joint Railway, which took control of 182 miles of lines, spread across the northern half of East Anglia. It survived the transition to the LNER and subsequently to British Railways, but pruning began in the 1950s and by the mid-1960s, less than a hundred years after the trains had arrived, most of rural Norfolk was once again without a railway service. Freight lingered on in a few places until the 1980s. The only rural route to be spared the axe, for some reason, was the line from Norwich to Sheringham via Wroxham and North Walsham.

Today, thanks to the North Norfolk Railway, the idiosyncratic and determinedly independent M&GNJR is more than just a memory. This preserved line has brought back to life the section of the M&GN between Sheringham and Holt, and has created in the process a railway that combines the flavour of that company with the great days of the LNER. The route of the line is through the typical Norfolk landscape of heathland, woods and coast, under a huge expanse of sky. The start of the journey is in Sheringham's magnificently restored station, a short walk and light years away from the minimalist platform and shed that is the terminus for scheduled services from Norwich. From here the line runs along the coast to Weybourne, a small and formerly remote station now dwarfed by the company's workshops. It turns inland to the old-fashioned and elegant market town of Holt.

The North Norfolk Railway operates a variety of steam and diesel services, which offer visitors the chance to experience a traditional taste of Norfolk, as well as the true spirit of the rural railway.

▲ *A re-born Sheringham station is the start of a journey on the North Norfolk Railway. Platform paraphernalia and enamel signs in Eastern Region colours set the scene.*

▼ *Ancient diesel railcars are as much a part of the preservation scene as steam locomotives. The North Norfolk regularly operates a little 1958 four-wheel rail bus, seen at the time of its introduction as a possible saviour for under-used branch lines. Despite its somewhat bouncy ride, this vehicle, seen here beside the coast, offers excellent views of the Norfolk landscape.*

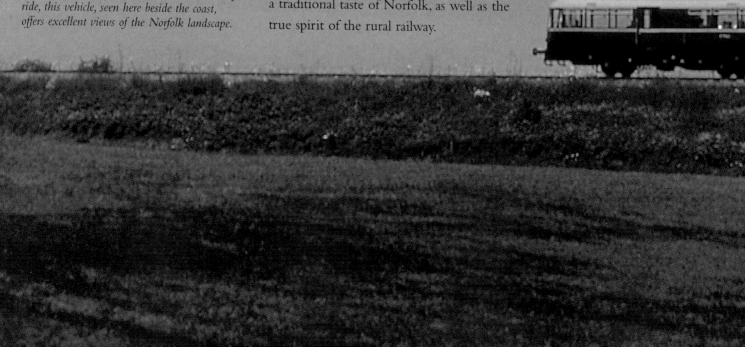

Fishermen at Work Baiting, Sheringham.

► Known for its lobsters and crabs since the eighteenth century, Sheringham has long been a busy fishing centre, despite having no harbour. Here, in 1908, local fishermen bait their pots.

▼ Sheringham station under British Railways, when much of Norfolk's rural network was still in place. A diesel multiple unit waits to depart.

► This Edwardian postcard illustrates the great days of the Midland & Great Northern Junction Railway, as an express from Cromer to Leicester and Birmingham races along the single track near Weybourne, hauled by one of the characteristic coffee-coloured locomotives. Nowadays the preserved trains of the North Norfolk Railway use this track, but at a very much slower speed.

TOY TRAINS

Detailed engineering models of trains exist from the early days of railways but, strangely, simple toys did not appear until the mid-nineteenth century. The earliest examples, made in Germany from printed tin, were crude and had little in common with real trains. Train sets powered by clockwork, designed to run on rails rather than carpets, and accurately modelled, appeared at the end of the century, again mostly made in Germany. British-made sets were pioneered by Bassett-Lowke, but the real breakthrough came in the early 1920s when Frank Hornby launched his first 0-gauge trains, the start of an ever-expanding clockwork and electric range that brought railways into homes throughout the land. The smaller 00 gauge followed in the late 1930s, again inspired by Continental models. Since then the toy train has been an essential part of childhood. For many, the basic train set inspired a long-lasting passion for model railways, and a lifelong enthusiasm for the real thing.

▼ *Model railways, and toy trains, come in all sizes and a variety of scales, the detail and finish determined by price. For most people, the train set is laid out, played with and put away again, but others build permanent layouts, often in a shed or the attic. Many also aspire to a garden railway. This 0-gauge Southern Railway example, photographed in 1949, was clearly the owner's pride and joy.*

▲ *Model villages, popular tourist attractions since at least the 1920s, very often included model railways. This 1950s postcard shows a train crossing a fine bridge at Bekonscot Model Village in Beaconsfield, Buckinghamshire.*

▲ *This charming Edwardian photograph shows a small boy with a magnificent toy train, including a goods wagon advertising the Eccles Co-Operative Society, a surprising touch in what is obviously a studio setting. It is likely the train was a photographer's prop, but the child seems more interested in the camera.*

▶ *Bassett-Lowke was one of the great names for toy trains and model engineering. Their extensive catalogues had much to offer the armchair enthusiast.*

◀ *Hornby's extensive 0-gauge range of colourful tinplate trains, with its vast choice of accessories, was the ideal toy railway. Here, laid out in a garden setting, is a Hornby interpretation of a branch line terminus somewhere in eastern England in about 1949.*

▶ *Railway images were very popular in the 1920s and 1930s in children's books and as subjects for children's illustrations. Typical is this early card showing Bo-Peep and her sheep being firmly turned away from a toy train.*

BASSETT-LOWKE LᵀᴰD

An Attractive All-purpose Model
STANDARD 6-COUPLED TANK

● ALL ELECTRIC MODELS, FOR THE PURPOSE OF GOOD CONTACT, HAVE
WHEELS OF CAST IRON INSTEAD OF ANTI-FRICTION METAL

YOU should have at least one of the railways' "Maids of All Work" on your layout. We are proud of the handsome appearance of our 0-6-0 model, which is available in both L.M.S. and S.R. livery, besides the L.N.E.R. model illustrated. It is a powerful model, fitted with a first-class mechanism, either clockwork or electric, and the provision of outside cylinders enhances its external appearance considerably.

SPECIFICATION	● PRICES.
	Length over buffers 9¾ in. Weight 2 lb. 4 oz.
FRAMES AND SUPERSTRUCTURE.—Pressed from lithographed steel plate.	
CLOCKWORK MOVEMENT.—Best quality 6-coupled with reversing gear and brakes. Cast wheels, of anti-friction alloy.	No. 3305/0. Clockwork .. .. .. £5 17 6 Purchase Tax £1 7 1
ELECTRIC MOVEMENT.—D.C. model. Standard spur drive mechanism 12 volts. Cast iron wheels are fitted.	No. 5305/0. Electric spur drive 12 volts
FINISH.—L.M.S. and L.N.E.R., black with red lines. S.R., black with green lines. Suitable lettering and numbering.	

Page 8

COWS · ONLY · ON THIS · TRAIN MADAM

St Margarets to Buntingford

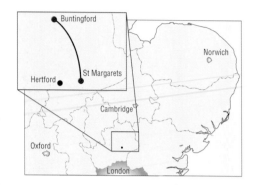

The Ware, Hadham & Buntingford Railway was one of many mid-Victorian lines that never fulfilled the hopes of its local supporters and never repaid the money invested in it. Authorized in 1858, it took five years to build and it was only thanks to considerable help, first from the Eastern Counties Railway, and then from that company's successor, the Great Eastern, that the line – which in the event never went to Ware – was completed. It was always worked by the GER, which took control in 1868. The route, from St Margarets on the Broxbourne to Hertford line, meandered through pretty countryside and small villages. Traffic was never heavy, and the branch was an early victim of competition from buses. In 1960 diesel railcars replaced steam, in an effort to reduce costs and make operations more flexible, but to no avail. The branch was closed to passengers in November 1964, and freight traffic came to an end just under a year later.

The route was attractive and rural, giving the railway classic branch line appeal. After crossing the Lee north of St Margarets, it followed the course of the Ash to Hadham, crisscrossing the river and its wooded banks. Beyond Hadham, a more open landscape took it to the winding valley of the Rib, which it followed to Buntingford. After the line's closure, much of the infrastructure was removed – hastened by vandalism – and so not much remains to be seen. Part of the lower section is now a footpath, and the surviving parts of the riverside routes can be explored from accompanying roads. Braughing and Buntingford stations still exist, as private houses.

▼ *In 1959, a few years before the line was closed, an old LNER tank engine is ready to depart from Buntingford on the slow, 13-mile journey to St Margarets via six intermediate stations. Passengers on this winter's day will be few and far between, but the riverside route will look pretty in the soft morning sunlight. The substantial station, seen in the distance, is now a house, but everything else has vanished beneath modern development.*

▼ One of the smaller intermediate stations was at Standon, photographed here on a quiet day in the 1950s. The timber buildings were demolished following vandalism after the line's closure, and today nothing of this remains.

G. E. R.
Buntingford

▼ Braughing was the next stop on the branch line after Standon, in the Buntingford direction. This card, posted in the 1950s, shows the old timber-framed grammar school. As is so often the case, the scene is completely deserted, except for a couple of dogs.

Braughing, Old Boys' School.

SAXMUNDHAM TO ALDEBURGH

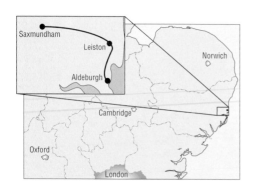

▼ *Aldeburgh station in the 1950s was a busy place, judging by the neatly lined up barrows. However, not many people have arrived on the train from Saxmundham, so there is plenty of time for staff to chat.*

In the middle of the nineteenth century, independent companies were building railways all over East Anglia. Two that were particularly active in Suffolk were the Eastern Counties and the East Suffolk, whose branch lines to Framlingham, Leiston and Snape were opened on 1 June 1859. The following year the branch from Saxmundham to Leiston was extended to Aldeburgh. Later, all these came under the control of the Great Eastern Railway. This ambitious company, which was subsequently absorbed into the LNER, was keen to develop holiday traffic in East Anglia, so excursions and through trains were run from London to Aldeburgh until 1939. To make the most of this traffic, Aldeburgh was given a smart station with a train shed and a long, single platform.

A resort since the early nineteenth century, Aldeburgh was famous for its Georgian terraces, fishermen's cottages, wide shingle beach and, above all, for its old-fashioned air of traditional seaside elegance. The railway contributed further to the town's popularity. Also important in railway terms was the development of Thorpeness, a holiday village built from scratch before World War I with a range of houses in a variety of styles, a large lake and a golf course. Naturally Thorpeness acquired a station, but it was a long way from the village, the railway's route at that point being well inland. Despite the continuing popularity of these resorts, the opening of the opera house at nearby Snape in 1948 and the continuing presence of a large engineering works with its own rail yard at Leiston, traffic on the Aldeburgh line declined steadily through the 1950s and 1960s, and closure came in September 1966.

▲ In June 1963 a two-coach, diesel railcar waits at Aldeburgh for the few passengers still using the railway. Freight traffic had stopped in 1959, and a crane is at work demolishing the remains of the goods yard.

G. E. R.

From _____

TO

ALDEBURGH

Aldeburgh, South Parade.

▲ In 1909, when this postcard was sent, Aldeburgh was a popular but undeveloped resort whose beach was evidently still used, for the most part, by local fishermen rather than by the visitors who are here seen ambling along South Parade.

Servicing the energy industry

Although it is now closed to passenger traffic, the Aldeburgh branch has been maintained as far as Leiston for the nuclear flask traffic for the Sizewell power stations, the first of which opened in 1966. Currently this amounts to an average of one train a week. As the track and infrastructure are still intact, including old-fashioned hand-operated level crossings with wooden gates, it is easy to follow this part of the route on nearby minor roads. With so much still in place, and yet with the atmosphere of a branch line of the past, there is a kind of Marie Celeste feeling about the line. For example, Leiston station has a platform and sidings, and the remains of station lamps, but the building itself is a private house and there are no passengers.

From Leiston south to Aldeburgh, things are much harder. There is not much to see of the line as it runs across farmland and then over the coastal heathland. Much of the route is inaccessible, but part of it is now a nature reserve. Visible but overgrown is the platform of Thorpeness's remote station, barely noticed by the passing golfers. Long gone are the old coach bodies that used to serve as station buildings, and in Aldeburgh itself there is little to see in railway terms.

▲ In the evening light, the station lamps should be coming on, but this one at Leiston has not been lit for forty years. Yet it is still there, along with the bracket that carried the totem name plate, now on display in some enthusiast's collection, perhaps.

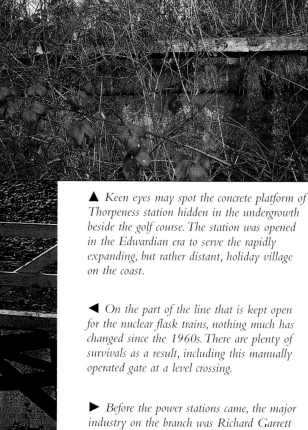

▲ Keen eyes may spot the concrete platform of Thorpeness station hidden in the undergrowth beside the golf course. The station was opened in the Edwardian era to serve the rapidly expanding, but rather distant, holiday village on the coast.

◀ On the part of the line that is kept open for the nuclear flask trains, nothing much has changed since the 1960s. There are plenty of survivals as a result, including this manually operated gate at a level crossing.

▶ Before the power stations came, the major industry on the branch was Richard Garrett of Leiston, engineers and makers of all kinds of steam engines. The large factory had its own railway connection, as is shown here in this remarkable, pre-World War I photograph of the staff pouring out for their tea break.

▼ At Leiston the rails are bright and the platform is complete but overgrown. At the time of writing, about one train a week passes through and it does not stop for passengers. The station buildings are now a private house. Beyond the crossing, the line continues as far as the loading bay for the Sizewell nuclear flask trains, just outside Leiston.

RAILWAY GARDENS

So widespread was the enthusiasm for gardening in late Victorian Britain that even the railways were inspired. The North Eastern and Great Western companies were pioneers in encouraging staff to decorate stations, both to make them more appealing for passengers and to instil a sense of local pride, but others soon followed. Others soon followed, and before long railway gardens became the subject of local and national competitions, judged by directors, senior officials and garden experts. Stations great and small all over Britain took part, some establishing fearsome reputations as winners year after year. Gardening skills became a necessary qualification for a station master, who typically revealed great ingenuity in creating his own combination of raised beds, tubs, hanging baskets, topiary, seats, fishponds and dovecotes, not to mention gnomes and other inhabitants. Colourful and elaborate planting schemes often incorporated the station name. Although it is seen much more rarely now, the station garden still exists and, even post-privatization, the station garden competitions live on.

▲ This Edwardian station master clearly knew where his priorities lay. No doubt his burgeoning planting schemes were dependent upon the greenhouse at his house near by, where colourful cottage and exotic species were carefully raised, ready for the annual competition.

▼ Railway gardens were not limited to the platform area or the immediate station surroundings, and sometimes were simply decorative lineside features. Nor were they solely the province of branch and minor lines. Here is a mainline garden, on the old Somerset & Dorset Joint Railway.

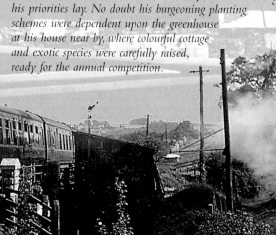

▲ The beautiful, well-tended garden at Stogumber station is a secluded oasis of tranquillity on the West Somerset Railway.

▼ Some station gardens were famous far beyond their immediate locality. A typical example was Ropley, in Hampshire, whose platform topiary left little room for passengers, luggage trolleys and normal railway comings and goings. In the early 1950s a local train drifts into the station, now part of the Watercress Line. Also preserved is the topiary, still flourishing on the same platform.

KELVEDON TO TOLLESBURY

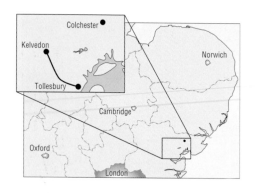

The grandly named Kelvedon, Tiptree & Tollesbury Pier Light Railway was a typical creation of the 1896 Light Railways Act, authorized in 1901. The first 9 miles were slowly built through rural Essex to the estuary of the river Blackwater and finally opened in October 1904. Three years later, the line was extended to Tollesbury pier. Cheaply built and operated, the railway featured stations with low platforms, no signalling to speak of, and a variety of ancient rolling stock acquired second or third hand. Tickets were issued on the trains. Run somewhat reluctantly by the Great Eastern Railway, it was at first successful, transporting jam, from Wilkinson's Tiptree factory, and prodigious amounts of shellfish harvested by the local fishing fleets. It is recorded that on one day the railway carried 110,000 oysters from Tollesbury to Kelvedon. It was this fish traffic that gave rise to the line's popular name, the 'crab and winkle'. However, the real hopes for the line, based on expanded use of Tollesbury pier, never materialized, partly because silting of the estuary made the pier inaccessible to ships of any size. The 1920s saw the end of traffic to the pier, which then quietly decayed until the floods of 1953 swept it all away. On the rest of the line, traffic was maintained through the LNER era and into the early years of British Railways, but by 1951 everyone had had enough, and passenger services were withdrawn. For some years, freight services were maintained as far as Tiptree, mostly for the jam factory, but these ended in October 1962. Since then the railway has all but vanished. Sold off piecemeal, the trackbed has mostly been ploughed out, and only a filled-in bridge, short stretches of low embankment and the occasional Station Road in a rural village reveal that there ever was a railway to Tollesbury.

▼ *The Tollesbury branch was well known for the random and often ramshackle nature of its rolling stock. This is apparent in this mixed-stock train in the 1950s, hauled by an old North Eastern Railway tank locomotive still in LNER colours.*

► In the autumn of 1949 two enthusiasts pose with the guard for a photograph in one of the line's bogie coaches, a vehicle used formerly on the Wisbech & Upwell tramway. They seem to be looking forward to a journey that was by then a relatively rare experience, for the railway saw few passengers in the last years of its life.

▼ At Kelvedon there were two stations, linked by a spur line. One was on the main line and the other, for the Tollesbury Railway, was on a lower level. Changing trains was, therefore, never straightforward. This 1948 photograph shows the light railway's Kelvedon station, where a train has just arrived from Tollesbury.

► Built cheaply across a flat landscape and mostly closed half a century ago, the Tollesbury branch has left few traces. Nearly all the trackbed has been ploughed back into the fields from which it came. A rare survival is a short stretch near Tolleshunt D'Arcy, a village in which there is a Station Road but no sign of a station.

▲ Having never fulfilled its promise, the extension to Tollesbury pier was abandoned in the 1920s. It was then left to its own devices, overgrown and quietly decaying, until the remains were swept away in the 1953 floods. Today there is little to indicate that Tollesbury ever had a railway.

MELLIS TO EYE

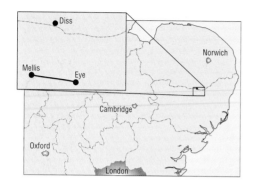

In 1848 the Eastern Union Railway opened its station at Mellis, on the main line south of Norwich. This inspired the citizens of Eye to seek their own branch line connection, a goal finally attained nearly twenty years later when the Mellis & Eye Railway opened its 3-mile line. From the start, it was operated by the Great Eastern. The GER introduced various economies to try to make the line viable, and these were continued by the LNER after 1923. However, a branch as short as this was never going to generate sufficient passenger traffic, and in 1931 passenger services were abandoned. Freight was a different matter, for Eye had a brewery, maltings and a busy cattle market, all of which ensured a steady supply of traffic, justifying a large goods yard with plenty of sidings. Indeed, the branch remained open for freight for over thirty years, finally closing in July 1964.

Exploring the remains of the Eye branch is a bit of a challenge. Being short and having no significant engineering features, it made little impact on the flat landscape. Some sections of the trackbed have been ploughed out, but the route can still be followed from the accompanying minor road. At Mellis, main line trains to and from Norwich roar past, but there is no station. Surviving buildings indicate where the junction was, and traces of trackbed can be seen on the way to Yaxley, an intermediate station opened by the GER to try to encourage traffic. Near by, a turreted bridge in engineering brick carries a minor road over the vanished line. The bridge that carried the A140 is long gone, but by the road is a short section of embankment, isolated like some ancient earthwork in the wide expanse of surrounding farmland. More traces can be seen on the approach to Eye, but Eye station and its once busy goods yard are now an industrial estate.

▼ *In the early 1960s the needs of local industries ensured that there was still some freight traffic on the Eye branch. Here a diesel shunts open wagons in the goods yard at Eye station. Today the site is occupied by an industrial estate, into which some buildings from the railway era are incorporated.*

G. E. R.

Eye

Eye Church and Grammar School.

OCULUS IN COELUM

SUFFOLK

EYE

▲ *Mellis station was never very significant, existing as it did mainly to serve the branch line. This view, on the main line looking towards Norwich, shows the station after the ending of passenger services in 1931. From then until closure, the Eye branch survived entirely as a freight line.*

▼ *Little of the Eye branch remains to be seen today. One of the few structures to survive is this bridge carrying a minor road near Yaxley. Impressively built from engineering brick, it features powerful fortress-like towers. A short stretch of trackbed leads up to it, but beyond it there is just a level field, with no sign of any railway ever having been there.*

▲ *Eye is an old market town that has had borough status since 1408. It had a castle, a priory and a great windmill, and it still has a fine fifteenth-century church, whose grand tower dominates the town. Adjacent to the church is the timber-framed grammar school, an enjoyable contrast in Suffolk building types.*

BRANCH LINE RAILCARS

Railcars, or self-propelled single coaches that could be driven from either end, came into use in the late Victorian era. They were built for branch lines and minor railways where facilities were limited and costs had to be kept to a minimum. Steam-powered models were often known as rail motors. From the 1900s various railcars were built with petrol or oil engines, succeeded in the 1920s by a range of rail vehicles based on road buses. More important were the diesel railcars of the 1930s, forerunners of the modern diesel multiple unit.

PRESTATYN TO DYSERTH BY MOTOR.

▲ *This old postcard shows a typical railcar of the pre-World War I era, as operated by the L&NWR on the Prestatyn to Dyserth branch in north Wales. Designed for use on lines with halts that did not have full platforms, this steam-powered railcar was equipped with its own set of folding steps.*

G.W.R. EXPERIMENTAL STREAM-LINED HEAVY OIL RAIL CAR.

◀ *The most famous of all railcars was this streamlined, diesel-powered vehicle introduced by the GWR from 1934. Designed to carry sixty-nine passengers at speeds up to 60mph, it made a significant contribution to the modern image projected by the company in the 1930s. These railcars remained in use for many years, and paved the way for the development of modern models by British Railways from the 1950s.*

▶ *The most basic type of railcar was the rail bus, a vehicle widely used on light railways in Britain and Ireland from the 1920s. The example here was operated on the Weston, Clevedon & Portishead Light Railway, a local company opened in 1897 and extended in 1907. Following liquidation, the line was taken over by Colonel Stephens, and this view at Portishead was taken during his reign. The line closed in 1940.*

▲ *Awaiting passengers for the Looe branch at Liskeard in 1969, this railcar is an example of the diesel multiple units introduced by British Railways from the 1950s. Designed to be operated from one driving position either singly or linked together as multiples, these vehicles, and their successors, have for decades been the mainstay of Britain's rural routes.*

▶ *Many railway companies produced their own versions of the railcar before and after World War I. This shows the Glasgow & South Western's rail motor, designed specially for short branch lines. There were a number of strange-looking hybrids such as this, precursors of the push-pull units that were so widely used from the 1920s.*

◀ *Some railcars were truly primitive, just a road vehicle simply converted to run on rails. This rail bus, with its charabanc-style raked seats, was operated for a short time by the Caledonian Railway along a section of the Ballachulish branch between Connel Ferry, near Oban, and Benderloch. A railway vehicle in the most rudimentary sense, lacking even buffers, it is somehow managing to tow a goods wagon, perhaps for passengers' luggage.*

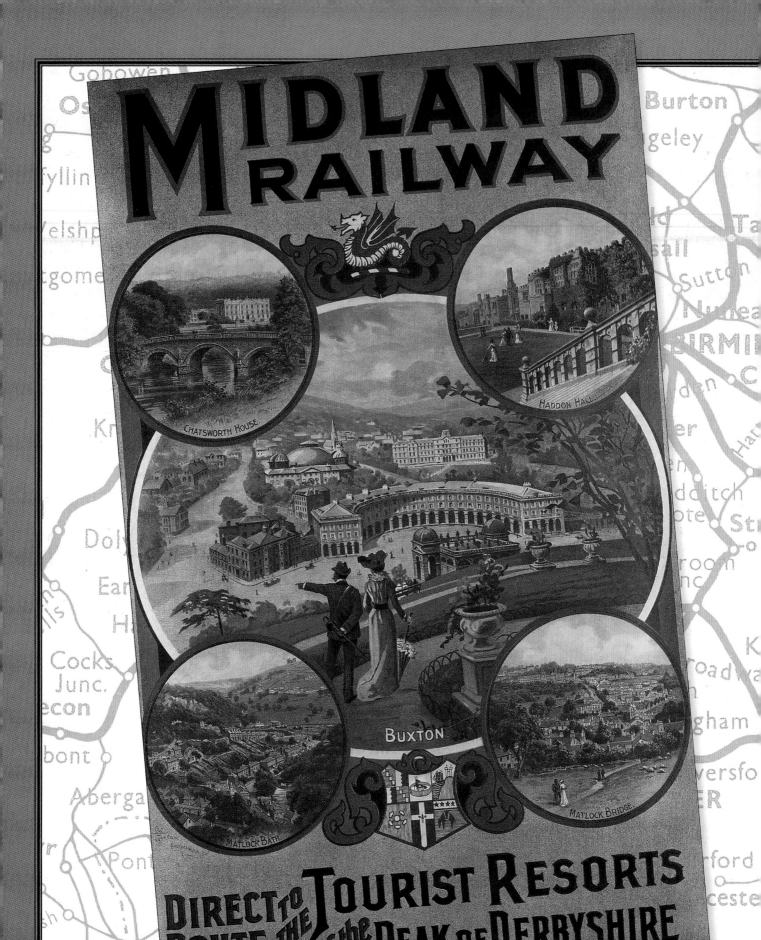

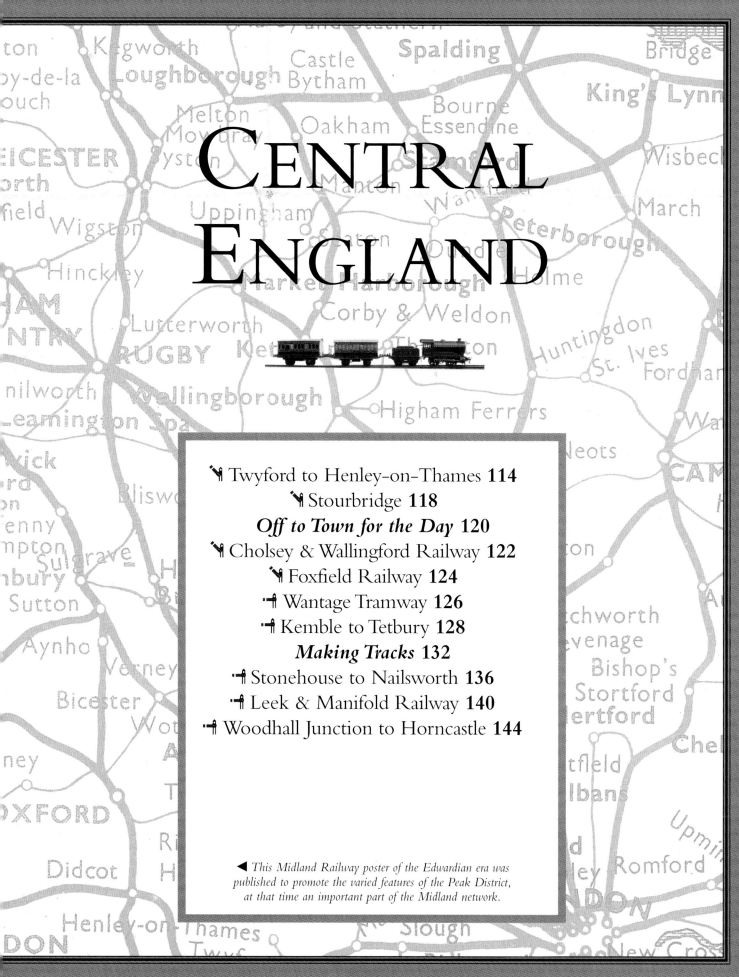

CENTRAL ENGLAND

Twyford to Henley-on-Thames **114**
Stourbridge **118**
Off to Town for the Day **120**
Cholsey & Wallingford Railway **122**
Foxfield Railway **124**
Wantage Tramway **126**
Kemble to Tetbury **128**
Making Tracks **132**
Stonehouse to Nailsworth **136**
Leek & Manifold Railway **140**
Woodhall Junction to Horncastle **144**

◄ *This Midland Railway poster of the Edwardian era was published to promote the varied features of the Peak District, at that time an important part of the Midland network.*

TWYFORD TO HENLEY-ON-THAMES

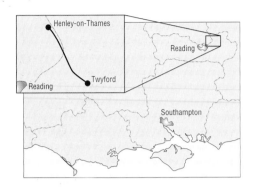

When the branch line from Twyford to Henley was opened by the GWR on 1 June 1857, it was a short, single-tracked, broad gauge railway serving a couple of sleepy Thames-side villages. Things then began to change fairly rapidly, thanks very largely to the railway. With increased leisure and the popularity of boating, cycling and rambling, there was inevitably a considerable demand for outings to towns and villages in the Thames valley. Henley and Shiplake fitted the bill perfectly, and so the train service flourished. Henley had, of course, been known for its regatta since 1839, but the railway broadened the town's appeal and extended its season as a Thames-side resort. In addition, the opening of the railway encouraged commuting to London and so, in the latter part of the Victorian era, Henley grew from a small village to a substantial town. By 1898 the track, already relaid to the standard gauge, was doubled, the stations at Henley and Shiplake were enlarged and a new one was opened at Wargrave. An extension to Marlow was planned, but this idea was abandoned by the GWR because of strong objections from rowing clubs, concerned about the impact of this proposed extension on the famous regatta course.

▼ *In 1954 Shiplake was still a real station, complete with signal box, staff and a splendid lineside garden, seen here as a riot of summer colours. A young boy – perhaps he is a train enthusiast or perhaps he is waiting for a friend or relative – watches a grimy GWR pannier tank haul its short train into the platforms.*

▲ *Established in 1839 and given its royal status in 1851, Henley's regatta is now a major international event in the sporting calendar. In 1886, when this photograph was taken, it was relatively parochial but none the less attracted thousands of spectators.*

▼ *Henley's Royal regatta has long been both a social and a sporting occasion. In 1939 it was described as 'vivid with bright dresses and sunshades, a blaze of rich colour mirrored in the water and set off by the cool greens of the trees'. In the Edwardian era, as this postcard shows, dressing for Henley was already a social necessity for the crowds who came by special trains.*

Henley on Thames Railway Station, Arrival for Regatta.
Sidney H. Higgins, Publisher, Henley on Thames.

115

Matters remained the same through to the British Railways era. In the early 1960s there were over thirty-five weekday trains each way, with through services to and from London at peak times for the commuter traffic. However, this was a period of change for railways generally, and Henley was no exception. The 1960s saw the branch reverting to single-track operation and the ending of freight services. The goods yards were removed and, to satisfy the commuters, were replaced by car parks. Commuters also ensured that direct London services survived until 1977.

A Thames-side journey

The journey is only a little over 4 miles, but it is still an enjoyable branch line experience. Twyford has a typical 1880s GWR station, with the Henley services operating from a bay platform. A sharp curve takes the train away from the station, and then the line runs more or less due north. At Wargrave it meets the Thames and, soon after, crosses the river by Shipley lock. From here the train is never far from the Thames and there are plenty of riverside scenes to enjoy between Shiplake and Henley. Henley's station is right beside the river, centrally placed for the town. Formerly a grand station with a train shed and long platforms designed to handle excursion traffic, it has recently been rebuilt on a smaller scale. It is now more in keeping with the simple shuttle service operated by modern diesel railcars, successors to the famous streamlined railcars of the 1930s that were developed by the GWR for branch lines such as Henley.

▼ *Even in the 1950s Henley's grand late Victorian station saw plenty of traffic. The shuttle to and from Twyford, still a steam-operated service, was continuous, with several trains an hour. There were through trains to and from London at peak hours, and excursions during the season to this popular resort. At this point, there was still plenty of freight, and the station goods yards were busy.*

▼ *The Henley branch has seen many types of branch line train. By the 1970s the standard vehicle, as on so many branch and rural lines, was the single-coach diesel railcar, seen here on the sharp curve that leads into Twyford station.*

STOURBRIDGE

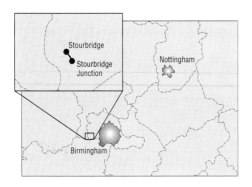

One of the most surprising branches still in use today is the short line from Stourbridge Junction to Stourbridge Town, an unexpected survivor from the devastation of the 1960s and still every inch a classic branch. The railcar comes and goes every few minutes from the bay platform at the Junction station, which itself has an enjoyably old-fashioned atmosphere, underlined by the signal box and the old GWR benches. This branch, opened by the GWR in 1879, has a long history of single-vehicle operation, by railmotors, auto-trains and generations of diesel railcars. In 1880 it was extended beyond Stourbridge Town station to join an old tramway, with sidings serving rolling mills, a gas works and other local industries. It was probably this freight traffic that kept the branch open in the 1960s. Now all that is long gone, buried beneath the bus depot, and the line ends at the buffers at the recently rebuilt Town station, a proper brick building in an attractive style, complete with ticket office and patterned brick platform. The journey, which takes only 3 minutes to cover the ¾-mile route, is well worth the detour. The railcar, complete with driver and guard, swings away to the left along pleasantly grassy tracks as it leaves the Junction station, and then drops steeply down into a secret cutting, flanked by old suburban houses. It goes under a bridge, kinks through some curves and then stops at Town station. At 75p (at the time of writing) for a day return, this must be the cheapest branch line journey in Britain.

▼ *The signal and the extra tracks have gone, and the low-level entrance and ticket office has been rebuilt, but in most other ways Stourbridge Junction still looks much the same. Here, in 1955, a GWR auto-train waits to depart for the short journey to Stourbridge Town, maintaining a tradition unchanged for decades. The modern diesel railcar leaves from the same platform. Little today is different, and even the bench just visible on the left is still there.*

▶ In Edwardian England, Stourbridge was a pleasant market town and still detached from Birmingham, although the smarter suburbs had begun to encroach. In 1909, when this card was posted, the Promenade Gardens, complete with bandstand and fountain, was a fine place to be on a warm Sunday, far away from Black Country industries and the local glassworks. The message is curious: 'Seem to be stranded here for the present. All cars are crowded.'

PROMENADE GARDENS STOURBRIDGE

◀ In 1975 Stourbridge Junction still had its signal gantry and British Railways enamel station name, dating from the 1950s. Only the diesel locomotive gives away the date. Today the signal box is still in use, but everything else has gone. The branch curves away beyond the signal on its descent to Stourbridge Town.

▼ The shortest, and possibly the cheapest, genuine branch line that is still part of the national network ends at Stourbridge Town's handsome and relatively new brick station, still fully staffed. It is a pleasant surprise on such a minor line not to be greeted by the standard vandalized and unattended bus-type shelter.

OFF TO TOWN FOR THE DAY

▲ *Eagerly awaiting the train at some country station, and proudly posing for the camera, this smartly dressed Edwardian group is off on an outing. There are children of all ages and plenty of adults, but the nature of the group is not clear, and there are no clues as to their destination. The only certainty is that they are going to have a good day out.*

What the railway offered above all else was a new sense of freedom for people who hitherto had rarely travelled beyond the bounds of their own town or village. From the very beginning, railway companies offered excursions and day trips, and the habit of the day outing became well established in the Victorian era, encouraged by the great exhibitions, the expansion of markets and shops, the popular sporting events and particularly by the Bank Holidays Act of 1871, which made it easier for families to spend a day out together, in town or by the sea or in the country.

The day trip appealed to men, to families, to social clubs, to school and Sunday school parties as well as to women, who now felt safe to travel on their own or with other women friends. The branch line network helped to make all this possible by offering both a range of services to local towns and places of interest, and through connections to the big cities.

▼ *It is a summer's evening in 1932 at Bawdrip halt, a remote station in Somerset. Two ladies, well dressed and carrying heavy bags, walk away down the platform after a shopping trip to Bridgwater, or perhaps Taunton. At this unmanned station deep in the Great Western's rural network, the guard will now have to close the doors and send the train on its way.*

▲ Resolven was a station to the north of Port Talbot, in that dense mass of railways that once filled the valleys of south Wales. A family group, very well turned out and widely ranged in age, is about to board the train, one of the new steam railcars that the GWR had developed for use on branch and minor lines. A wedding, or some other family celebration, is probably the reason for the outing on this sunny day in about 1905.

◀ The train is about to depart. A young lady, looking slightly nervous but nonetheless elegant, is setting off on a day trip, perhaps visiting friends. Her clothes indicate that this photograph dates from the 1950s. At that time, 'ladies only' compartments were still available, a legacy of the Victorian era.

CHOLSEY & WALLINGFORD RAILWAY

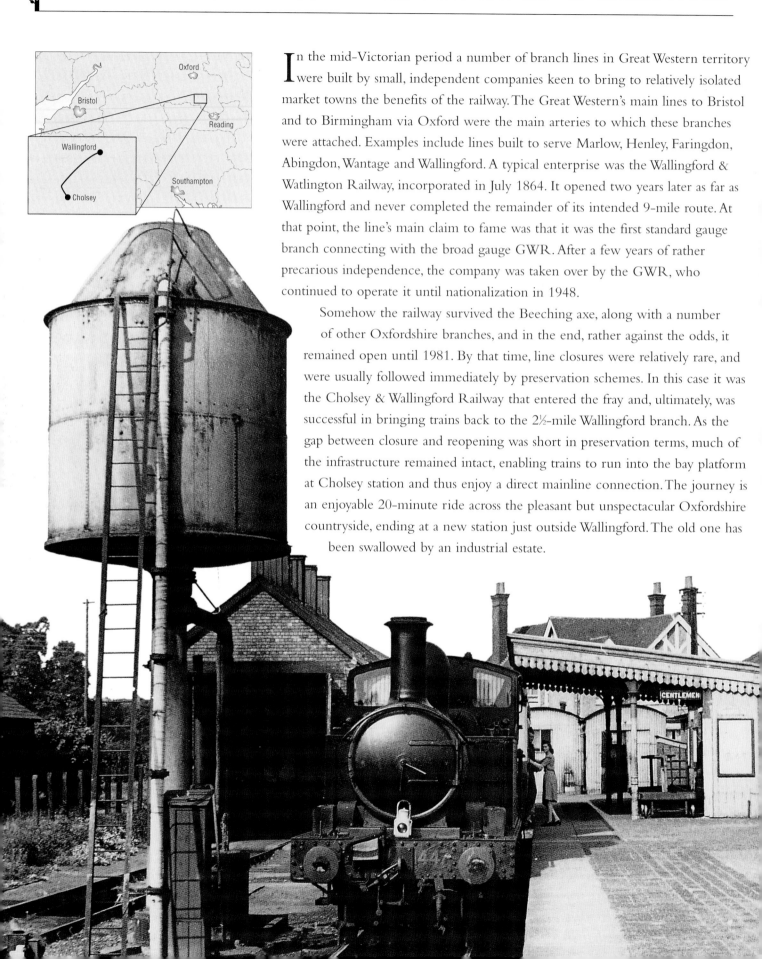

In the mid-Victorian period a number of branch lines in Great Western territory were built by small, independent companies keen to bring to relatively isolated market towns the benefits of the railway. The Great Western's main lines to Bristol and to Birmingham via Oxford were the main arteries to which these branches were attached. Examples include lines built to serve Marlow, Henley, Faringdon, Abingdon, Wantage and Wallingford. A typical enterprise was the Wallingford & Watlington Railway, incorporated in July 1864. It opened two years later as far as Wallingford and never completed the remainder of its intended 9-mile route. At that point, the line's main claim to fame was that it was the first standard gauge branch connecting with the broad gauge GWR. After a few years of rather precarious independence, the company was taken over by the GWR, who continued to operate it until nationalization in 1948.

Somehow the railway survived the Beeching axe, along with a number of other Oxfordshire branches, and in the end, rather against the odds, it remained open until 1981. By that time, line closures were relatively rare, and were usually followed immediately by preservation schemes. In this case it was the Cholsey & Wallingford Railway that entered the fray and, ultimately, was successful in bringing trains back to the 2½-mile Wallingford branch. As the gap between closure and reopening was short in preservation terms, much of the infrastructure remained intact, enabling trains to run into the bay platform at Cholsey station and thus enjoy a direct mainline connection. The journey is an enjoyable 20-minute ride across the pleasant but unspectacular Oxfordshire countryside, ending at a new station just outside Wallingford. The old one has been swallowed by an industrial estate.

▼ Like most preserved lines, the Cholsey & Wallingford Railway operates Santa Specials during the Christmas season. Here, on a mild winter's day, one of the railway's small fleet of tank locomotives hauls a substantial train of three carriages and a brake van across the flat Oxfordshire farmland.

◄ A touching scene on the single platform at Wallingford in the early 1960s, as a girl says a fond farewell to her boyfriend, who may have been the only passenger on the train. He is off to Cholsey along the short branch, and then to who knows where.

▲ An important town since the Roman period, Wallingford once boasted fourteen churches. It suffered during the Civil War, being the last Royalist stronghold to surrender. However, as this old postcard suggests, there is still plenty to see, including the seventeenth-century town hall and the Georgian terraces around the market place.

FOXFIELD RAILWAY

Branch lines built purely or primarily for industrial and freight use have been a feature of the railway network since the start of the nineteenth century. Of these, the vast majority were built to service collieries in the various coalfields all over Britain, the transport of coal being for many railway companies a vital source of revenue. Collieries often had their own railway systems, many of which were absorbed into the National Coal Board on nationalization. A typical colliery branch is the one opened in 1893 from Blythe Bridge to Foxfield, in the north Staffordshire coalfield. Closed in 1965 together with the pit, this line has since been reopened as a preserved railway with a definite industrial emphasis. At the time of preservation, scenes of the kind shown below were still common, but since the devastation of the coal industry in the 1980s the colliery railway is almost extinct.

This has given Foxfield an even greater relevance, for it now represents not just a part of railway history, but also a vanished way of life. It depends on the carriage of passengers between Caverswall Road in Blythe Bridge, and Dilhorne Park in Foxfield, but many of the vehicles, the locomotives and, of course, the setting, maintain the memory of a great local industry.

▶ *In July 2003 a former GWR tank, in the colours of the National Coal Board, hauls a line of mineral wagons past the remains of Foxfield colliery, re-creating the once familiar conjunction of pithead winding gear and steam railway. The Foxfield Railway maintains a vital link with the social history of the area.*

▲ *Foxfield Railway's terminus at Caverswall Road is adjacent to Blythe Bridge station. As this is on the national network, access is easy. In addition to the preservation of a once self-contained railway system, Foxfield has been able to reflect its early history by assembling large numbers of wagons and a significant collection of industrial locomotives dating back to the 1870s.*

WANTAGE TRAMWAY

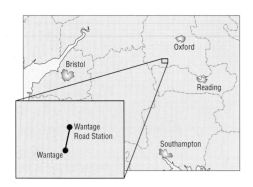

The Great Western Railway's line was built well to the north of Wantage, leaving the town without a railway. The GWR opened a station called Wantage Road, 'Road' being a nineteenth-century euphemism for a station miles from the town it claimed to serve. The citizens of Wantage were not satisfied and campaigned for a branch line. In 1875 the Wantage tramway was opened. Cheaply built, mostly along the edge of the main road, this basic railway was initially horse-drawn. Soon steam trams of various kinds arrived, and then in 1878 the company purchased the locomotive 'Shannon', which was destined to stay with the tramway throughout its existence. Once into its stride, the company operated an efficient service, meeting trains at Wantage Road and carrying ever-increasing amounts of freight, notably coal, corn, groceries and building materials. In 1905 nearly 55,000 passengers were carried in elaborate tramcar-like vehicles, and 5,000 wagons were moved up and down the line. Successful and profitable, the tramway even paid its shareholders a generous dividend. After World War I, however, everything changed. Road transport became more competitive, and in 1925 passenger carrying ended. Freight traffic continued, and the line remained in profit, albeit at the expense of track and vehicle maintenance. Everything came to an end on 21 December 1945, when the last train staggered along the by now almost impassable track. After closure, the remains of the tramway were quickly obliterated.

▼ *On 22 October 1873 a public meeting was called in Wantage under the chairmanship of Colonel Sir Robert Loyd Lindsay to campaign for a tramway link between the town and the GWR's main line, 2½ miles to the north. This led directly to the building of the tramway, which opened in October 1875. Always distinctive and full of character, the Wantage Tramway ran beside the road for much of its route. In its early days, it relied on steam tram engines, of the kind seen below.*

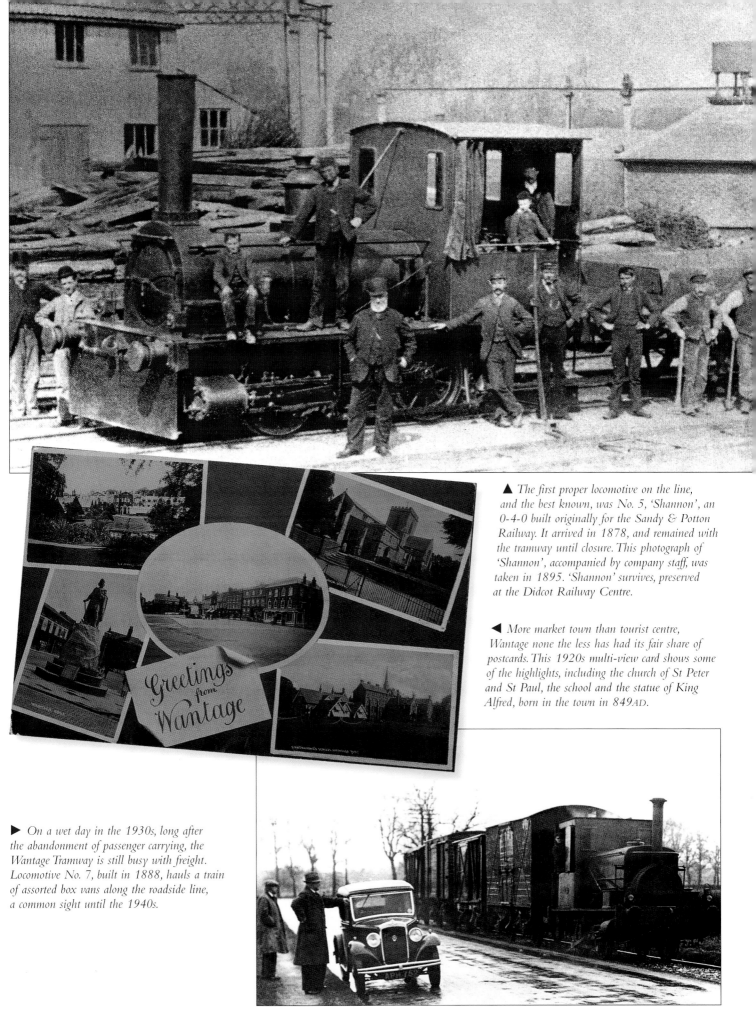

▲ The first proper locomotive on the line, and the best known, was No. 5, 'Shannon', an 0-4-0 built originally for the Sandy & Potton Railway. It arrived in 1878, and remained with the tramway until closure. This photograph of 'Shannon', accompanied by company staff, was taken in 1895. 'Shannon' survives, preserved at the Didcot Railway Centre.

◄ More market town than tourist centre, Wantage none the less has had its fair share of postcards. This 1920s multi-view card shows some of the highlights, including the church of St Peter and St Paul, the school and the statue of King Alfred, born in the town in 849AD.

► On a wet day in the 1930s, long after the abandonment of passenger carrying, the Wantage Tramway is still busy with freight. Locomotive No. 7, built in 1888, hauls a train of assorted box vans along the roadside line, a common sight until the 1940s.

KEMBLE TO TETBURY

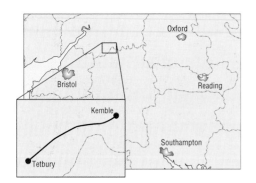

Kemble station, now much used by commuters to London, is a richly decorative stone building in a vaguely Tudor style with many Cotswold references. The station has long been famous for its gardens, a tradition that lives on, albeit with plastic flowers in the hanging baskets. It was built by the GWR in 1872, replacing an earlier wooden structure whose temporary nature was determined by difficulties with a local landowner who insisted that no permanent passenger facilities could be built on his land unless he was given an impossibly large sum of money. This wooden platform allowed passengers for Cirencester to change at Kemble. After the death of the landowner, the present station was built, its grandeur somehow making up for the shortcomings of its more basic predecessor.

In 1889 a second branch, to Tetbury, opened, making Kemble a three-way junction. While the Cirencester branch curved away to the east, the Tetbury branch started at a bay platform on the western side of the station. At the end of the Tetbury platform, a huge water tank, which still survives at the station, supplied not only locomotives but also the GWR railway works at Swindon, some 14 miles away.

The Tetbury branch was typical of countless Victorian minor railways in that it was built with enormous local enthusiasm and never fulfilled the hopes of its supporters. Its route, passing through the undulating Gloucestershire countryside, included a surprising number of minor halts, some of which were characterized by such unusual names as Jackament's Bridge and Trouble House. Other stops, Rodmarton and Culkerton, were opened to serve minor settlements. In the case of Rodmarton, the village lay some distance away from the railway.

▼ *Overcrowding was never a problem on the Tetbury branch. In May 1963, with closure on the horizon, one of the little four-wheel diesel railcars developed by British Railways for use on minor branches waits at Culkerton while the driver checks whether there are any passengers lurking in the Gents. By this time, few passengers were using the branch, and the stations had a neglected air.*

▲ *In the 1950s the branch was still operated by steam trains, one of which is waiting at Tetbury station in the distance. This shows the approach to the station, past the engine shed and water tower. Today, the site survives, with railway features intact.*

Despite its rural nature, the branch enjoyed a long life, first in the care of the GWR and subsequently with British Railways, which tried to keep it open by using little diesel railcars. In 1961 there were ten trains each way on weekdays, taking 25 minutes to cover the 7-mile journey. Most of these trains were timed to connect with London expresses. In 1964 British Railways gave up the struggle, and closed both the Tetbury and the Cirencester branches.

Following the branch today

Today, the line from Kemble to Tetbury is easily followed from the adjacent A433. The route is clearly marked by a line of trees and occasionally by a low embankment on the hillside and, sometimes, in a valley to the south. Intermediate halts and bridges have gone, but sections are walkable on paths that, although they are unofficial, are clearly regularly used.

The railway entered Tetbury on a meandering route, following a minor stream. The station, which was set in a valley below the town, has gone, but the site survives as a car park, pleasantly surrounded by meadows, footpaths and the occasional bench. Old sleepers are set into the paths. Overshadowing it all is a towering goods shed in dark engineering brick, now abandoned and decorated with graffiti. A short walk up the hill leads to Tetbury's town centre, where handsome houses and elegant streets surround the old town hall and covered market.

▼ *Tetbury station was a typical GWR building with a wide platform canopy. By the early 1960s, when this photograph was taken, it had seen better days, reflecting the low level of maintenance applied to loss-making branch lines at this time. The little diesel railcar is ready to depart for Kemble, nearly empty as usual.*

▲ *A famous feature of Kemble station is the large and decorative water tank, which supplied both locomotives and the railway works at Swindon. The platform for the Tetbury branch was to the left, beyond the mainline platform.*

▼ *Westonbirt School and the famous arboretum are just to the south of Tetbury. This aerial view shows the main building, originally Westonbirt House. Designed by Lewis Vulliamy, it is a magnificent 1860s interpretation of late sixteenth-century domestic architecture on a grand scale.*

CHIPPING STEPS, TETBURY.

WESTONBIRT SCHOOL, TETBURY, G

379.

▲ *The Chipping, or market steps, have been a famous Tetbury feature since the late eighteenth century. Years ago farm hands and domestic staff offered themselves for employment on market day here. This old card, posted in 1924, says: 'This is a darling place.'*

MAKING TRACKS

In the Victorian era railway companies began to produce maps and guidebooks to encourage wider usage of their lines. By the 1920s this was a major business, with railway companies offering the public through-the-window journey guides and a vast range of walk and ramble booklets based on local stations. The closures of the 1960s left thousands of miles of abandoned trackbed all over Britain, much of which quickly reverted to agriculture and private ownership. In the 1970s books, and organizations devoted to the exploration of old railways, laid the foundations for the establishment of a national network of footpaths, cycle tracks and bridleways on old railway lines. The charity Sustrans, founded in Bristol in 1977 and driven by a desire to overcome problems posed by the relentless growth of road traffic, campaigned for the building of a network of cycle routes over Britain, many based on former railways. Its Bristol & Bath Railway Path was the starting point for the 10,000-mile network nearing completion.

RAMBLES in ESSEX

BRITISH RAILWAYS

1/-

▼ *The Bridport branch today is typical of many branch lines after closure: the route is a mix of official footpath, unofficial footpath whose use is tolerated by owners, and inaccessible private land. Here, the line curves towards Powerstock, a section popular with walkers.*

▶ *The 'Big Four' established the tradition of publishing walks guides in the 1920s and this was continued by British Railways. With its colourful cover, clear text and simple maps,* Rambles in Essex, *issued in 1950, is a typical example.*

BROMLEY: KESTON UPPER LAKE

RAMBLE N.

A Zigzag Walk from Hayes to Westerham

IT takes about half-an-hour to get from London Bridge to Hayes, and as you emerge from Hayes station you may well gasp at the sudden and complete change from town to country.

After climbing out of the station-approach you find yourself at once on a common of heather, bracken and gorse, with a bewildering diversity of footpaths going in all directions. You may spend a very happy hour or two searching among its two hundred acres of loveliness for the Neolithic hut-circles which prove how densely populated this now lonely land was in Pre-Roman days.

When I was last there in the month of March, there were brimstone and tortoiseshell butterflies

— 92 —

— 93 —

▲ *SPB Mais, a well-known writer and rambler, produced a number of guides for the Southern Railway in the 1930s.* Southern Rambles, *published in 1938, featured a range of walks based around the suburban network, including this 'Zigzag Walk from Hayes to Westerham'.*

▶ *East of Castle Douglas the route of the Kirkcudbright branch is, briefly, an official footpath, a section that includes a fine stone bridge. Within a mile or so, the trackbed is private and inaccessible. Always seek permission in advance from the landowner to walk on sections in private ownership.*

▼ *One of the many long-distance cycle routes established by Sustrans is C2C, which crosses northern England from coast to coast. Part of it is along the former Cockermouth, Keswick & Penrith Railway. Here, the path crosses a former viaduct near Threlkeld.*

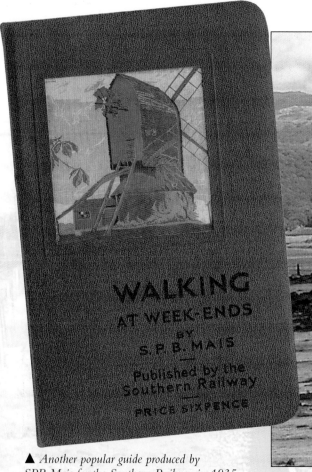

▲ Another popular guide produced by
SPB Mais for the Southern Railway in 1935
was Walking at Week-ends, a selection of
longer walks based on SR stations in southern
England, from Dover to the New Forest. The
striking cover illustration was by Gregory
Brown, a well-known poster artist of the time.

▼ The New Forest path and cycleway follows part of the former line from Brockenhurst westwards
to Ringwood. A good surface, a fine stone railway bridge adorned with greenery, and grazing New
Forest ponies make this an attractive route, ideal for families.

▲ *The Mawddach Trail follows the route of the former Barmouth to Dolgellau railway right alongside the splendid Mawddach estuary, an ideal, and level, introduction to some of the best scenery in west Wales.*

▲ *Many routes interconnect and many have been specially prepared to be easily accessible from major cities and conurbations. Typical is the Upper Don Trail, west of Barnsley in Yorkshire. Here, the railway origins of the route are obvious from the long, straight cutting. Clear signage is an important principle of the national cycle network.*

STONEHOUSE TO NAILSWORTH

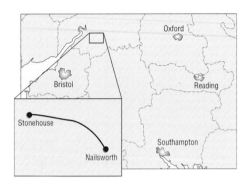

Although they were deep in GWR territory, Gloucester, Stroud and Bristol were also part of the Midland Railway's tentacle-like network. Indeed, the Midland had ambitious plans to invade Southampton via the Cotswolds, and the line to Nailsworth might have been the first stage of that assault. In the event, all that was ever built was the short branch from Stonehouse, constructed by the independent and locally sponsored Stonehouse & Nailsworth Railway and opened in 1867. As was so often the case with these small companies, there was too much optimism and not enough money, so the railway was in financial difficulties within a few months of opening. The Midland Railway stepped in and a take-over was arranged in 1878. At the time, Stroud and Nailsworth, traditional wool towns, were major centres of textile production, and the railway seemed to be viable. In fact, freight did turn out to be significant, keeping the branch open until 1966. Passenger services had ended in June 1949, along with most of the old Midland Railway interests in the region, including their station at Stroud, Wallbridge. Long before Beeching, British Railways could see that running competing services over the same route was likely to be a waste of time, money and resources.

Nailsworth is a pleasant old town, squeezed into the meeting point of three steep river valleys. All that river water supplied power for the mills, but it also made access difficult. The branch line, therefore, was built close by the road that already ran along the narrow valley.

▼ *In 1965 the regular pick-up goods train, hauled by a British Railways Standard locomotive, drifts past Ryecroft station. The platform has gone, the goods shed is abandoned and the whole station looks sad and run down. At this point there had been no passenger traffic for sixteen years, although a few enthusiasts' specials had penetrated the branch.*

▲ *This view of the goods yard at Nailsworth was taken in the early 1960s. An elderly locomotive is shunting wagons into the goods shed, an indication of continuing freight activities towards the end of the line's life. Today the distant two-storey goods warehouse and the railway hotel survive, but everything else in the photograph has gone, buried beneath modern housing developments.*

From railway track to cycle track

Today, the line is still there, converted into a cycle track. This offers an enjoyable and secluded route between Stonehouse and Nailsworth, shielded from the noisy road and the developing industrial and domestic buildings by woodland, which in spring is heavy with the scent of wild garlic. Although it was a short, relatively minor branch line, the railway builders invested in substantial stations, at Ryecroft, Dudbridge, Woodchester and Nailsworth. Of these, the most magnificent was at Nailsworth, a richly decorative High Victorian Gothic palace in local stone, with plenty of Cotswold details. Luckily, this survives. Along with its platform, it is in private hands but is easily appreciated from the cycle track and the surrounding roads. The building has many attractive features, notably the arched entrance arcade in Romanesque style, whose short columns and flowery capitals give it the look of a medieval cloister. The cycleway, well below the level of the station and platform, follows the old goods lines into what was a substantial goods yard. Here, a large brick warehouse survives, overlooked by a handsome stone building that is decoratively labelled Station Hotel. This goods yard was to have been the starting point for the Midland Railway's line southwards towards Southampton.

▼ *This photograph captures perfectly the atmosphere of a freight-only branch line near the end of its life. The grassy track, the hissing locomotive waiting while the fireman opens the old crossing gate, the abundance of encroaching nature and the little vegetable patch in the foreground with the beans growing well all add to the picture of a way of life gone for ever.*

Near Nailsworth Glo'stershire.

▲ 'Near Nailsworth, Glo'stershire': an artistic view of the wooded river valleys that meet at the town. Although the image is probably Edwardian, the card was posted in 1935. Today, parts of the cycleway along the route of the branch have a similar feeling, but cyclists are unlikely to encounter a milkmaid.

▲ Nailsworth station survives as a private house. This splendid stone-built structure in a kind of Cotswold Gothic style underlines the Victorian enthusiasm for even minor railways.

▼ An old LMS locomotive shunts the daily goods at Dudbridge in 1963. For nearly twenty years from 1949, the Nailsworth branch and the link to Stroud from Dudbridge were freight-only lines, and scenes such as this were commonplace. Dudbridge station is now a private house.

LEEK & MANIFOLD RAILWAY

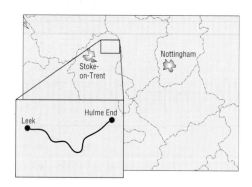

▼ *This 1990s photograph shows the curving route of the former Leek & Manifold Light Railway as it follows the river Manifold along the valley. Also apparent in this view is the particular quality of the rugged limestone landscape, its unchanging nature and its inaccessibility. It is only by walking or cycling along the route that all this can be appreciated.*

The Leek & Manifold Valley Light Railway, to give this quaint line its grand title, was born out of the late Victorian enthusiasm for using railways to open up parts of Britain that were hitherto inaccessible to visitors. The Manifold Valley, part of a wild landscape on the borders of Derbyshire and Staffordshire, was just such an area, first penetrated in 1899 by the building of a line from Buxton to Ashbourne. Already in existence was the North Staffordshire Railway's Churnet valley line through Leek, and that company, somewhat reluctantly, was persuaded to support two new railways, first a branch eastwards from Leek to Waterhouses and the stone quarries at Cauldon Low, and second a narrow gauge line along the Manifold valley from Waterhouses to Hulme End.

Building started, and in 1904 the 9-mile-long, 2ft 6in gauge line opened up the glorious scenery of the valley to visitors. They came, but not in their thousands, for the railway was a classic case of a line from nowhere in particular to nowhere in particular, via some splendid scenery. With eight intermediate stops, the train took 40 minutes to cover its short route. As a result, it never fulfilled its hopes and never repaid its debts. In 1923 it was absorbed, along with the North Staffordshire Railway, into the LMS, which was not very enthusiastic either.

◀ *A major feature on the route is Thors Cave, accessible on a footpath from the station below. This 1907 postcard is one of a series published by the North Staffordshire Railway to promote their routes.*

▲ *The Leek & Manifold Railway opened on 27 June 1904. The first train, comprising both its locomotives and most of the rolling stock, was clearly overcrowded.*

In March 1934 the LMS closed the Leek & Manifold, which was still operating with the two locomotives, four passenger carriages and eight freight vehicles that it had started with thirty years earlier. After closure the line mouldered away until, in 1937, the route was presented by the LMS to Staffordshire County Council. They converted it into a footpath, surely setting an early precedent for this now popular way of bringing a railway back to life.

A spectacular limestone gorge

The well-surfaced route now sees far more visitors than it ever did in its railway days, and in the season it is crowded with cyclists and walkers enjoying what is still the only way to see the Manifold valley. A cycle-hire base at Waterhouses makes exploration of the line straightforward.

From its start at Waterhouses, by the handsome wooden building that once served the standard-gauge connecting line from Leek, the route is steadily downhill, allowing ample opportunity to admire the surrounding hills with their rock formations and caves, many of which are accessible via footpaths. At Wetton Mill, refreshments are available. Beyond Wetton a short tunnel, now on a minor road, is a useful reminder of the route's railway past. From here, the line followed a more open valley to its terminus at Hulme End, where the old station building is now a visitor centre and shop. At this northern end of the branch line there was never any railway connection, and little to see or do, so most visitors probably had a brief stroll then took the train back up the valley. Today, walkers and cyclists do exactly the same, discovering, of course, that it is uphill all the way back.

▼ *The railway's two locomotives worked all the trains throughout the lifetime of the line. Here, in 1933, a few months before closure, locomotive No. 2, 'JB Earle', is serviced at Hulme End. Even at this stage, everything is still smart and tidy, a reflection of the faithful following that this eccentric railway enjoyed.*

▲ While the railway was built primarily for passengers, it did its best to carry freight, and played its part in the national process of milk collection and distribution. Here, at Ecton in 1910, heavy milk churns are manhandled on to the single box-wagon behind the locomotive, a vital service for isolated farms.

◄ Hulme End's former station, the northern terminus of the line, is now home to the Manifold Valley Visitor Centre. The well-restored building houses a shop, information centre and displays on the history of the railway. The style of the timber building is typical of the railway's distinctive architecture, little of which survives.

► The path built along the trackbed in 1937 has always been popular and is maintained to a high standard. It is used by walkers and cyclists of all ages throughout the year, and on summer weekends can be very crowded. Here, in winter, there is still plenty of activity. The path is popular with families for, at 9 miles, it is relatively short and the good surface makes for easy cycling. Riding down from Waterhouses is quick and easy, but the return can be hard work, especially into the wind.

WOODHALL JC TO HORNCASTLE

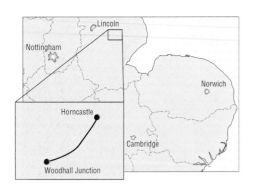

Many Victorian branch lines were entirely local enterprises, built to satisfy the demands of the industry and business in the area and run with a degree of independence. The Horncastle Railway was just such an enterprise, set up in 1854 by local businessmen who wanted to link their town to the national network. Initially they asked the Great Northern to build the line but, when that company refused, they went ahead and did it themselves. The 7-mile branch to the main line at Kirkstead (or Woodhall Junction, as it was later known) opened in 1855. Despite the pessimism of the Great Northern, which actually worked the line and took fifty per cent of the receipts, the railway regularly made a profit and the local shareholders regularly received dividends. Until 1915 there was even a through coach from London. Confronted with this unusual situation, the Great Northern naturally changed its tune and tried on several occasions up to 1920 to buy the company, but the Horncastle Railway remained independent until it was absorbed into the LNER in 1923.

▼ *It is the late 1950s and passenger services have been withdrawn, but the branch is still busy with freight. A dirty and unkempt Ivatt Class 4 locomotive waits to take the local mixed freight out of Horncastle yard. This kind of activity was a regular sight until the closure of the line in 1971.*

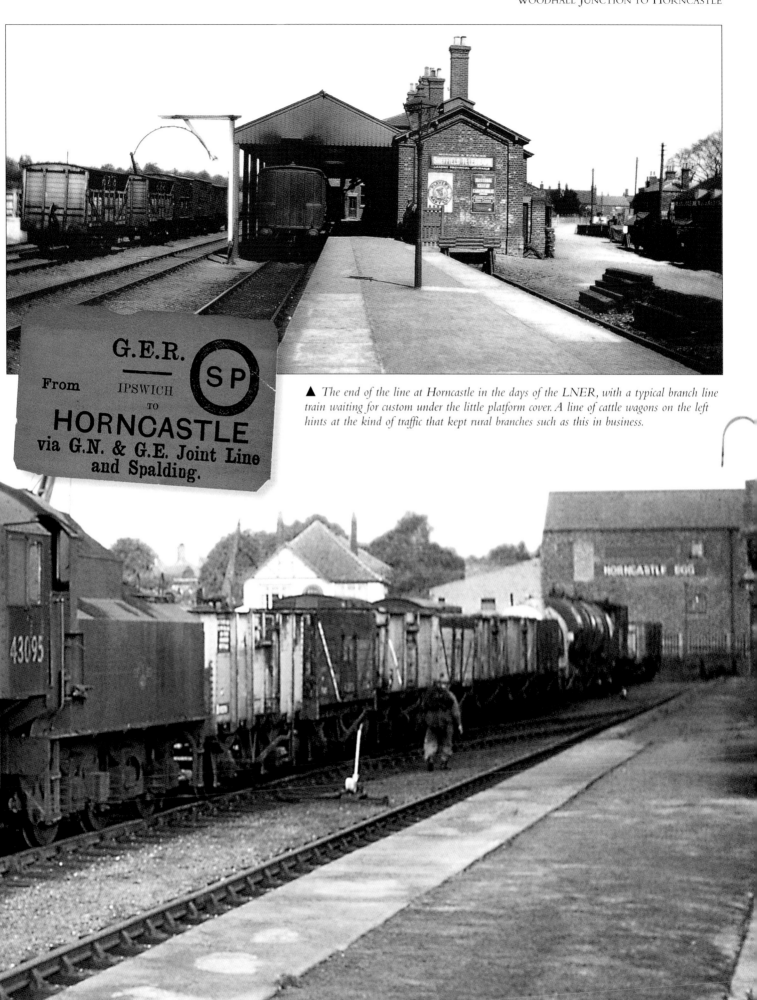

G.E.R.
SP
From   IPSWICH
TO
HORNCASTLE
via G.N. & G.E. Joint Line
and Spalding.

▲ *The end of the line at Horncastle in the days of the LNER, with a typical branch line train waiting for custom under the little platform cover. A line of cattle wagons on the left hints at the kind of traffic that kept rural branches such as this in business.*

The secret of the line's success was considerable freight traffic and the burgeoning popularity in the late Victorian period of Woodhall Spa as a resort. The exploitation of health-giving bromo-iodine waters (discovered by chance during a search for coal) and the rising enthusiasm for golf put the place on the map. By the 1940s all this was over, and the railway was in decline. Services were worked by old survivors from the days of the Great Northern, including a set of articulated carriages and various locomotives that had seen better days. British Railways carried on for a few years more and then withdrew passenger services in September 1954, despite strong local opposition. The branch remained open for freight until 1971.

▼ *An Edwardian view of Woodhall Spa station, with its rural main street. A cart piled with baggage is on its way to or from one of the smart hotels catering for the popular appeal of the spa's waters.*

The Spa Trail

Since closure, the branch has been given a new lease of life as a path for walkers and cyclists, known as the Spa Trail, part of the Viking Way from Oakham to Barton-on-Humber. The trackbed crosses this flat, peaceful landscape, with little else to hint at the comings and goings of the railway in its heyday. Horncastle station is long gone, but Woodhall Junction survives, with other relics of the railway, as a private house.

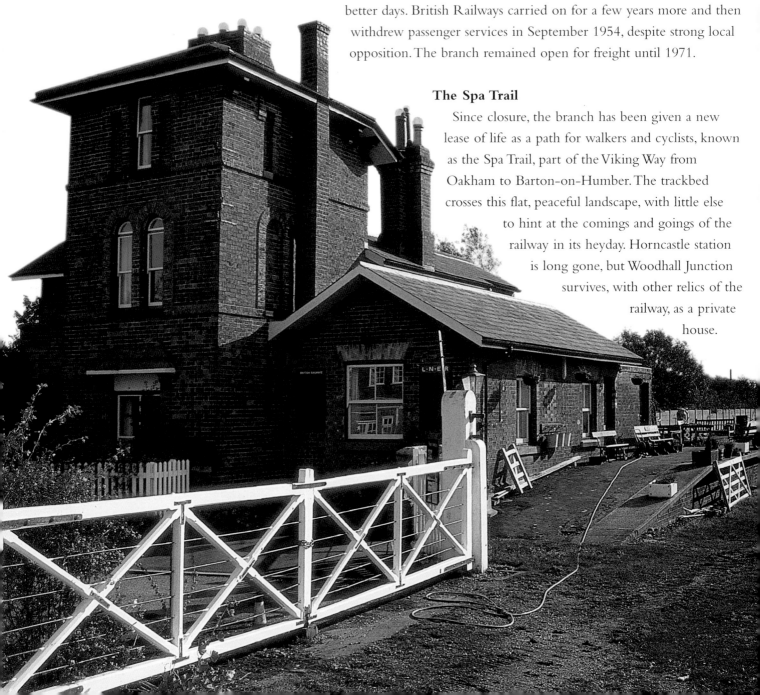

▲ Seen here in winter sunshine and with a light covering of snow, the Spa Trail crosses the open Lincolnshire landscape, marking the route of the Horncastle branch. In other circumstances, a level railway with little significant engineering would probably have disappeared back into the landscape.

EAGLE LODGE HOTEL, WOODHALL SPA.

◀ At Woodhall Junction, the Horncastle branch and the former main line linking Lincoln and Boston live on, except for the track and the trains. The station buildings are now a private home, generously adorned with railway relics.

▲ In February 1910 Mrs Mirrlees, no doubt staying at Woodhall Spa to take the waters, sent this card of the Eagle Lodge Hotel to her daughter, with the message: 'This is where I am staying. Isn't it a smart house.' The development of Woodhall Spa as a health hydro turned the little town into a resort.

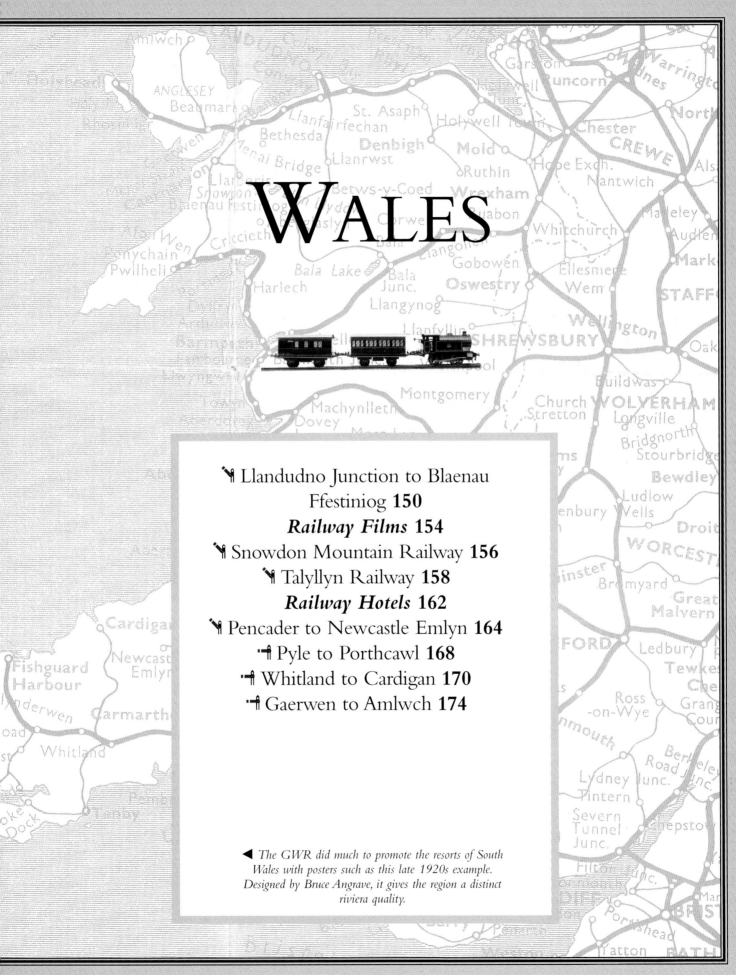

WALES

Llandudno Junction to Blaenau
Ffestiniog **150**
Railway Films **154**
Snowdon Mountain Railway **156**
Talyllyn Railway **158**
Railway Hotels **162**
Pencader to Newcastle Emlyn **164**
Pyle to Porthcawl **168**
Whitland to Cardigan **170**
Gaerwen to Amlwch **174**

◀ *The GWR did much to promote the resorts of South
Wales with posters such as this late 1920s example.
Designed by Bruce Angrave, it gives the region a distinct
riviera quality.*

LLANDUDNO JC TO BLAENAU FFESTINIOG

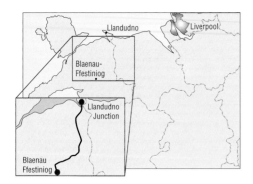

As a centre of the slate industry, Blaenau Ffestiniog has a long railway history. First came the narrow gauge Ffestiniog Railway, whose 13-mile line opened in 1836 to transport slate to Porthmadog harbour. Passenger carrying started in 1865. Next came the Conwy & Llanwrst company's line south from Conwy, a laborious, expensive undertaking that took nearly twenty years to complete, even with the backing of the mighty L&NWR. The following year the GWR's rival line from Bala in the south arrived, its 22 miles having taken ten years to build. So, by the early 1880s, Blaenau had three stations, all inspired by the slate trade. Ironically, by that time the slate industry was in terminal decline. The Ffestiniog closed in 1946, only to be progressively reopened as a preserved tourist line. The Bala line closed in 1961, although a short section was kept open until recently to service the nuclear power station at Trawsfynydd. The Conwy Valley line, as the route between Llandudno Junction and Blaenau Ffestiniog is known, survives primarily as a tourist route serving Betws-y-Coed and other parts of Snowdonia.

Today the Conwy Valley line is one of Britain's most exciting railway journeys. From Llandudno Junction it follows the sweeping curves of the river Conwy, climbing into the hills through a landscape that becomes more dramatic mile by mile. By the 1880s tourism in this part of Wales was developing fast, and the L&NWR encouraged this traffic by building a hotel at Betws-y-Coed. This is still an important stop for visitors and walkers. Beyond Betws-y-Coed the railway follows the steep and rocky valley of the Lledr, forcing its twisting route up through the hills.

▼ *In 1966 steam was still to be found at Blaenau Ffestiniog. A pair of LMS 4MT tank engines await their duties against a typical background of slate spoil tips.*

▼ Blaenau Ffestiniog is a setting without equal in Britain, thanks to the slate spoil landscape. All around are relics of the slate industry and the complex infrastructure of railways that serviced it. Throughout the nineteenth century Welsh slate was exported worldwide.

This was the section that cost its builders dear, in both time and money, for the route required numerous tunnels and viaducts, most notably the seven-arched Lledr viaduct, or Cethyn's Bridge, built in a primitive, rocky style to match its surroundings. The twists and turns come ever sharper, and eventually the train plunges into the long tunnel beneath Moel Dyrnogydd. The noise reverberates from the rough-hewn walls and the passage through the tunnel seems interminable, giving a real sense of burrowing through solid rock. At last, daylight returns and the train emerges into the extraordinary landscape of Blaenau Ffestiniog, a town almost surrounded by broken grey hills, the mountainous piles of spoil from the once thriving slate industry whose remains are scattered all about.

The station is the end of the Conwy Valley line but, as it is now shared by the narrow gauge Ffestiniog Railway, it can be the start of another exciting journey, this time down to the sea at Porthmadog. Together, the lines offer a multi-faceted nineteenth-century railway experience, a route running from coast to coast through mountains that presented the kind of seemingly impossible challenge so appealing to Victorian railway builders.

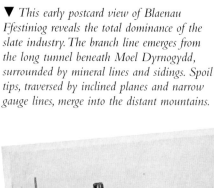

▲ *An old postcard shows the railway's scenic route along the Lledr valley. During this part of the journey the train crosses and re-crosses the fast-flowing river against a backdrop of towering mountains.*

▼ *This early postcard view of Blaenau Ffestiniog reveals the total dominance of the slate industry. The branch line emerges from the long tunnel beneath Moel Dyrnogydd, surrounded by mineral lines and sidings. Spoil tips, traversed by inclined planes and narrow gauge lines, merge into the distant mountains.*

CRIB AU & FRIDD-Y-BWLCH, BLAENAU FESTINIOG.

► *The qualities of the landscape that the Conwy Valley line made accessible to tourists and walkers were actively promoted by the London & North Western Railway, desperate to claw back some of the money poured into the building of the line. A number of official L&NWR postcards show scenes around Betws-y-Coed, including this one of Swallow Falls, posted by a visitor in 1908.*

▼ *In 1998 a modern, single-coach class 153 sprinter has emerged from the long tunnel on the approach to Blaenau Ffestiniog to reach the dramatic climax of a memorable journey.*

SWALLOW FALLS, BETTWS-Y-COED.
L. & N.W. RAILWAY.

RAILWAY FILMS

Some of the earliest films, made in the 1890s, feature trains, often seen from the lineside. Even more popular were sequences shot from the locomotive footplate. One of the first adventure films was about a train robbery. Since then there have been many films in which trains, and railway settings, play major roles. Famous 1930s examples include *Oh! Mr Porter* and *The Lady Vanishes,* while the classic of the 1940s is *Brief Encounter.* There are countless films with important railway sequences, from *Murder on the Orient Express* to James Bond. In Britain, the railway preservation movement has given film makers and television directors ample opportunities for filming railway scenes in period dramas.

▼ ▶ *The only significant branch line film is* The Titfield Thunderbolt, *whose poster, designed by Edward Bawden, is shown below. Made in the 1950s, just as British Railways was about to devastate its local network, it tells the story of the struggle to save a branch line. A splendid social comedy, the film had many memorable performances, but the real hero was the old Liverpool & Manchester Railway locomotive, 'Lion', seen on the right during filming at Combe Hay, near Bath, in June 1952.*

EALING STUDIOS PRESENT
A MICHAEL BALCON PRODUCTION

Stanley HOLLOWAY Naunton WAYNE George RELPH John GREGSON DIRECTED BY Charles CRICHTON

The Titfield Thunderbolt

with Godfrey TEARLE Hugh GRIFFITH Gabrielle BRUNE Sidney JAMES

IN TECHNICOLOR

PRODUCED BY Michael TRUMAN ORIGINAL SCREENPLAY BY T.E.B. CLARKE

FRANK LAUNDER and **SIDNEY GILLIAT** present

FRANKIE HOWERD & DORA BRYAN in

THE GREAT St. Trinian's TRAIN ROBBERY

George Cole
Reg Varney
Graham Crowden
Richard Wattis

Raymond Huntley
Desmond Walter-Ellis
Eric Barker
Godfrey Winn

EASTMAN COLOUR

◀ Loosely inspired by the real great train robbery, which took place in 1963 on the Glasgow to London Royal Mail train, this light-hearted film was filmed on the Longmoor Military Railway in Hampshire.

▶ The Railway Children is probably everyone's favourite railway film, judging by the number of times it appears on television. Beautifully adapted from EE Nesbit's book and filmed on the Keighley & Worth Valley Railway, the film is a railway classic. However, one has to ask what a 1930s GWR tank engine is doing in an Edwardian melodrama set in Yorkshire!

◀ Feature films that need railway sequences frequently make use of the great variety of locomotives and rolling stock on preserved lines all over Britain. Here, a scene for the James Bond film Octopussy is being filmed at the Nene Valley Railway, well known for its collections of European locomotives – in this case a Swedish one.

SNOWDON MOUNTAIN RAILWAY

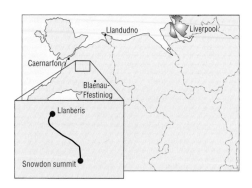

▲ *Still in use are four steam locomotives that were supplied new to the railway in 1896. A further three, built to the same design by the same Swiss makers, were added to the fleet in 1922. There are also four modern, British-built diesels, but these have none of the romance associated with a steam-powered ascent.*

The late Victorian period was marked by a great enthusiasm for mountains, mountain scenery and mountain exploration. Railway companies responded by building lines into mountainous and hilly country, particularly in Wales, the Lake District and Scotland. The next stage, following the Swiss experience now familiar to the many thousands who had explored that country and its mountains by train, was to build railways up the mountains. There were numerous schemes, affecting most significant mountains, including Ben Nevis, but in the end the only true mountain railway on the British mainland was that built to the top of Snowdon. The route to the mountain had been opened up in 1869 by the Carnarvon & Llanberis Railway's branch line and, after some delays, the railway to the top was completed in 1896 by the grandly named Snowdon Mountain Tramroad & Hotels Company. It was a Swiss-inspired operation, using Swiss locomotives and the Swiss Abt system of rack-and-pinion track, by which the locomotive hauls its way up the steep slope with cog wheels that engage in the toothed track. By this means, the 2ft 7½in gauge Snowdon Mountain Railway climbs 3,140 feet in the 4½ miles from Llanberis to the summit. The journey is a truly Victorian experience of epic dimensions, as the ancient, panting locomotive slowly pushes its single carriage up the steep track, accompanied by the clattering of the cogs. And all around is the most spectacular scenery, which even on a wet and misty day is filled with the drama, light and colour so beloved by Victorian painters. The tradition, established in the Victorian era, of taking the train to the top, having some refreshments and then walking down, is still widely followed. The remarkable thing is that the train, and the whole experience, have altered little in the hundred-plus years that have passed since the opening.

▶ *Until the Grouping of the 'Big Four' railway companies in 1923, the Snowdon Mountain Railway was actively promoted by the LNWR as part of its support for its Welsh tourist lines. This romantic view of Snowdon in winter, a time when the trains were probably not running, is from a series of official promotional postcards issued by the LNWR before World War I. The card, posted in 1914, was sent by a boy at boarding school to his mother, giving the usual school news.*

SNOWDON SUMMIT IN WINTER
L. & N.W. RAILWAY.

COPYRIGHT.
SWDN. 19.   ARRIVAL OF TRAIN FROM SNOWDON.   LILYWHITE LTD.,
                                                                            TRIANGLE, HALIFAX.

◀ *Haymaking goes on in the background as a Snowdon train arrives at Llanberis in the 1920s. The passengers, well wrapped up, make their way to waiting cars and to the branch line train back to Caernarfon. This postcard bears a special Summit of Snowdon postmark and the message: 'Wish you were here with us!'*

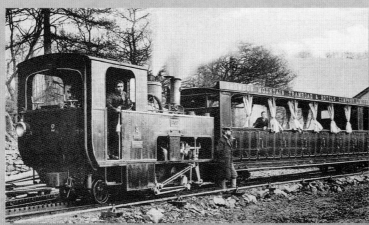

◀ *A view of the Snowdon train soon after the opening of the line, showing the Swiss-built locomotive 'Enid' at the start of what was to be a long life. The delightfully curtained, but windowless, carriage bears the full name of the original company that built and operated the line.*

▼ *The train's journey up the mountain is memorable for both passenger and spectator. Travelling on the train is thrilling, with an excitement underlined by the effort of the locomotive, but even more dramatic is the sight of the tiny train struggling up through the glorious landscape of Snowdonia.*

TALYLLYN RAILWAY

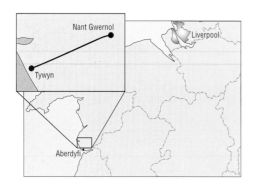

▼ *This 1930s view shows the Toy Railway, as the Talyllyn was frequently called in its publicity material, at the height of its pre-war popularity as a tourist line. The carriages are full, and old slate wagons have been brought into use, long before the days of Health and Safety regulations. The card includes this message from Pat to Philip: 'How you would love to go up the mountains in this funny little train. I wish you could see the engine, it would make you laugh.'*

In a land famous for its narrow gauge lines, the best-known name in Welsh railway history is probably the Talyllyn. Like many other similar lines that were opened in the nineteenth century, the Talyllyn Railway was inspired by the slate industry. In the 1860s slate was still a major part of the Welsh economy, and huge quantities were being sent all over the world from ports on the north and west coasts of Wales. In many areas the problems of getting the slate from the quarries to the ports were considerable, owing to the extremely difficult nature of the terrain. The answer lay in the small-scale, cheaply built, local mineral railway. Authorized in 1865 to link the slate quarries at Bryn Eglwys, near Abergynolwyn, with the coast at Tywyn, the 7-mile-long Talyllyn Railway opened just over a year later. By this time the line being built northwards from Aberystwyth to Pwllheli along the Welsh coast was nearing completion, and by 1867 Tywyn also had mainline connections with other parts of Britain. Tywyn became, therefore, an important centre for the slate traffic, with cargoes being transferred from the narrow gauge railway to the main line.

Although the Talyllyn was built as a freight line, the carriage of passengers started in 1866. The railway continued to operate throughout the rest of the nineteenth century, despite the fact that the slate industry was by this time in terminal decline. In 1911 the line and the quarries were sold to Sir Henry Haydn, and under his guidance the emphasis switched towards tourism. Through the 1920s and 1930s, the tourist potential of the line was actively promoted, often in conjunction with the GWR, the company operating the mainline services along the Cambrian coast and inland from Machynlleth.

Towyn   Off by the Toy Railway

▼ 'Edward Thomas', a locomotive dating from the 1920s, takes water at Dolgoch on a summer's day in 1955. The Talyllyn Railway was by then in its fourth year of preservation and was already enjoying great popularity as a tourist attraction. Great improvements had been made to the locomotives, vehicles and infrastructure, setting the standard for other enthusiast-operated railways.

► In this 1920s postcard, the train pauses on the bridge at Dolgoch to enable passengers to look at the falls. This romantic image is typical of the publicity material used by the Talyllyn Railway during a period when tourism had become the mainstay of lines such as this that were increasingly under threat from road traffic.

Pont Dolgoch.

▼ The railway preservation movement started in Wales in 1950, when the Talyllyn was rescued from oblivion by a group of enthusiasts. This photograph from August of that year shows one of the first trains at Tywyn Wharf station.

It was during this period that the phrase 'the Toy Railway' was developed, and on contemporary posters and postcards this name was used instead of Talyllyn Railway. In 1950 Sir Henry died, and the Talyllyn Railway threatened to follow him, having become very run down and under-used during the war years.

A first for preservation

Faced with the possible closure of the railway, a group of enthusiasts, including the pioneer canal and railway historian Tom Rolt, formed a preservation society. Within a year, and despite the decrepit nature of the track and the infrastructure, services of a kind were running once again, using the railway's original locomotives and vehicles. The appeal of the line, then as now, is that it has survived as something of a time warp, providing an insight into the Welsh slate railways of the 1860s. The Talyllyn made history as the first railway in Britain to be saved for preservation by volunteers and enthusiasts, establishing a precedent and setting a pattern that has since been followed by like-minded enthusiasts all over the country. The Talyllyn was, indeed, a small acorn from which a very large and influential oak tree has grown.

Today, well over half a century later, the line is still thriving as one of the Great Little Trains of Wales, offering its visitors a delightful ride through hills and woods inland from Tywyn to Nant Gwernol. The journey starts at Tywyn Wharf, and the train passes houses and industrial sites before the town is left behind. Soon green fields surround the track, dominated by distant views of Cader Idris, a reminder that much of the route is in the Snowdonia National Park. A highlight of the route is Dolgoch, the site of the waterfalls that have been such a major feature of promotional campaigns past and present. Dolgoch viaduct is the line's major engineering feature. From here to the terminus at Nant Gwernol, set high above a rocky ravine, the journey is spectacular and exciting.

▲ *A smart Talyllyn locomotive backs towards its carriages at Tywyn in the late 1990s, at the height of the busy tourist season. This picture makes clear the small scale of the railway, with the tunnel-like road bridge just framing the locomotive.*

▼ *Through much of its 7-mile route the Talyllyn passes through a lush and delightful setting of woods, trees and river valleys, against a mountainous background. This 1990s photo of the train in its landscape makes abundantly clear the popularity in the past of phrases such as the Toy Train.*

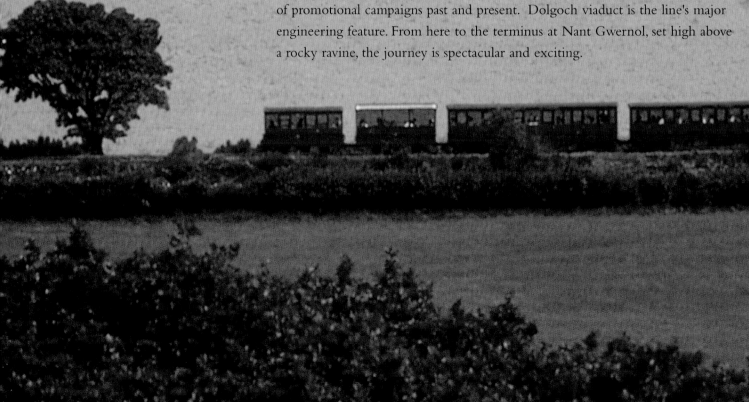

◀ It is the 1950s and the Talyllyn is coming back to life as a tourist railway, appealing to all ages. By now, a trip on the train was an established part of many family holidays in the region, particularly for those staying in caravans or on campsites. At this point, the Cambrian coast main line was still busy, bringing many people to west Wales.

▼ The overgrown track and the general air of dereliction and decay suggest this photograph dates from the early days of preservation. By contrast, the passengers who have got out to stretch their legs and pass the time of day with the driver of 'Dolgoch', are smartly dressed – as they would normally have been for an outing in the early 1950s.

RAILWAY HOTELS

The link between railway and hotels was established in the late 1830s, and railway companies continued to develop their hotel interests through the Victorian period. Most served important city termini, but others were built in ports. As tourism became more important, so railway hotels increasingly served seaside and golf resorts. Others were set up in areas of scenic beauty, such as Devon and the Lake District. Ultimately, the railway companies owned or operated over 100 hotels, both large and small, all over Britain. In the twentieth century, although some newer hotels enjoyed a great reputation for comfort and modernity, the overall number was steadily reduced. By 1962 there were just thirty-seven, and in 1981 the twenty-nine that remained as part of British Rail were sold off. Few branch lines boasted railway-owned hotels, but there were examples at Moretonhampstead and Strathpeffer. However, usually even the smallest branch line terminus boasted a hotel of some kind, and these played a significant role in promoting and supporting both their location and the railway that delivered the guests to their doors.

◀ *After the Grouping of 1923, the 'Big Four' – GWR, SR, LMS and LNER – created a new image for the railways, emphasizing efficiency, service, modernity and elegance. Stylish design and typography was part of this image, as reflected by this LMS poster.*

▲ *The GWR bought the Manor House at Moretonhampstead in Devon in 1929 and quickly developed it into a flagship country house hotel, hoping to repeat the success enjoyed by the long-established Tregenna Castle at St Ives. At the time, the GWR was famous for its modernist Art Deco look, applied here to the Manor House.*

► *A delightful example of a small resort hotel was the Lynton Cottage, depicted in this Edwardian postcard. With its Arts and Crafts styling, thatched terrace and splendid gardens, this must have been a popular destination for tourists travelling to the town on the narrow gauge Lynton & Barnstaple Railway.*

Lynton Cottage-Hotel. Lynton. North Devon.

BEN WYVIS HOTEL.
Illustrated Booklet Free, also, if asked for, Pamphlet on Strathpeffer.

Suites, Lounge, Lift, Electric Light, Garage, Golf, Fishing. Most convenient Touring Centre. Private Walk to the Wells, Pavilion, and Spa Gardens.

STRATHPEFFER SPA.
Telegrams: Ben Wyvis.
Telephone: Strathpeffer 38.

◄ *The spa town of Strathpeffer, in the Scottish Highlands, was famous for its hotels. The grandest was the Ben Wyvis, set high above the town but well placed for the railway station. Strathpeffer's popularity in the early part of the twentieth century owed much to the railway, whose publicity material emphasized not only the spa, but also the appeals of landscape and golf.*

23573 Felixstowe. Felix Hotel.

► *One of Felixstowe's grandest hotels, the Felix was built in the late Victorian era in the polychrome, gabled style favoured by the Great Eastern Railway. The style reflected the close ·historical and physical links that East Anglia has with the Netherlands.*

Pencader to Newcastle Emlyn

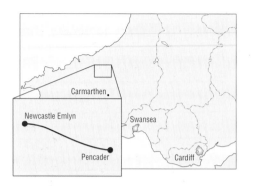

The story of the Newcastle Emlyn branch, like so many others in Victorian railway history, is complicated by over-ambitious expectations. In 1854 the Carmarthen & Cardigan Railway was authorized to build a line to connect those two towns, with a route via Newcastle Emlyn. Work started, and the first section, from Carmarthen to Conwil, opened in 1860. Financial problems brought work to a standstill, and even closed the railway for a while. More money was raised, and the line reached Pencader in March 1864 and Llandysul a few months later. There it all came to an end and a receiver was appointed. In 1867 services started in

a half-hearted manner, using locomotives hired from the GWR. The railway then struggled on until 1881, when it was wound up and bought by the GWR. Within a few years another railway had reached Cardigan, and so the Great Western was left with an unfinished line that ended in a small town in the middle of nowhere. To make the best of a bad job, the company decided to complete the line as far as Newcastle Emlyn, and in July 1895 the railway planned so optimistically forty years earlier as a main line opened as a minor branch from Pencader. This sorry tale is typical of numerous Victorian railway ventures, and it explains why so many over-enthusiastic shareholders lost their money.

The Newcastle Emlyn branch enjoyed a quiet life for the next fifty years, relying entirely on local passenger and freight traffic. The town of Newcastle Emlyn benefited from the railway, being connected, albeit in a roundabout way, to the national network. From Pencader there were trains to Carmarthen and northwards to Aberystwyth. The GWR remained in charge until nationalization.

▲ *To the north of Pentrecwrt the river Teifi enters a steep valley, which involved the railway builders in some expensive engineering. There is a short tunnel, now inaccessible, and alongside the river a deep cutting, which ends by this large stone bridge. This massive structure, a memorial to Victorian railway builders, carries a minor road high above the trackbed.*

▼ *This 1952 photograph, rich in period detail, shows the branch in the last year of passenger services. A single-coach train basks in the sun at Newcastle Emlyn while the locomotive simmers quietly. There is no one to be seen, and nothing is happening, but presumably the Bedford lorry on the platform has met the train to collect or deliver goods. The faded station sign uses the old-style name.*

British Railways kept the branch running for a while, but in September 1952 it abandoned passenger services. Freight continued for a time, and then the story came to an end.

Along the valley today

The route follows the valleys of two rivers, the Tyweli and the Teifi. The best way to explore the branch is to go to Henllan and take a trip on one of the trains operated by the Teifi Valley Railway. This company has acquired several miles of the trackbed and is building a narrow gauge preserved line westwards from Henllan. Services operating over the section that is open to Llandyfriog offer fine views of the river valley and its wooded banks.

Elsewhere along the route, the trackbed is often visible from parallel roads as a low embankment flanked by trees, running in a straight line across the landscape. Bridges and other railway structures survive. There is not much of the railway to see in Newcastle Emlyn and, at the other end of the branch, Pencader Junction is hidden in woodland deep in the river valley. However, there is no easy access to much of the trackbed either, as most of it is on private land.

Bridge Street and Adpar
Newcastle Emlyn.

▲ *The old-fashioned atmosphere of Newcastle Emlyn is captured in this Edwardian postcard. Bridge Street, now much busier, leads to the crossing of the Teifi. The town takes its name from the so-called New Castle built in the fifteenth century, a few remains of which can still be seen.*

▶ *The narrow gauge tracks of the Teifi Valley Railway lead westwards from Henllan through the woods towards the river. This preserved line plans to extend its route towards Newcastle Emlyn. The style of the railway today has more in common with the industrial and quarry lines of Wales than with the old days of the rural GWR.*

G. W. R.

Newcastle Emlyn

▼ *On a winter's afternoon the bare trees make easily visible the low embankment that carried the railway in a straight line across the fields of the Tyweli valley. Throughout its route, the branch followed river valleys, and in many places similar stretches of embankment can be found, occasionally pierced by a little bridge over a stream or track. When following an old railway line in the landscape, the secret is to remember that no straight lines occur in the landscape in nature.*

PYLE TO PORTHCAWL

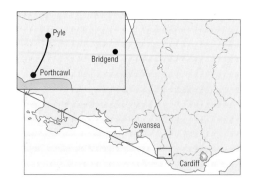

The railways came to Porthcawl at an early date, inspired by the rich deposits of coal in the area. The first seems to have been the Dyffryn Llynfi line, opened in about 1828. This 17-mile tramway linked Dyffryn colliery with Porthcawl harbour. Others in the area included the Llynfi Valley Railway and the Ogmore Valley Railway, lines sponsored by local ironmasters and colliery owners. In 1866 these lines merged as the Llyfni & Ogmore Railway, which in turn came under GWR management ten years later. By this time Porthcawl had developed as a major coal port, a position it enjoyed until it was eclipsed by the rapid rise of Barry harbour at the end of the nineteenth century. In 1898 the GWR closed Porthcawl harbour, but by that time tourism had begun to take over. The harbour was converted into an esplanade, and Porthcawl began a new and prosperous life as a resort. Hotels and other holiday facilities appeared, and during the 1920s and 1930s the resort enjoyed a fashionable existence, with through trains from London and connections with the major south Wales expresses. After World War II, holiday camps and caravan parks began to appear and the railway continued to prosper. As late as 1961 there were over twenty-six weekday trains each way between Pyle and Porthcawl, taking 12 minutes for the journey. However, this was the line's swansong and it soon surrendered to the car, the bus and the lorry. Closure for passengers came on 9 September 1963, and for freight two years later.

Inevitably with so short a line, much has been lost, particularly at the Porthcawl end. Part of the railway's route into the town is a walkway, and traces of trackbed and embankments can be seen in the farmland north of the town. A few bridges survive, isolated reminders of a once busy railway.

▼ *The station at Porthcawl was rebuilt in 1916 by the GWR on the site of the former coal harbour. By then the tourist trade was developing fast, so the station was built with long platforms to handle the holiday specials. Here, in the summer of 1962, a year before the line's closure, just a small group of passengers await their train.*

► When its life as a coal port ended, Porthcawl re-invented itself as a resort, helped and encouraged by the GWR. Promenades were built on the site of the old harbour, and hotels flourished. In the 1930s, when this postcard was published, Porthcawl was a successful and fashionable resort, as reflected by the spaciousness and elegance of the promenades and the Art Deco architecture.

THE TWO PROMENADES, PORTHCAWL.
W.1998

► The route of the railway can still be traced in the countryside but, on a line with few significant engineering features, actual remains are few and far between. An old box-van body, at one time used as a feed store or animal shelter, moulders in a field just to the south of the junction with the main line at Pyle.

▼ The only intermediate stop on the line was Nottage Halt, which served a cluster of farms and houses just north of Porthcawl. Here, the old platform survives, with its edging of grey engineering bricks still in place. The well-defined trackbed is now used for farm access.

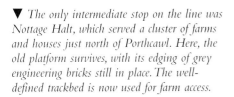

WHITLAND TO CARDIGAN

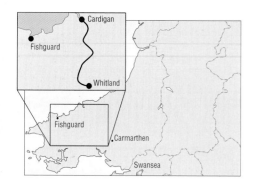

There were a number of schemes from the 1850s onwards to build railways to Cardigan. The Carmarthen & Cardigan Railway, incorporated in 1854, planned to link the two towns, but in the event only part of its route was built and Cardigan remained isolated from the railway network until 1886, when the Whitland & Cardigan Railway was opened. This was itself an extension of an existing line, built by the Whitland & Taf Vale Railway to Crymmych Arms twelve years earlier. Never really independent, Cardigan's railway was operated from the start by the GWR, which took control from 1890. At that time, this old market town, with a long history as a vital crossing point on the Teifi, was beginning to attract tourists, many of whom were drawn to the site of the castle, where the first national eisteddfod was held by Rhys ap Gruffyd, then the ruler of south Wales. The castle itself, built by Richard I, was destroyed during the Civil War. Cardigan was also once a busy port, but this trade had been lost because of the silting up of the river estuary. Fishing was still important, and visitors were beginning to explore the coastline and beaches near by. The railway was therefore seen by the town as a lifeline, and a new source of revenue. In the event, it was never really busy but it remained the town's main link with the outside world until the 1920s.

The railway was an essentially local enterprise. The 27-mile journey took over an hour and a half, with nine intermediate stops between Whitland and Cardigan. Several were halts serving small, isolated communities. Having reached Whitland, travellers were still a long way from Carmarthen, the nearest town of any size. Up to the 1930s the pace of life in rural west Wales made this unimportant, but the spread of road transport in the 1950s changed that, and by the early 1960s there were only three or four trains each way on weekdays, carrying few passengers.

▼ *On 8 September 1962, a couple of days before the closure of the line, a two-coach train pauses at Glogue halt while the locomotive takes on water. It is a busy scene, with many coming to see the train for the last time. Even a dog has stopped to watch. Today the grass-covered platform survives, along with parts of the crossing gates, now smartly painted.*

PICTURESQUE CARDIGANSHIRE
KILGERRAN CASTLE

▲ This Edwardian card of Kilgerran Castle highlights one of the major architectural features of the route. Wonderfully sited above the Teifi, this Norman castle, rebuilt by Edward III, was a royal residence in the fifteenth century.

G. W. R.

KILGERRAN

▼ On a leisurely afternoon in 1961, a train for Whitland waits in Cardigan station. There is plenty of time for chatting while the guard's van is loaded. By this time, few passengers were using the line, and the journey was too slow to attract a new generation of tourists already committed to the freedom offered by the car.

▲ East of Cardigan the trackbed is now an official path. For a while it follows the tidal Teifi, a popular route to a nature reserve on marsh and estuary land south of the river.

◄ This old postcard, probably based on a photograph from the 1930s, shows Cardigan's High Street, with plenty of period detail. A busy harbour established Cardigan's wealth, but it had silted up long before the coming of the railway. By then, farming, fishing and tourism were the mainstay of the town, and its railway.

▼ Near Login, a former halt two stops up the line from Whitland, gates still mark the site of the level crossing. On a bright morning in early spring, it is easy to imagine the local train trundling out of the woods and whistling as it approaches the crossing. In scenes such as this, the Cardigan branch survives in the landscape.

HIGH STREET, CARDIGAN.

217738

The line was an early candidate for closure, which took place on 10 September 1962, shortly before the publication of Dr Beeching's report. Freight lingered on a few more months.

Despite its unremarkable life, the Cardigan branch offered passengers a delightful journey, as the train wound its way along wooded valleys, following the meanderings of little streams that made their way northwards towards the grander valley of the Teifi. It was a journey that showed the landscape of west Wales at its best. Had it survived, it would be a popular tourist railway.

Looking for clues

Tracing the railway brings to life some of that journey, even though much of the route is remote and inaccessible. Like the journey itself, it is a slow process, for only minor roads follow the line, and in a random way. However, the sites of most of the various stations and halts can be found. In Cardigan itself nothing remains of the railway, and the site of the junction near Whitland is impenetrable. But in other places, railway buildings and structures can be identified. At Llanglydwen, for example, the station buildings still overlook the old coal yard, a reminder of the importance of the coal trade even to a minor railway. And at Glogue, where the platform survives, the scant remains of the crossing gates are carefully preserved and freshly painted. Elsewhere, the railway's leisurely route through the landscape is indicated by surviving embankments and the remains of bridges. The line's final approach to Cardigan, following the curve of the tidal Teifi through what is now a nature reserve, is a footpath. This short section shows how the whole route would make an excellent footpath and cycleway, but sadly much of it is privately owned and so detailed exploration is not possible.

▼ *At the end of its life, the railway slips quietly towards oblivion. On the last day of passenger services, a train for Whitland waits in Cardigan's single platform, the usual two carriages hauled by one of GWR's ubiquitous tank locomotives. Only a few people have turned out to watch the ending of an era. A well-dressed family group in the distance, probably seeing off visiting relatives, is using the railway as it had always been used, as the mainstay of community life.*

GAERWEN TO AMLWCH

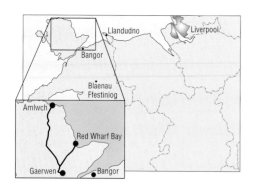

One of Britain's best-known railways is the line to Holyhead, engineered by George Stephenson and opened throughout in 1850. The most significant part was that built by the Chester & Holyhead Railway, incorporating as it did grand and revolutionary viaducts at Conwy and across the Menai Straits. In 1859 this became part of the L&NWR, the forerunner of the LMS. Eight years later, an independent company, the Anglesey Central Railway, opened a branch from Gaerwen on the main line to Amlwch. This was followed by another branch, to Red Wharf Bay. In 1876 these were bought by the L&NWR for £80,000, and in 1923 they all passed into the care of LMS. The branches were generally served by trains from Bangor, on the mainland.

Lack of traffic, and particularly the shortage of hoped-for tourists, made the Red Wharf Bay branch an early closure victim. Passenger services were withdrawn in 1930, and freight in 1950. Amlwch, however, was a different story. Its busy harbour, combined with some local industry, its fine beaches and the sea baths at Bull Bay, gave lasting appeal to a town first developed by the Romans to take advantage of the nearby copper deposits. As a result, train services were maintained well into the British Railways era, and the end of passenger services did not come until December 1964. Even at that point, the line did not die completely, as it remained open for many years to carry traffic from a chemical works near Amlwch.

▼ *Amlwch was a pretty station with some decorative cast-iron details, platform flower beds, and a station name board with letters made from rope. This scene shows a few passengers about to board the diesel railcar for Bangor. Here, as elsewhere in Britain, these vehicles were introduced in the early 1960s to try to keep the branch alive – but to little avail.*

▲ *A wet day at the simple wooden terminus station at Red Wharf Bay, probably in the late 1940s. Passenger traffic had gone in 1930, but freight lingered on until 1950. By now run down and untidy, the station building, still in LMS colours, is dominated by the Portland Cement advert.*

▼ *Issued by the L&NWR before World War I, and overprinted on the reverse by that company for use as a receipt for correspondence, this card of Bull Bay and the castle was part of an official series promoting tourism in north Wales, with the general heading: 'Visit North Wales for a charming holiday.'*

▲ *As the Amlwch branch approaches the junction at Gaerwen, all seems nearly normal. The track and the points are there, and the signal waits. Only the encroaching gorse shows there have been no trains for years.*

▼ *In the late 1950s the line was still steam operated. The train is ready to leave, the guard checks his watch, but the place is deserted.*

Closed, but not lost

Despite being closed for over fifty years, the short branch to Red Wharf Bay can still be traced in the landscape. Remote, rural and generally inaccessible, the route can be followed from minor roads. Bridges are in place, but the trackbed is often an impenetrable jungle. The most visible section is on the approach to Red Wharf Bay, where an embankment crosses fields either side of a former level crossing.

The line to Amlwch is much more unusual. The branch has been closed for some years, following the end of the chemical factory traffic but, unexpectedly, everything is still in place, track and sleepers, crossing gates, signs and signals. In some places, it looks as though the trains could still run, while in others the track has been buried beneath encroaching greenery, gorse, shrubs and a variety of flowers, including bluebells and valerian. The stations have mostly become private houses, but the line still runs past the old platforms. One, at Pentre Berw, has been restored and is now decorated with old signs. Even the old military branch north of Rhosgoch still has its tracks. As a result, the branch line has an almost eerie presence all the way from the chemical works north of Amlwch, through the town with several level crossings, and then winding its way across the landscape to the junction at Gaerwen, where a signal stands as though waiting to let trains out on to the main line, busy with traffic to and from Holyhead. Much of the route is inaccessible and private, but following it is easy, from minor roads, tracks and footpaths. It is a rare treat to explore a closed branch with a sense of railway reality. One day the trains may even return.

► *Amlwch has an ancient tidal harbour which, by the time this card was printed in the 1930s, was as much picturesque as practical. Here, at low tide, it is filled with three coastal trading vessels and a couple of small steamers. The photograph is probably older than the postcard.*

► *Despite years of closure, the Amlwch branch has all its track and infrastructure. Even the notices are still in place. Near Gaerwen the single line begins, but trains would have a hard time forcing their way though the plantlife that has taken over.*

► *In the last fifty years much of the line to Red Wharf Bay has disappeared, but in some places there are still visible traces. This section of embankment, now the province of sheep, crosses the surrounding farmland on the approach to Red Wharf Bay.*

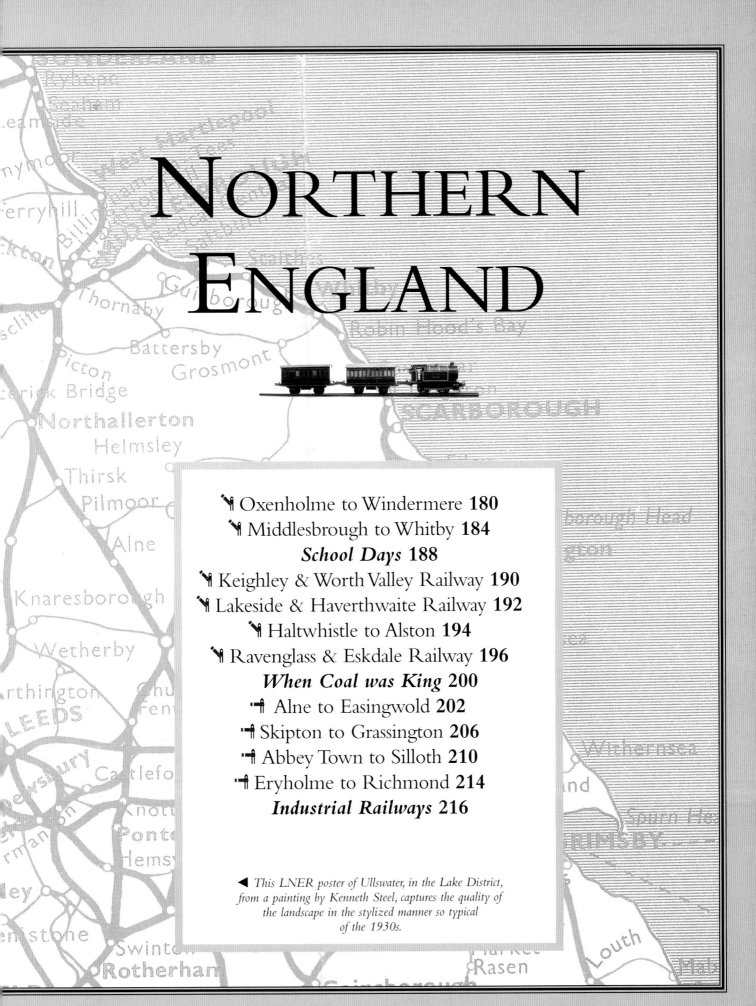

NORTHERN ENGLAND

Oxenholme to Windermere **180**

Middlesbrough to Whitby **184**

School Days **188**

Keighley & Worth Valley Railway **190**

Lakeside & Haverthwaite Railway **192**

Haltwhistle to Alston **194**

Ravenglass & Eskdale Railway **196**

When Coal was King **200**

Alne to Easingwold **202**

Skipton to Grassington **206**

Abbey Town to Silloth **210**

Eryholme to Richmond **214**

Industrial Railways **216**

◄ *This LNER poster of Ullswater, in the Lake District, from a painting by Kenneth Steel, captures the quality of the landscape in the stylized manner so typical of the 1930s.*

OXENHOLME TO WINDERMERE

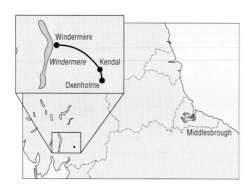

When the Lancaster & Carlisle Railway reached Oxenholme in 1846, the people of Kendal felt left out and aggrieved. They therefore promoted their own 10-mile branch line, the Kendal & Windermere Railway, which was completed in 1847. In the process they invoked the wrath of local poet William Wordsworth, who, fearful that his beloved Lakeland was going to be desecrated, wrote a strongly worded sonnet ranting against the railway. This early example of nimbyism notwithstanding, and despite erratic time-keeping, the line was soon successful. It established Windermere, which at that time was no more than a small hamlet called Birthwaite some distance above the lake, as a popular resort.

From the station, a handsome building in Lakeland stone with a porte cochère and a glazed roof, the town spread down to the lakeside, a classic example of a railway creating a resort out of very little. As traffic expanded, so the station grew to match it, with ever-lengthening platforms to handle the holiday excursions that came from all over Britain. By 1879 the mighty L&NWR was in control, and the line continued to thrive through the LMS period and into the time of British Railways. As late as 1965, a scheduled named train, the Lakes Express, ran direct to Windermere from London. All this came to an end in the 1970s with the completion of the full electrification of the West Coast main line. From then on, Windermere was served by a shuttle service of diesel railcars, and the surroundings inevitably decayed as station buildings were taken out of use or closed.

▼ *In 1907 Windermere station was a grand place, already much extended by the L&NWR to fulfil the needs of the many specials that brought thousands of visitors to this Lakeland gateway. The photographer has picked a quiet moment during the afternoon to capture the atmosphere of the station. The bookstall, with its stocks of newspapers, magazines and Frith's popular photographs of Lakeland scenery, is ready for the next wave of excited travellers.*

◄ *Railway companies spent much time and effort promoting their resorts. The L&NWR was famous for its series of scenic view cards of places accessible via their services. This one shows the boat landing stage at Bowness. It offers 'delightful boating excursions and great sporting opportunities to anglers'.*

BOATLANDING STAGE, BOWNESS, LAKE WINDERMERE.
L.&N.W.RAILWAY.

► *British Railways continued to promote Windermere and the Lake District as holiday destinations. This June 1961 leaflet, with its appealing drawing of a lake steamer, was designed to encourage the use of Holiday Runabout Tickets, which offered a wide range of journeys in the Lake District and along the Lancashire and Cumbrian coasts. The idea was 'an attractive form of Holiday Travel for passengers who wish to return to their own homes each day'. They could take their bicycles and their dogs, both of which cost the same as a child under 14, and they could travel on Windermere steamers.*

PLEASE RETAIN THIS PROGRAMME FOR REFERENCE
F.212

HOLIDAY RUNABOUT TICKETS
(GO AS YOU PLEASE)

AREA No. 2
LANCASHIRE COAST
AND
LAKE DISTRICT

SECOND **30/-** CLASS

CHILDREN UNDER 14, HALF FARE
TICKETS ARE NOT TRANSFERABLE

AVAILABLE FOR SIX DAYS

SUNDAY TO FRIDAY
30th JULY to 4th AUGUST 1961 (inclusive)
OR
6th AUGUST to 11th AUGUST 1961 (inclusive)

FROM

LIVERPOOL
AND STATIONS SHOWN HEREIN
Unlimited travel on any train between any stations within the area.

BICYCLE TICKETS 15/-	DOG TICKETS 15/-
Issued in conjunction with the above	

F.212

LONDON MIDLAND

◄ *This L&NWR postcard, showing islands on Lake Windermere, was posted in London in November 1906. The message on the back is unusual: 'Splendid view of the King & Queen of Norway, the Prince and Princess of Wales and the Duke and Duchess of Connaught. Fortunately it remained fine for them.'*

ISLANDS ON LAKE WINDERMERE
L. & N.W. RAILWAY.

Windermere station, the gateway to the lakes, became notably run down, with only a single track still in use. This changed in the 1980s with the building of a new little station slightly to the north. Meanwhile, its grand Victorian predecessor became a supermarket, but managed to retain some of its original style.

The Windermere shuttle

Despite the many reminders of one-time glories, a journey to Windermere is still a classic branch line experience. Passengers for the branch leave the Virgin express at Oxenholme station and cross to the bay platform, where the shuttle service waits. The route as far as Kendal is a steady descent into the valley of the Kent, with splendid views of surrounding hills and fells, which rise to 2,000ft and more. Beyond Kendal and the crossing of the Kent, the line climbs to Burneside, a town famous for its paper mills. Until the 1960s these helped to maintain freight traffic on the branch. Next stop is Staveley, high above the village. In a landscape of increasing splendour, the line soon reaches its climax with a view ahead of the main Lake District peaks and ranges. From here, the train drops through fellside bracken and woodland towards the terminus at Windermere, with occasional glimpses far below of the lake and perhaps the boats that connect at Lakeside with the Lakeside & Haverthwaite preserved railway (see pages 192–3).

▼ *In the 1950s and early 1960s Windermere was still a busy station, with plenty of holiday specials filling the long platforms and a wide network of local services. The glazed train shed of the original station stands in the background, and on the right are goods sheds built from rough stone in a typical Lakeland style. Little of this can be seen today.*

▲ After years of services in slightly decrepit diesel railcars, the Windermere branch now has smart new trains. Seen here in 2001, a class 175 multiple unit is ready to depart from Windermere's minimalist station. The remains of the old station building, now a supermarket, stand in the background.

756. The ferry boat on Windermere.

◀ A vehicle ferry still operates across the lake, linking Bowness on the eastern side with Sawrey, famous as the home of Beatrix Potter. This card shows the ferry in earlier days, carrying what seems to be a very fine 1930s touring car.

MIDDLESBROUGH TO WHITBY

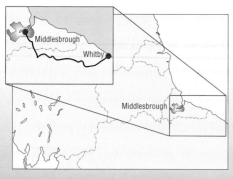

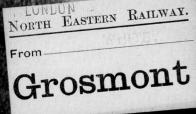

▼ *Larpool viaduct strides across the river Esk to the west of Whitby. It was built in 1885 to carry the railway south to Scarborough on a dramatic route along the coast. When this photograph, showing a local service on its way along the valley from Whitby, was taken in the early 1960s, the whole network was under threat. Today the line survives precariously, and the viaduct carries a footpath and cycleway.*

The Esk valley line from Middlesbrough to Whitby is today one of Britain's most famous branch lines, partly because of its history and the magnificence of its landscape, and partly because of its perennially uncertain future. Whenever there is a discussion about the viability of rural routes, this line is mentioned. At 35 miles, it is a long branch, and that is one of the problems. Maintenance is expensive, and traffic levels are unpredictable and hard to sustain. Also, it was never built as a branch. Until the 1960s the route was an integrated part of a whole network of lines, and Whitby itself was the meeting point of three busy railways.

Whitby's history is complex. First, in 1836, there was the Whitby & Pickering Railway, whose 24-mile line was initially partly worked by rope haulage. Next, after a long planning and building period, came the Whitby, Redcar & Middlesbrough Union's line from the north, opened in 1883. In 1885, after an equally long battle with finances and construction problems, the Scarborough & Whitby Railway's line from the south arrived. Whitby, as a result, flourished, as a port and fishing centre, and as a place for tourists to visit. By the 1890s the North Eastern Railway was in control and in due course this became part of the LNER. From 1948 British Railways maintained the network, but by 1965 the supporting routes had closed and the Esk Valley line was left as a long and complicated branch. The section from Grosmont to Pickering has been preserved as the North Yorkshire Moors Railway.

◀ *It is the summer of 1971 and a diesel multiple unit carrying a group of rail enthusiasts pauses at Commondale, a station high in the North York Moors. Boarded up and disused, the station buildings retain their original lamps. Today this and other moorland stations are popular with walkers, and much has been done to promote walks that start from stations on the Middlesbrough to Whitby line.*

▶ *Hundreds of postcards celebrate the attractions of Whitby and its harbour, for the town has long appealed to visitors. The harbour, built on the estuary of the Esk, is a fine sight, framed by tiers of old buildings. A famous whaling port, it was also the starting point for Captain Cook's voyages of exploration. The popularity of Whitby jet jewellery put the town on the map in the 1800s, as did its association with Bram Stoker's* Dracula.

North Eastern Railway.

From KNARESBRO.

WHITBY

▲ *The Esk Valley line is for most people all about landscape, and many who use the line today take the train as the best way to enjoy the diversity of scenery that the line offers. Moorland, woods, river valleys and fantastic views are all part of this remarkable journey. Here, near Danby, the line follows the Esk through an old-fashioned landscape of small fields bounded by hedges, carpeting the hills with green. Old lanes follow the traditional field pattern, and the railway appears to be a natural part of the picture.*

▶ *A class 101 diesel multiple unit pauses at Kildale in 1960, shortly after the introduction of these modern vehicles to the Whitby line. The open door might suggest that someone has misjudged the length of the platform and will have to make a jump for it. Today, Kildale is a moorland station popular with walkers, but the trains are much shorter and generally fit on to the platform.*

Taking the Esk Valley line today

Initially, until it escapes the industry and suburbs of Middlesbrough, the journey is unremarkable. However, beyond Nunthorpe the North York Moors come into view, and the landscape continues to improve steadily as the train climbs to the 550ft level, reaching its summit on Kildale and Commondale moors. The train now drops down towards the Esk valley as the moors give way to woods and farmland, passing a series of stations serving remote hillside communities for whom the train is still the best way to go to school and work, and for shopping in town. In winter it is often the only way.

Following the Esk, the line criss-crosses the river, whose course is in some places through gentle fields and at others through wild ravines. At Grosmont the station is shared with the steam trains of the North Yorkshire Moors Railway. After more crossings of the Esk, at this point a substantial waterway, the train winds its way towards its destination along the north bank of the river. It passes beneath the great viaduct at Larpool, which used to carry the line southwards to Scarborough, and then Whitby comes into view. The harbour and the tidal estuary are filled with small boats, while high above the town stand the red stone ruins of the abbey. It is a glorious end to a remarkable journey.

SCHOOL DAYS

In opening up the hinterland of Britain, the branch line network offered new freedoms and mobility to millions, removing in the process the conventional boundaries of rural life. Many aspects of family, social and working life were changed for ever. Thanks to the train, children could be educated away from home, and so the village school lost its dominant position in the rural community. The railway offered families the chance to send their children away to school, on a daily basis or as boarders. At the same time, the railway offered schools not just the chance to attract more pupils but also the possibility of outings and school trips. As a result, from the end of the nineteenth century, railway companies began increasingly to arrange school specials, school tickets and other activities related to the needs of schools and schoolchildren. Inner city schools could send their pupils in speed and safety to outlying playing fields, and at the start and end of terms, or at half-term, stations were thronged with uniformed children being sent unaccompanied on journeys all over Britain. When faced with the massive evacuation of children from the cities at the start of World War II, the railways were able to draw on their long experience of transporting schoolchildren.

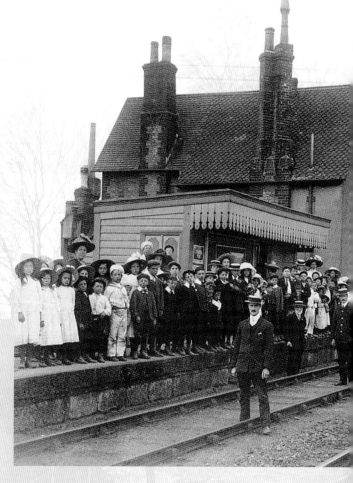

▼ *A late afternoon train pauses at Morebath Junction halt, and two schoolgirls, clearly sisters, leave the remote platform to walk home after attending school in Taunton or Tiverton. In the 1950s, long before the era of the school run, going to school often involved a journey on a train or bus, and many thousands of children undertook journeys like this every school day all over Britain.*

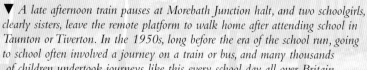

▶ *St Katharine's School, Wantage, shown here in an Edwardian view, was a feature of the town and a fitting reflection of the Victorian enthusiasm for education. It is unlikely that many of the pupils travelled to this school on the Wantage tramway, but school specials were a feature of many branch lines.*

St. Katharine's School Wantage

▼ *A remarkable group stands on the platform at Stanbridgeford, a station on a cross-country line east of Leighton Buzzard. Presumably they are waiting for a special train to take them on an outing. Smartly dressed children of all ages, teachers, parents and station staff pose for the Edwardian photographer to commemorate a special occasion.*

BRITISH RAILWAYS

BR 29101/2

RESERVED FOR SCHOOL GIRLS

▼ *It is August 1965 and the train has just left Ravenglass. On the platform is a school group, casually dressed and waiting for their teacher to sort out the tickets before they set out, perhaps for an educational trip on the Ravenglass & Eskdale narrow gauge railway. In another part of England, another narrow gauge railway, the Romney, Hythe & Dymchurch, still runs school specials.*

RAVENGLASS

KEIGHLEY & WORTH VALLEY

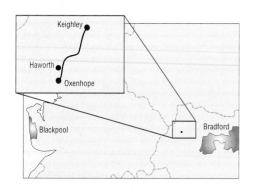

The route of the Keighley & Worth Valley Railway, along a steep-sided valley off Airedale, was made familiar to millions by the film *The Railway Children*. When it reopened as a preserved steam railway in 1968, it made history as the first standard gauge line sold to a preservation society and helped to establish the principle of the private tourist railway operated and manned by volunteers. It also pioneered the classic 1950s British Railways branch line look. Its subsequent success has been helped by the connection with the national network at Keighley.

In many ways the Keighley & Worth Valley Railway has always been dedicated to tourism. Opened as an independent operation in 1867, it was supported by the giant Midland Railway and was absorbed totally by that company in 1881. By then Haworth was already popular as a Brontë shrine, and it was this growing tourist business that gave the line its *raison d'être*. Local needs, and local freight, mostly for the textile mills, encouraged the line's promoters to continue to Oxenhope. Freight traffic also came on to part of the line after the opening in 1884 of a new through route linking Skipton and Halifax, which joined the branch just south of Keighley. In many ways a classic branch, the line lingered on through LMS and British Railways days, closing in 1962. A natural candidate for preservation, the branch caters for tourists and the needs of local residents. Just under 5 miles long, it climbs through the heart of Brontë country, stopping at several well-restored stations en route to Oxenhope. Haworth, convenient for the Brontë Parsonage Museum, is the railway's headquarters.

▼ *Oxenhope station is the railway's carriage and wagon depot. This atmospheric photograph, taken in 1969, shows the early days of preservation on the line. Typical of this era was the eccentric mixture of vehicles and the somewhat ad hoc nature of operation. Small boys respond to the universal appeal of a steam locomotive, even though steam had only just disappeared from the national network.*

Railway Station.

Haworth,

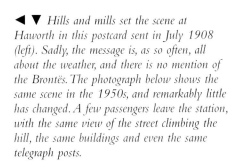

◀ ▼ *Hills and mills set the scene at Haworth in this postcard sent in July 1908 (left). Sadly, the message is, as so often, all about the weather, and there is no mention of the Brontës. The photograph below shows the same scene in the 1950s, and remarkably little has changed. A few passengers leave the station, with the same view of the street climbing the hill, the same buildings and even the same telegraph posts.*

▲ *The reopening of the branch as a preserved railway was a major event, establishing a pattern for the future. Against a background of sturdy stone mills, a crowd clusters round the locomotive during the opening ceremony at Keighley in 1968. At this point, the K&WVR had its own livery, but since then preserved railways have tended to adopt more historically correct schemes.*

LAKESIDE & HAVERTHWAITE RAILWAY

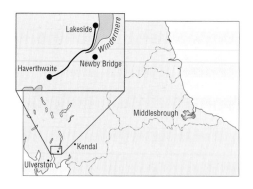

57† 5,000— 9 | 14. TO
LAKE SIDE
From the Furness Railway.

▼ *In 1973 the Lakeside & Haverthwaite Railway reopened 3 miles of the former Furness branch amid considerable local celebration, as seen here. A train pulls into Lakeside station, hauled by a locomotive in Caledonian Railway colours, perhaps re-creating the great excursions of the past.*

Despite the objections of William Wordsworth and others, the Lake District was successfully penetrated by a number of railway lines. The line from Oxenholme to Windermere was followed by two more, reflecting the ambitions of the local Furness Railway, established in 1844. The company was involved in the building of the branch to Coniston, completed in 1859, and was directly responsible for the branch from Ulverston to Lake Side (as it was styled then), at the southern end of Windermere. This line, opened in 1869, was designed from the outset to connect with steamer services on Lake Windermere. Lake Side station was, therefore, an ambitious building in yellow sandstone, complete with tower, glazed elevated train shed connected directly to the quayside, and a restaurant, which proved to be so popular it had to be enlarged. The station itself was built to handle large excursion trains, a mainstay of the line. From 1872 the steamer services on the lake were operated by the Furness Railway, a pioneer in such tourist-related activities. In the Edwardian era, the company was famous for its integrated rail, road and boat services. This tradition was maintained by the LMS, and to some extent by British Railways but, faced with increasing competition from road traffic, the branch was closed in 1965. The line to Coniston, which had never been as popular, had already closed some years earlier.

In 1973, 3½ miles of the branch were reopened as a preserved line by the Lakeside & Haverthwaite Railway. At Lakeside it is once again possible to take a meal in the station restaurant or a boat up to Windermere, perhaps for a trip on the branch line to Oxenholme (see pages 180–3).

◄ *Published by the Furness Railway to promote its tourist routes, this card of Rydal Water was posted in 1904 by a couple on holiday to their son away at school. The message is typically parental: 'I hope you are having a right good time and that you have got to the top of the class.' In many ways the Furness Railway was a pioneer in the development of tourist traffic, which it saw as a means of reversing the decline in revenues from the carriage of haematite from quarries near Barrow, a trade that had collapsed in the 1870s.*

Furness Railway. RYDAL WATER—Frosty Morning. VIA LAKE SIDE STATION (WINDERMERE).

▲ *In 1960 Lake Side was still a busy excursion terminus, as is shown in this view of the station from the signal box. Visible are the long platforms demanded by excursion traffic and, in the distance, the glazed train shed and decorative station buildings, some of which survive today.*

► *On a summer's evening in the 1950s a long excursion train is ready to depart from Lake Side filled with passengers, perhaps from the Manchester area, who, it is hoped, were looking back with tired pleasure on their day on Windermere. The smart locomotive is a LMS Patriot class, named 'Home Guard'.*

HALTWHISTLE TO ALSTON

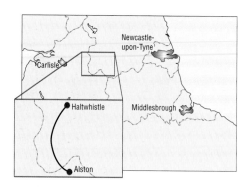

Most branch line closures took place in the 1960s, but there were a few that escaped the Beeching axe only to perish ten years later. A famous example was the Alston branch, kept open against all odds because in a bad winter it was sometimes the only access to Alston, England's highest market town, but eventually closed in May 1976. This spectacular line, whose twisting 13-mile route along the Tyne valley climbed high into the hills south of Haltwhistle, was opened in 1852 by the Newcastle & Carlisle Railway. Coal was one of the reasons for its creation, justifying the heavy engineering and the resultant high construction costs. Notable were the bridges and viaducts, the most famous of which was Lambley, a strikingly narrow and elegant stone structure whose tall arches carried the line over the South Tyne's rocky gorge. Its poor condition was one of the reasons given for the line's closure. Since then the viaduct has been restored and now carries a footpath. The branch was also famous for its stations, handsome Tudor-style structures that reflected both the tough landscape and the region's history. The best of these was Alston, designed by Benjamin Green, a proper terminus station with glazed train shed and plenty of architectural flourishes.

While the branch was dying, a preservation society was waiting in the wings. In 1983, a 2¼-mile section from Alston to Kirkhaugh was reopened as the South Tynedale Railway, England's highest narrow gauge railway. This popular little line now has ambitions to take its trains all the way down to Haltwhistle.

▼ *An old LNER J39 goods engine draws breath at Alston in the 1950s, having hauled a heavy excursion train up the branch. The covered train shed and the attached engine shed were demolished in the 1960s. However, the main buildings still stand, now fully restored.*

▲ 'Naklo', a Polish locomotive, hauls its rake of smartly painted and locally built carriages along the short stretch of the old Alston branch brought back to life by the South Tynedale Railway. Their aim is to extend the 2ft gauge line and eventually reopen the whole route.

▼ With Slaggyford Viaduct in the background, a diesel multiple unit climbs through spectacular scenery towards Alston, shortly before the closure of the branch in 1976. The route was one of England's great rail journeys.

RAVENGLASS & ESKDALE RAILWAY

Miniature, as distinct from narrow gauge, railways were a phenomenon in Britain through the first half of the twentieth century, with many examples running round circuits or along short stretches of track at seaside resorts, in public parks and country house gardens, and among the attractions at fairgrounds and holiday camps. Most were essentially local, but a few offered scheduled or regular services over considerable distances. Of the latter, one of the best known is the Ravenglass & Eskdale, whose 7-mile route inland to Dalegarth from Ravenglass on the Cumbrian coast is now one of the premier tourist attractions in north-west England. However, behind present-day success lies a complex, chequered history.

The railway was opened in 1875 as a mineral line, to carry iron ore and haematite from mines near Boot down to the coast. It was built to a 3ft gauge, to allow for the heavy traffic. Passengers were carried from 1876, mainly to increase revenues as the predicted iron ore traffic was not sufficiently forthcoming. Plagued by financial problems, the railway closed in 1908. In 1915 it was bought up by Bassett-Lowke, the engineering and model railway company, who relaid it to a 15in gauge and reopened it as a tourist line on which they could demonstrate their products. Helped by some quarry traffic, the railway kept going until 1958, when it closed again. At this point, a preservation group stepped in, bought the remains at auction, and set to work to turn it into a great success as a tourist railway.

▼ *This photograph, taken in 1990, captures the distinctive look and spic-and-span image of the modern Ravenglass & Eskdale. The LNER-style 'River Mite', a locomotive built in 1966, hauls its train out of Ravenglass. This engine, and its two much older sisters, the 'River Irt' of 1894 and the 'River Esk' of 1923, are named after local waterways.*

◄ ▲ *Three photos from a private album celebrate a journey on the Ravenglass & Eskdale in the 1930s and reveal the nature of the railway at that time. In those days open wagons were the order of the day, with glass windscreens to keep the weather at bay. Despite these rather basic conditions, most people seem to be having a good time.*

▶ *In 1906, when this postcard was sent, the Ravenglass & Eskdale was still a substantial narrow gauge line, with the 3ft gauge built for the iron ore traffic in 1875. The train is standing at Eskdale Green, three stations down from Boot, then the northern terminus. The card, posted in Boot, says: 'Came by express. Just going off to see the falls.' Two years later, the railway closed.*

◄ *'The Eskdale Express approaching a Bridge where the Main Road crosses the Railway.' This is the grand title of this 1930s postcard, which also refers to the 'picturesque quality of this unique little Railway'. More important in historical terms is the size of the bridge in relation to the track, which reveals it was made for a much bigger railway, the original 3ft gauge mineral line opened in 1875.*

The Ratty experience

Always an independently minded operation, the Ratty, to give it its popular name, is now well known as a forward-thinking company, building and maintaining its own locomotives and vehicles, and pioneering radio-controlled signalling and traffic management on small-scale railways. Locomotives have also been built at Ravenglass for export, notably to Japan.

A real railway, despite its diminutive size, the Ravenglass & Eskdale offers visitors a complete railway experience. Apart from the journey itself, through the magnificent landscape of Cumbria, there are workshops and a museum to visit, shops and restaurants, a water mill at Muncaster that grinds its own flour, a pub and, for those who want to stay longer to explore both the region and its railways, a pair of camping coaches. Splendid scenery and dramatic hill country flank the route up to Dalegarth, and many walkers make good use of the line. At Ravenglass there is direct main line access from the spectacular Cumbrian coast line between Carlisle and Barrow.

▼ *Another 1930s view shows the railway in the landscape setting that has always given the line its particular appeal. Crowded open wagons and a sunny summer's day allow the passengers to make the most of their outing as the train makes its way towards Eskdale.*

▶ Open wagons are still part of the Ravenglass & Eskdale experience and in the right conditions add to the excitement of the journey. In the summer of 1976, which many will remember as one of the hottest and driest of recent times, a crowded train makes its way past Muncaster Mill.

▼ Against the glorious backdrop of the bare Cumbrian hills, the train winds its way along the valley near Muncaster Mill, which by contrast seems almost excessively green. Only the crowded open wagon behind the locomotive gives away the scale of this line. It is this quality of landscape that makes a journey on the Ravenglass & Eskdale unlike any other.

COAL

Through the 1800s and up to the 1950s, Britain was a coal-fired country. The burning of coal, in various forms, powered industry, drove ships and railways, and heated homes, offices, shops, schools, churches and hospitals. The transport of coal from the mines to the docks and other distribution centres was, therefore, the major incentive for the building of railways, on both a local and a national scale. The financial success of many railway companies depended on the coal trade. From the 1850s the annual tonnage carried by rail rose steadily, reaching a peak of 225 million tons in 1913, with much of that being exported to markets all over the world. While the bulk of this traffic was transported to docks and depots, coal was also an essential domestic commodity. Every town, village, hamlet and farm needed coal, and this was delivered to local yards and stations by the wagon load. The wagons, owned by the railways, the collieries or the coal merchants, had to be emptied quickly and returned, so the movement of coal trains was continuous.

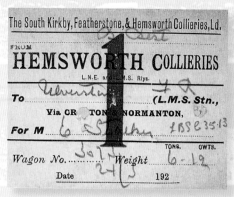

▲ *On every journey, every wagon had to carry a label showing its ownership, its route and destination, and the weight of coal carried. By this means haulage fees could be calculated and recorded, along with the location of the wagon. In the pre-computer age, this process required a massive bureaucracy, with all the information being collected and recorded by hand.*

▼ *The main areas of coal production were the Midlands, north-east England, south Wales and Scotland, but there were also significant deposits in Somerset and Kent. The scale of demand and improvements in deep mining technology meant that relatively small deposits could be exploited. A typical small pit was Norton Hill, in the Somerset coalfield.*

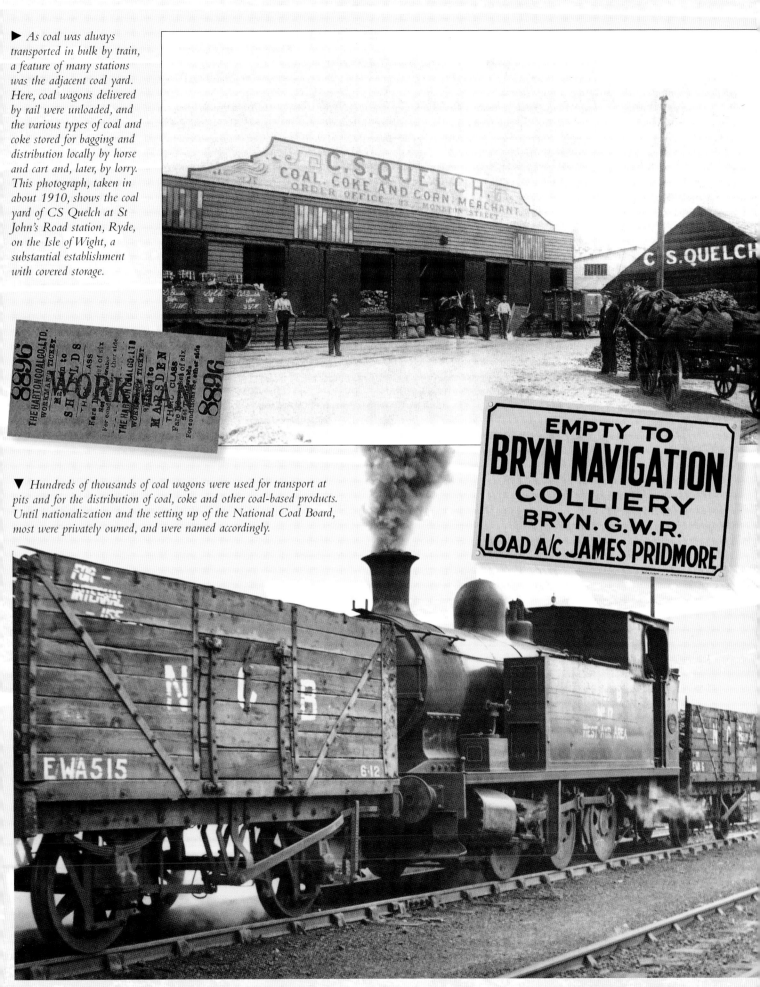

► As coal was always transported in bulk by train, a feature of many stations was the adjacent coal yard. Here, coal wagons delivered by rail were unloaded, and the various types of coal and coke stored for bagging and distribution locally by horse and cart and, later, by lorry. This photograph, taken in about 1910, shows the coal yard of CS Quelch at St John's Road station, Ryde, on the Isle of Wight, a substantial establishment with covered storage.

▼ Hundreds of thousands of coal wagons were used for transport at pits and for the distribution of coal, coke and other coal-based products. Until nationalization and the setting up of the National Coal Board, most were privately owned, and were named accordingly.

ALNE TO EASINGWOLD

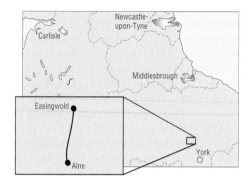

A dangerous mixture of enthusiasm and optimism inspired the building of many minor railways in late Victorian Britain. It was a time when every town of any stature had to be part of the ever-expanding railway network. Easingwold was just such a place, a small market town with a population of about 2,000 and some ambitious local businessmen who believed that trade could not develop properly without a railway. They set to work, raising support and money for the building of a branch line to connect Easingwold with the busy main line of the North Eastern Railway less than 3 miles away at Alne, another small market town, to the north of York. Authorized in August 1887, the Easingwold Railway was completed in July 1891, with construction costs of £17,000.

The Easingwold Railway was from the start fiercely independent. It owned its own locomotives, two small tank engines, which continued to haul trains up and down the short line for much of its life. When these were in need of repair, replacements were hired from the NER. Carriages, mostly old four- or six-wheel vehicles, were acquired as cast-offs from larger companies. In the end, the NER operated the line, but the company remained independent. It survived the grouping of 1923, never becoming part of the LNER, and in 1928 underlined its independence by renaming itself the Easingwold Light Railway. More remarkably, it escaped the all-encompassing net of British Railways when the network was nationalized in January 1948. Perhaps it was too small and insignificant to attract the attention of the Whitehall bureaucrats. By then passenger traffic had dwindled to almost nothing, and in November 1948 the passenger service ceased. Freight, however, kept the line alive for another decade, with British Railways locomotives hauling the wagons to and fro. On 27 December 1957 the last train ran along the overgrown tracks of the Easingwold Railway.

▼ *It is the summer of 1952, and Easingwold Railway maintains its independence into the era of British Railways. By then passenger carrying had ceased, but at least one of the line's antiquated carriages was still in use, seen here shunted against the buffers. In the background, cattle wagons show that the line was still busy with agricultural traffic.*

▼ *Towards the end of its life, the branch to Easingwold, by then threatened with closure, was popular with railtours. At Alne, in the summer of 1957, passengers on the Yorkshire Coast Railtour scramble to mount the open wagons in which they will travel. Such scenes of simple enthusiasm, once commonplace, are inconceivable in the Health & Safety age.*

▲ *A typical Easingwold train, an ancient carriage and one of the railway's two tank locomotives, waits in the bay platform at Alne, beyond the tracks of the East Coast main line. Both vehicles carry the Easingwold's name and livery. On this warm day the driver and a lady friend pose for the camera.*

Lost, but not forgotten

Nearly half a century after its closure, the lightly engineered Easingwold Railway might have been expected to have disappeared into history. Surprisingly, this is not the case.

There is no station today at Alne, and trains on the East Coast main line thunder through the huddle of buildings that indicate where the station, and the junction, were once sited. From there the route across the flat Yorkshire landscape is initially hard to trace, and much of the trackbed has been ploughed out. On the approach to Easingwold, however, it is well defined, raised above the surrounding fields and partly hidden by bushes. New housing has now spread over the once extensive station site at Easingwold, but in the middle of this development, part of which is called Station Court, is the old station house, which was once the station hotel, a richly decorative and strongly built stone structure dated 1892, as well as a range of former offices and station buildings. These grand structures, reflective of the local ambition and pride that brought the railway into existence, are a fine memorial to a line that was famous for its independence.

▲ *Most of the Easingwold Railway has vanished back into the fields, but unexpected traces can still be found. This old 1950s van body is quietly decaying by a farmyard not far from Easingwold. The doors indicate that this was an early type of container, transported on flat wagons. The route of the line was by the distant line of trees, across the field on the left.*

◄ *The best memorial to the branch is the Old Station House, formerly the station hotel at Easingwold. Though now surrounded by modern housing, this grand building reflects the pride with which the line was constructed.*

▼ *The track and platform are overgrown, but a few trains still run. In this 1957 photograph, staff and onlookers wander away, while three people stand waving at the departing train. As passenger carrying had long since ceased, they are probably saying farewell to a visiting railtour group. The photographer must have been standing on the guard's van. The house on the right was once the station hotel.*

SKIPTON TO GRASSINGTON

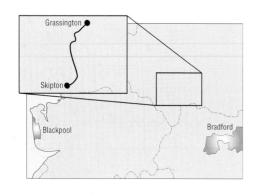

The railways came early to Yorkshire, long before the dales were popular with visitors. Minerals and freight were the primary inspiration. Another factor was the ambition shared by several companies to build the best route between the industrial towns of Lancashire and the north-east. The origins of the Grassington branch lay in just such a scheme, planned by the Liverpool, Manchester & Newcastle Junction Railway in 1846. This, and other schemes in the 1860s and 1880s, came to nothing, and it was the end of the century before the Yorkshire Dales were invaded by railways.

In 1895 the Yorkshire Dales Railway was formed to build a line from Embsay, near Skipton, to Darlington. In 1902 it was opened as far as Grassington. It never went any farther, for by that time these expensive cross-country routes no longer made economic sense. While the Yorkshire Dales Railway remained independent until 1923, the branch was always operated by the Midland Railway. Branch line services were augmented by through coaches to and from Bradford, making possible onward travel to London and other major cities. However, the line was never busy and regular passenger services were withdrawn in 1930. Ironically, this was just before the great rise in the popularity of walking in general and in the Yorkshire Dales in particular, and so the branch continued to be used by excursion trains.

▼ *In the summer of 1968, a year before closure, the Dalesman railtour train creeps along the overgrown track into Grassington station, with operations being directed by the smartly dressed station master. A few spectators, including the inevitable small boy, enjoy the rare sight of a passenger train at Grassington. With so many lines closing in the 1960s, special railtours such as this became a common event.*

▲ Local freight survived on the northern section of the Grassington branch for nearly forty years after regular passenger services ended in 1930. Here, in 1966, a British Railways Standard Class 4MT locomotive, with a few open wagons in its care, waits to depart from Grassington's still intact station. Weeds and grass cover the track, a reminder that few trains came this way during the last years of this part of the line.

▶ Grassington has long been one of the most popular of the Wharfedale villages, as reflected by this Edwardian view of the famous seventeenth-century bridge. Lead mining established the town's wealth, but tourism took over in the late Victorian period, greatly encouraged by the railway.

The Wharfe below Grassington Bridge.

▼ *From Swinden quarry southwards, the line is in fine shape, thanks to the continuing traffic from the limestone quarry. In 1979, when this picture was taken, the 1,100-tonne trains, with their special hopper wagons, were usually hauled by pairs of class 31 diesels, as shown here. Always a massive operation, the line has now carried over 4 million tonnes of stone.*

Freight was another matter, with the extensive traffic from a limestone quarry at Swinden, near Cracoe, a few miles south of Grassington. Closure of the section of the line from Swinden to Grassington came in August 1969, but from Skipton to Swinden the branch remains open, catering for much-expanded quarry traffic.

The lost and the living

From Swinden quarry to Grassington, cuttings, embankments and bridges make it simple to trace the route. With the great increase in road traffic, the Yorkshire Dales need more, not fewer, railways and there have been schemes to reopen the line to Grassington. At the other end of the branch, the Embsay & Bolton Abbey Railway has opened as a preserved line a section of the old Midland Railway route to Leeds. The atmosphere of this steam railway is similar to that of the Grassington branch in its heyday, while the Grassington branch today is home to massive stone trains hauled by modern diesels.

▼ *The line now ends at Swinden quarry, visible here in the distance, across the main road. After a short break, the old trackbed appears, now a home for geese and goats, happily grazing where the trains used to run. A bit farther on, a couple of stone bridges survive.*

ABBEY TOWN TO SILLOTH

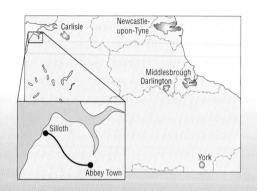

Through the 1850s a network of railways was built westwards from Carlisle along the southern shore of the Solway Firth. First, in 1854, came the line to Port Carlisle, along which – until 1914 – passengers were carried in a horse-drawn tram. Next was an extension to Silloth, opened in 1856. A line went north across the firth to Annan on a spectacular 2-mile viaduct. Supported on 193 piers, this was one of the great engineering achievements of the 1860s. Another link went southwards to Aspatria. This, in effect, turned the Silloth line into a short branch from Abbey Town.

Silloth at that time had busy docks and supported various local industries, including fishing. Despite all this, however, the line did not thrive, and in 1880 it was taken over by the North British Railway, resulting in the unusual situation of a railway situated in England being run by a Scottish company. Eventually, trade picked up as visitors were increasingly drawn to this remote region for its beaches, its wild landscape and its golf courses, and Silloth began to develop as a resort. A handsome small town built on a grid pattern, Silloth made the most of this new business. At the same time, the docks expanded, along with the local industries, notably flour milling. More freight traffic was attracted to the railway and so, by the end of the nineteenth century, the station and its extensive goods facilities covered a considerable acreage. During World War II a big airfield outside Silloth also brought an increase in traffic.

▼ *Seeking out remains from Silloth's railway days is difficult, as little survives. Adjacent to the dock, however, is this old fence of weathered railway sleepers, looking not unlike a piece of environmental sculpture.*

▶ *Criffel Street, Silloth, as depicted on a 1904 postcard, at the height of the town's popularity as a resort, with plenty of elegant visitors and their carriages parading up and down. The distinctive architecture and the grid pattern of the streets can clearly be seen. To the left is the green, which spreads north towards the sea and the beaches. Little has changed today, except that the hotel is now called the Golf.*

Cockermouth, Keswick and Penrith Railway.

TO

SILLOTH

INTRODUCTION OF
LIGHT-WEIGHT
DIESEL PASSENGER TRAINS

—

AMENDED
TRAIN SERVICE

CARLISLE

and

SILLOTH

and intermediate stations

29th NOVEMBER 1954
until further notice

(Subject to alteration)

In November 1954 the Silloth line saw new-style diesel multiple units being used for the first time on a British branch line. It was widely believed that the combination of their modern look and the rapid, clean and comfortable journeys that they offered would bring passengers back to the railways. However, by the end of that decade, traffic on the Silloth branch line was in decline, and in September 1964 the line was closed, along with the remaining parts of the Solway Firth network. Local opinion was determinedly against the closure, and there were protests and a even a sit-down on the line, but all to no avail.

Fading into history

Having been laid across a predominantly flat landscape, the railway has for the most part disappeared back into farmland. Little remains of Silloth station, although the docks survive in use and the flour mill is still busy. Traces of the trackbed can be seen from nearby minor roads, and some bridges survive, often isolated in the landscape. Most of the intermediate halts, usually adjacent to former level crossings, have become private houses. At Abbey Town, not far from the remains of the red stone abbey, the former junction has vanished almost entirely, absorbed back into the farmland.

▲ *The Silloth branch was the first in Britain to have its steam trains replaced by the new diesel railcars, pioneers of a type of passenger vehicle that was soon to become universal on lesser and branch lines all over Britain. This British Railways leaflet advertises their introduction on 29 November 1954.*

► *An aerial photograph of Silloth, taken in the 1950s, reveals the grid pattern of the streets, the large dock basin, the extensive network of railways around the station, and the large park-like green, with the beach beyond.*

▼ *Silloth's station and its extensive facilities, which included lines serving the docks and the flour mill, have almost all vanished, except for this building on the old platform. The main station building, to its left, was at one point converted into flats, but is now empty and abandoned.*

▼ *The old and the new, sitting side by side at Silloth station in the 1950s, when diesel railcars were a novelty. In the background is the flour mill, to the left the docks, the mainstays of the line through much of its history.*

ERYHOLME TO RICHMOND

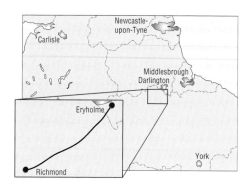

Rival companies and numerous mergers make the railway history of the north-east of England in the 1840s and 1850s very complex. Buried in this confusion is the story of the Richmond branch, authorized by the Great North of England Railway in 1845. Before the branch was complete, the GNER had been absorbed by the Newcastle & Darlington Junction Railway, which in turn became part of the York, Newcastle & Berwick Railway. Matters were simplified in 1857, when these and other components formed the North Eastern Railway.

By then the Richmond branch had been open for eleven years. Generously built, and marked by fine stone buildings in an extravagant Victorian Gothic style, many designed by GT Andrews, the branch was a memorable, if underused, route to one of England's finest market towns. World War I brought a great increase in traffic with the development of Catterick Garrison, served by a 4-mile branch from the Richmond line. Indeed, the army kept the railway busy until the 1950s. By the British Railways era there were thirteen trains each way on weekdays, and extra unadvertised services took troops from Catterick to Darlington. As was the case with many branches, decline set in in the 1960s, and passenger services ceased in March 1969. Freight services, mostly for the army, survived for another year.

Today, there are plenty of remains to look out for, and much of the 9-mile route can be tracked on minor roads. Notable are stations at Scorton and Moulton: both are now private houses, but still boast their platform clocks.

▼ *Remarkable among branch line termini, Richmond station is a masterpiece of Victorian Gothic by GT Andrews, rich in buttresses, arches, gables, mullion windows and other medieval details. In matching style is the train shed, with its angled twin-span roof and its delicate cast-iron supports and herringbone timberwork. Seen here in the 1960s, this magnificent building dwarfs the little diesel railcar waiting at the single platform. After the closure of the line, the station became a garden centre. This in turn has now gone, and the building stands empty but still complete, a glorious reminder of the ambitions, and the extravagance, of early Victorian railway companies.*

▲ In 1954 the 12.25pm for Darlington stands ready to depart. At this point, the Richmond branch still enjoyed a busy service.

► Many of the qualities of Richmond are apparent in this Edwardian view, including the keep of the Norman castle and the bridge over the Swale. The station was across the bridge to the left.

Richmond from Terrace

NORTH EASTERN RAILWAY.

RICHMOND.

▲ The Richmond branch featured finely built and decorative stations, some of which survive as private houses, along with their platforms. This is at Scorton, where the trackbed is seen stretching away into the distance and the old platform has long been grassed over.

INDUSTRIAL RAILWAYS

Thousands of branch lines were built all over Britain solely for industrial and freight usage. Indeed, the earliest railways were industrial lines, linking coal mines, quarries and ironworks to ports or canals. The railways soon established themselves as the best carrier for bulk products, and at the same time developed the efficient and comprehensive national freight networks that were the backbone of railway economics. By the end of the nineteenth century, and until the 1950s, most factories and production areas had railway connections as a matter of course. Those not adjacent to main lines were connected by branch lines, some of which were both long and complex in their operations. From the early days, special locomotives were built for industrial use, and famous names such as Hunslet and Barclay were still making steam locomotives for industries at home and abroad until the 1960s. Even today, after decades of road competition, there are miles of industrial lines. Transporting bulk commodities such as coal, stone, oil, cement, timber and chemicals, they are still very much part of the modern railway infrastructure.

E.R.O. 33899

TRAFFIC IS WAITING FOR THESE WAGONS
UNLOAD IMMEDIATELY PLEASE

▼ *Until its devastation in the 1980s, the coal industry was the mainstay of the railways. Collieries had their own railway networks, operated by aged industrial tank locomotives. Steam survived long after it had gone from British Railways. Here, in 1979, 'Warrior', an ex-War Department locomotive, struggles to haul a rake of loaded wagons away from Bickershaw Colliery, Leigh, near Manchester.*

► The transport of stone of all kinds has always been, and remains, a major area of railway activity. Many miles of branch line railways were built to service stone quarrying activities. In the early days slate and iron stone were particularly important, along with the transport of ballast, used for track laying, and building materials such as Portland and Bath stone. Later, stone products, particularly cement and concrete, became more significant. In this picture, taken in 1966 at an iron ore quarry near Wellingborough, Northamptonshire, a tank locomotive shunts quarry wagons.

◄ Many industrial lines were narrow gauge, for economy and ease of operation. From the 1840s in Purbeck, Dorset, numerous narrow gauge lines were opened to transport clays for onward carriage to harbours such as Poole. The most important was the Furzebrook Railway, or Pike's Tramway, which closed in the 1950s.

▼ Many industries had their own railway networks and their own vehicles. Typical was the brewing industry, which depended on the railway for supplies of raw materials and the transport of the beer. At the Bass brewery in Burton-on-Trent, one of its own locomotives collects wagons from the main line in 1958.

ISLE OF SKYE
GO NORTH THIS YEAR
TRAVEL BY RAIL

BRITISH RAILWAYS

SCOTLAND

🚂 Fort William to Mallaig **220**

Branch Line Locomotives **224**

🚂 Bo'ness & Kinneil Railway **226**

🚂 Leadhills & Wanlockhead Railway **228**

🚂 Castle Douglas to Kirkcudbright **230**

🚂 Roxburgh to Jedburgh **234**

Old Railway Carriages **236**

🚂 Killin Junction to Loch Tay **238**

🚂 Ballinluig to Aberfeldy **240**

🚂 Dingwall to Strathpeffer **242**

Railwayana **244**

🚂 The Mound to Dornoch **246**

Humorous Postcards **250**

◄ *The Isle of Skye and its spectacular scenery featured in this British Railways poster of about 1949. There were, and still are, two routes to Skye by train, via Mallaig and via Kyle of Lochalsh.*

FORT WILLIAM TO MALLAIG

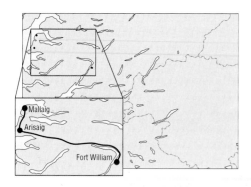

At 41 miles long, the line from Fort William to Mallaig can hardly be called a branch, yet this westward extension of the West Highland route from Glasgow has all the important branch line characteristics. Fish was the inspiration for building a railway across the wild and inaccessible landscape of the western Highlands, and it was the battle for the fish trade between two Scottish railways, the Caledonian and the North British, that brought it into being. The railway reached Fort William in 1894, and it took another seven years, and a huge expenditure, to extend it to Mallaig. The heavily engineered route includes countless rock cuttings, steep gradients and viaducts, and eleven tunnels.

For some time fish and freight fulfilled the line's expectations, and passenger carrying was almost a secondary consideration. However, since the 1950s the line has in effect been a railway 'Road to the Isles' and has had to rely increasingly on tourism. Today, the emphasis is on the journey itself, rather than the destination, with the train being seen as a mobile viewing platform that makes its way through some of Scotland's most awe-inspiring scenery. It also passes through a region closely associated with Bonny Prince Charlie and the 1745 Jacobite rebellion. It was at Glenfinnan on 19 August 1745 that the clans declared themselves for the prince and the Stuart cause. It was the pursuit of tourists that inspired British Railways to introduce the scheduled steam-hauled trains on the Mallaig line in the late 1980s. These services proved highly successful and, now marketed as 'The Jacobite', they continue to operate in the summer months.

▼ *In a magnificently wild and snowy landscape, a steam train crosses the 21 arches of Glenfinnan viaduct. Built on a curve, this pioneering concrete structure is a favourite with photographers. It is 1987, the start of regular steam-hauled services on the line, and a Stanier Black Five is setting the pace for the future.*

◀ 'Evening light over Ben Nevis from Corpach' is the title of this early postcard, a typically romantic view of the great mountain that towers above Fort William and the line to Mallaig, which passes through Corpach. It is a glorious scene, enlivened by the little boat in the foreground.

▼ The impetus for building the line to Mallaig over such hard terrain was the desire to capture some of the fish traffic, a major source of income for railways until the 1950s. A busy fishing harbour before the coming of the railway, Mallaig expanded rapidly after 1901. This 1920s card, 'The Morning Catch', shows fish being auctioned prior to packing for transport by train.

EVENING LIGHT OVER BEN NEVIS FROM CORPACH

THE MORNING CATCH, MALLAIG, INVERNESS-SHIRE.

One of the greatest railway journeys in the world

The route is a continual series of excitements, from the start in Fort William under the shadow of Ben Nevis to the finish at Mallaig, with views over the fishing boats in the harbour to the islands beyond. In between is the crossing of the Caledonian Canal on the famous 1901 swing-bridge, the delightful run alongside the shore of Loch Eil, the climb into the mountains for the crossing of the Glenfinnan viaduct and the views of Loch Shiel. Then comes the twisting route along the rocky valley of the river Ailort to Lochailort, the Atlantic views across the bays of Loch Nan Uamh, the inland journey through woods to Arisaig and finally the sandy beaches of Morar. The Mallaig section of the West Highland line is often promoted as one of the great railway journeys of the world. On a sunny day when the train and the landscape are bathed in that special and ever-changing Scottish light and colour, that claim is certainly justified.

▼ *On a glorious spring day in 1988, a dirty class 37 diesel locomotive, in late British Rail colours, trundles its two-coach train past Loch Eil, on the way to Mallaig, through scenery that makes this one of the world's most exciting rail journeys.*

◀ *Fort William station in the 1950s was a busy place, with plenty of freight and passenger activity, including the nightly sleepers to and from London. Here, a former LNER K2 locomotive stands on the quayside while passers-by pay more attention to whatever is going on in the harbour. Still standing then was the old station, an eccentric stone-built structure with a spire, a tower, a steeply pitched roof and a big lunette window over the entrance. This was all demolished in 1975.*

▼ *Mallaig is another stone-built station, but more in the manner of a house with gables. This 1974 photograph shows well the generous platform awnings, since removed. The class 27 locomotive is reversing its rake of carriages out of the platform, on the way to the carriage sidings, where they will be prepared for the journey back to Fort William.*

▲ *Apart from steam services and specials, long, locomotive-hauled trains are a thing of the past on the Mallaig line. Today, services are operated by the ubiquitous sprinters. A typical example is seen here in the early days of privatization. All around the station are overgrown reminders of better days.*

BRANCH LINE LOCOMOTIVES

Rarely designed for heavy traffic, branch lines were usually cheaply built. As a result, they were lightly engineered and often included sharp curves, which limited the kinds of vehicles that could use them. Many were built by independent companies, some of which had their own locomotives, but most lines were operated by larger companies with fleets of locomotives. Inevitably, older engines were sent to work out their last years on branch lines, a pattern maintained throughout the age of steam. By the 1950s, branch lines and remote rural railways had become a kind of mecca for train enthusiasts, filled as they were with veterans, often dating back to the time of Queen Victoria. From the Edwardian era, auto-trains and push-pull units were developed for branch line use, forerunners of the diesel railcars that became universal from the mid-1950s. Nevertheless, elderly locomotives lingered on until the end of steam on British Railways.

▲ *In the 1950s the Dornoch branch, virtually the most northerly in Britain, was home to the last surviving Highland Railway tank locomotives in regular service. One of these little engines, built in the early 1900s, is seen leaving Skelbo with a mixed train from Dornoch.*

▼ *Detached as they were from the mainland, the railways of the Isle of Wight were always individual. The original independent companies had their own locomotives, but once the network was under the control of bigger organizations such as the Southern Railway and British Railways, it ended up with a mix of locomotives dating back to the 1860s. A typical 1864 veteran is no. 13, 'Ryde', seen looking very smart at St Helens in 1929.*

◀ Narrow gauge railways often had distinctive locomotives, and none more so than the Leek & Manifold Valley line. This railway had two locomotives, finely built but strange-looking vehicles that, with their huge headlights, would not have seemed out of place in India. These two engines served the railway throughout its short life, from 1902 to 1934. Some narrow gauge locomotives moved around from line to line, but in essence they always carried the individual look of the line for which they were originally built.

▶ A simple solution to the problems of single-track, low-cost branch line operation was the auto-train, a linked locomotive and carriage that could be driven from either end. These vehicles were used extensively on Great Western and Southern branches, thus keeping in action locomotives that would otherwise have been scrapped. A number of these auto-trains have been re-created on preserved lines, including this example photographed on the West Somerset Railway in the 1990s.

◀ Some railways stayed in business by being run as cheaply as possible. Typical was the Kent & East Sussex, part of Colonel Stephens' light railway empire. Everything on this line was second- or third-hand, and so it became well known for its unusual locomotives and vehicles that had been collected from sidings all over Britain. Shown here at Rolvendon in the 1930s is an elderly saddle tank locomotive that ended up in Kent. Its long life had started many years earlier with the London & South Western Railway.

Bo'ness & Kinneil Railway

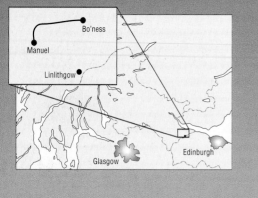

The Bo'ness & Kinneil Railway is based on a former branch built by the North British Railway. This ran northwards from Manuel, on the main Edinburgh and Glasgow line, to the shores of the Forth. Serving collieries and claypits as well as carrying passengers, the branch survived until 1965. Railway development started early in this area, and a considerable network was established in the 1840s. Much of it ultimately came under the control of the North British company.

Reopened in part by the Scottish Railway Preservation Society, the line is today as famous for its buildings as for its trains. Gathered from all over Scotland, these include the great iron train shed built for Edinburgh Haymarket station by the Edinburgh & Glasgow Railway in 1842, the adjacent 1879 station from Wormit in Fife, a Highland Railway footbridge from Murthly and a Caledonian Railway signal box. The railway's modern buildings have been designed to match traditional and vernacular styles. The line runs for over 3 miles to Birkhill, where the station, another re-creation, incorporates cast-iron awning brackets from Monifieth, near Dundee. With its buildings, locomotives and vehicles, and exhibition displays, the Bo'ness & Kinneil aims to tell the story of Scotland's railways and their impact on the landscape and culture of the local area.

◄ This postcard, posted in 1923, shows Market Street, Bo'ness. The clothes worn by the townspeople going about their business suggest the photograph was taken before World War I.

▼ One of the Bo'ness & Kinneil's most famous residents is 'Maude', a North British Railway 0-6-0 goods locomotive of 1891, seen here on the Avon viaduct re-creating a local freight train of the early days of British Railways.

LEADHILLS & WANLOCKHEAD

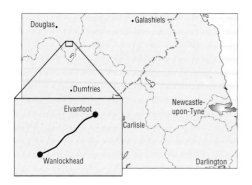

There is always something particularly appealing about railways in remote places, partly because their very existence is a reflection of the determination of Victorian engineers to conquer the challenges posed by extreme landscape. When such a line is long gone, it is sometimes hard to believe that it ever existed, or to understand why it was built. Just such a line is the Leadhills & Wanlockhead Light Railway, whose 8-mile branch from Elvanfoot, on the Caledonian Railway's main line northwards to Edinburgh and Glasgow, was completed in 1902. Building railways in hilly country was always demanding and expensive, but this line was something else, including as it did the highest summit (1,498ft) on any standard gauge line in Britain.

Minerals were the key to this unlikely enterprise. The bare hills that surround the source of the Clyde had been famous for lead mining since the Romans, and some of these mines remained active until the late 1920s. It was also a region long renowned for its gold deposits – hence its reputation as 'God's treasure house in Scotland'. Despite the effort put into its creation, the line was never a success. It was little used by the inhabitants of the scattered hill communities it served, and the hoped-for tourism failed to develop. As a result, the branch closed to passengers in 1938. Freight survived a while longer.

Forty-five years later, a preservation society, fired by the same spirit that built the branch in the first place, was formed to bring railways back to this remote region on the old Lanarkshire and Dumfriesshire borders. Today the Leadhills & Wanlockhead Railway offers an unusual and appealing journey, in locally made vehicles, on a mile of 2ft-gauge track south from Leadhills. There are plans to extend the line into Wanlockhead, where there is a museum of lead mining.

▼ *A number of railway lines constructed in Scotland in the early years of the twentieth century featured concrete viaducts of the kind pioneered by Sir Robert McAlpine, whose predilection for this material earned him the nickname Concrete Bob. Several were built on Caledonian lines, including this famous example on the Leadhills & Wanlockhead Railway at Risping Cleuch.*

▲ Mainly for aesthetic reasons, the curved concrete arches of the Risping Cleuch viaduct were faced with terracotta bricks, made at the Cleghorn brickworks in Glasgow. After the line's closure, however, these bricks began to drop off, prompting the spectacular destruction of the viaduct by explosives. The Leadhills & Wanlockhead Railway Society has now incorporated some of these terracotta bricks into its signal box at Leadhills.

◄ This postcard, issued in the Edwardian era by the Caledonian Railway, when the branch was still relatively new, was an attempt at encouraging tourists to visit Leadhills and Wanlockhead by train. While Wanlockhead can claim the highest house in Scotland, Leadhills boasts the monument and the curfew bell, featured here alongside a picture of the railway.

ON THE CALEDONIAN RAILWAY. LEADHILLS.

THE MONUMENT.

THE CURFEW BELL.

C.R. ENGINE WORKING ON LEADHILLS RAILWAY.

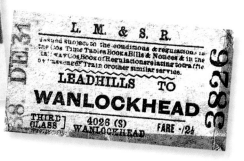

L. M. & S. R.

LEADHILLS TO WANLOCKHEAD

THIRD CLASS   4026 (S)   FARE -/2½
WANLOCKHEAD

3826

CASTLE DOUGLAS TO KIRKCUDBRIGHT

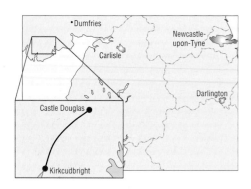

South-west Scotland is now a region virtually without railways. There is a line northwards via Dumfries, and a meandering and slow route southwards from Glasgow to Stranraer, but everything in between was obliterated in the 1960s. Gone is the old direct route from Dumfries to Stranraer, via Castle Douglas and Newton Stewart, and with it its branches to Portpatrick, Whithorn and Kirkcudbright. Gone is any sense that Dumfries was the hub of a major railway network.

The Kirkcudbright Railway received authorization for its 10-mile line to Castle Douglas in 1861, and it opened three years later. In 1865 it was taken over by the Glasgow & South Western Railway, which continued to operate it until the Grouping of 1923. At this period there were through trains from London, taking between ten and twelve hours for the 371-mile journey from St Pancras. It then became part of LMS until the formation of British Railways in 1948. Throughout this time extensive passenger and freight services kept the branch busy, particularly with fish traffic from Kirkcudbright's harbour. At the same time, there was a steady flow of tourists keen to explore the elegant streets of this handsome county town, whose busy and sharply tidal bay is overlooked by the ruins of sixteenth-century McLellan's Castle. It was from this harbour in 1622 that the first boatload of Scottish emigrants sailed for Nova Scotia. In the late 1800s painters from Glasgow regularly visited Kirkcudbright, drawn by the soft colours of the landscape, and Edward Hornel, one of the 'Glasgow Boys' group of artists, came to live here.

▼ *Towards the end of the line's life, in the early 1960s, a two-coach local train crosses the Tongland viaduct over the river Dee on its way to Castle Douglas and Dumfries. It is hauled by a British Railways Standard tank locomotive of the kind used on minor railways all over Britain at this time. At this point the Dee is still tidal and the hydro-electric power station just upstream of the viaduct is used to maintain the water level.*

▶ *Kirkcudbright station was a handsome stone building, in keeping with the architecture of the town, and domestic in its appearance. Today nothing remains but the memory of all the people who passed through its doors over a century of railway use – including those exciting Glasgow colourist painters at the end of the nineteenth century.*

Kirkcudbright

◀ *Kirkcudbright sits at the head of the tidal estuary of the Dee, a situation that explains both its importance as a fishing port and its appeal to visitors. This 1930s postcard shows this setting, and the compact nature of the town. The station was off the card to the left.*

▼ *Today Tongland viaduct's piers and approach arches are still standing, their weathered stone suggesting something far older than the railway age. South of the bridge, a low embankment, which still exists among the trees, carried the line towards Kirkcudbright. To the north, little remains to be seen until Tongland is left behind.*

The thriving artistic community that was established here still exists today. However, none of this was sufficient to keep the line open, and closure came in 1965, along with the rest of the network in this part of south-west Scotland.

Where to find the evidence

Since closure, much of the line has returned into the gentle green landscape whence it came. Despite this, plenty does survive and the route can be followed and readily identified from adjacent roads. A short stretch a little south of Castle Douglas is an official footpath, allowing for close inspection of bridges and other structures, which often feature attractive detailing in local stone. Some stations exist, now converted to private houses or offices, for example Bridge of Dee and Tarff. Some sections have been buried by road improvement schemes, but elsewhere, notably north of Tongland, the route can clearly be traced on the wooded hillside on the east side of the road. The main engineering feature was the viaduct that carried the line across the Dee to the south of Tongland. The approach arches and piers that carried this still stand, just to the north of the old arched road bridge. From here into Kirkcudbright the line becomes harder to distinguish, with much having been obliterated by housing and road schemes. Originally it came to an end in a big station yard overlooking the Dee's tidal estuary, to the north of the harbour and the town centre. Here, it is hard to find any evidence to indicate that Kirkcudbright once had a railway, let alone one that existed for just over a century.

▲ *In addition to bridges and other railway structures that survive, more transient things can occasionally be spotted. This iron gatepost included a patent closing mechanism to ensure animals could not stray on to the track.*

▲ Near Mollance the embankment that carried the railway is clearly visible, with the remains of a small bridge. Beyond the bridge the embankment has vanished, giving the concrete remains, now the province of sheep, a curious kind of abstraction. In the distance are the hills that provide a magnificent backdrop for much of the route.

◄ On a rather gloomy August day in 1961, the local for Dumfries stands ready to depart from Kirkcudbright, headed by an LMS tank locomotive. The railway garden is flourishing and well cared for, the beds neatly edged with angled bricks, but the cast-iron name plate on the seat back already seems to have been removed by someone, although closure was still four years away.

ROXBURGH TO JEDBURGH

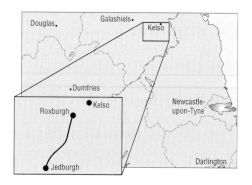

High in the list of regions of Britain most devastated by the railway closures of the 1960s is the Scottish Borders. A large area south of Edinburgh is now devoid of any rail service whatsoever. Included in the slaughter was the old North British line from Coldstream to St Boswells via Roxburgh, an area famous for its castles and abbeys. From Roxburgh a 7-mile branch ran south to Jedburgh, along the banks of the Teviot and Jed Water. Built independently and opened in July 1856, it was taken over by the North British Railway in 1860. Through the rest of the nineteenth century and into the twentieth, the line was the main gateway to this county town and royal borough, famous for its abbey and its castle, and its associations with Mary, Queen of Scots, who stayed here in 1566. Other famous visitors included William Wordsworth and Sir Walter Scott; the latter made his first appearance as an advocate in a criminal trial here in 1793. Another of the town's claims to fame is the invention of seven-a-side rugby.

The railway survived into the time of British Railways, but in August 1948 disaster struck as floods seriously damaged the track. Passenger services ceased at once, but basic repairs enabled freight trains to run until 1964. Today, in Jedburgh itself there is little sign of the railway. The site of the station and the goods yard has vanished beneath an industrial park, but the trackbed is apparent as it leaves the town past the rugby club's field. From this point, it is easily discernible in the landscape and, considering the early date of closure to passengers, there is plenty to be seen, including station houses and platforms at Nisbet and Kirkbank, both now private, and a platform at Jedfoot. Here, and elsewhere, the trackbed is a part of the Borders Abbeys Way. Never far from the river, the route is an enjoyable walk, especially on the approach to Roxburgh with the grand arches of the Teviot viaduct in the distance.

▼ *Freight services survived on the Jedburgh branch until the 1960s and were very regular in the late 1950s, when this photograph was taken of Jedburgh station yard. The locomotive waits while a porter loads goods into a wagon. One of Jedburgh's major industries was textiles, and the factories were busy users of the line. Today, nothing of this remains.*

◄ *Jedburgh station is buried beneath a modern industrial estate. It was never a grand station and, by the time this photograph was taken in the late 1950s, it had a tired air, a consequence of the ending of passenger services several years earlier.*

► *This romantic view of Jedburgh Abbey, set above the river, was issued as a postcard in the 1920s, one of a series called 'Ruined Abbeys'.*

▼ *All that remains of Jedfoot station are two platforms. One, flanking the trackbed that at this point is part of the Border Abbeys Way, is in good order, with stone edging. The other is decrepit and overgrown, but visibly formed from old sleepers set vertically. Near by is a pile of telegraph poles, abandoned when the line closed, and in the bushes are the remains of the level-crossing gates.*

Jedburgh Abbey

OLD RAILWAY CARRIAGES

When new and smart, railway vehicles run on the main lines. As they age, they are put to work on rural routes. Towards the end of their practical life they shuffle up and down branch lines. Finally, they are put to rest on distant and overgrown sidings, where they may quietly decay for years before the scrapyard or the bonfire finally beckons. However, since the dawn of railways, some vehicles have escaped that fate. These, usually just a grounded body without running gear, have retained a railway-based life as a tool store or mess van. Others have become waiting rooms or ticket offices on remote platforms. Now, such sights are rare, but fifty years ago the recycling of vehicle bodies on the railways was commonplace and practical.

Other vehicles escaped the railways altogether. From the 1920s old railway carriages were often used as cheap housing. Parked on bricks in a field or on a beach and given basic facilities, they helped to overcome housing shortages and, in the years before the Town and Country Planning Acts, acted as holiday homes. At that time, many railway companies sold old wooden carriage bodies for around £20, including delivery to the nearest station or rail head. There were hundreds all over Britain, but few survive today. Most have burnt down or have just fallen apart, while a few have been rescued and restored to run again on preserved lines. Still common, however, are the bodies of former goods vans, thousands of which were used as stores and animal shelters on farms all over Britain.

▲ *Made in about 1900, this wooden-bodied carriage used to run on the Somerset & Dorset Joint Railway, but when it was photographed at some unknown railway location in the 1950s, its running days were long over. Saved from the scrapyard and mounted on blocks, it had done good service, perhaps as a mess or dormitory van, but now, in a poor state of repair, it clearly faced an uncertain future. It was probably turned into firewood years ago.*

▼ *Retired railway carriages seem to have congregated in some places, particularly by the seaside. A famous location for such gatherings was Dungeness, and even today some survive in that rather bleak and windswept setting. These two spent their working lives on the London, Brighton & South Coast line.*

◄ *A former GWR carriage, in use as a house in rural Dorset. Such vehicles can be dated by style and construction, and the original numbers and markings can sometimes be traced under layers of paint. This carriage was built in 1903 and was moved here in the early 1920s.*

▼ *This early 1950s photograph shows a group of grounded carriage bodies in use as staff accommodation outside Ipswich station. Once common all over the network, sights such as this are now to be seen only on preserved lines.*

RAILWAY COTTAGE EYPE

▼ *Many farms all over the country still have the remains of railway goods vehicles quietly decaying in their fields and farmyards after a long and useful life as feed and tool stores or as livestock shelters. This cow looks quite at home with this former box-van in the corner of her Norfolk field.*

▼ *Old railway carriages can be found all over Britain, with many still earning their keep as holiday homes. This example, smartly presented in LNER colours, is delightfully placed beside a stream in Yorkshire, having acquired a pitched roof to protect it from the worst of the weather.*

KILLIN JUNCTION TO LOCH TAY

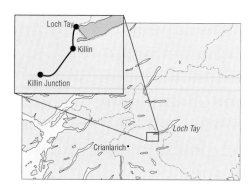

The appeal of the history and the landscape of Scotland, and Scottish rivers and lochs in particular, increased steadily through the latter years of the Victorian era, encouraged both by literature and by increasing accessibility. It was the expanding railway network that really opened the country up to visitors. Typical was the region around the river Tay, with Loch Tay itself being served by two separate railways. One was the 5-mile Killin Railway, opened in 1886 to link the western end of Loch Tay with the Caledonian Railway's main line westwards from Dunblane to Oban via Crianlarich. Operated by the Caledonian and later by the LMS, this was primarily a tourist line, with its terminus on the shores of Loch Tay by the steamer pier. When the steamer service was withdrawn in September 1939, passenger carrying beyond Killin also ended. The rest of the line lived on into British Railways' time and survived until September 1965.

Today there is much to be seen. The trackbed is visible, and walkable, to the site of the Loch Tay terminus. Killin station has gone, along with most of the route through the town. However, beyond the spectacular Falls of Dochart, one of the area's main attractions, the trackbed becomes a well-defined footpath that climbs gently through the surrounding forests to Killin Junction. Here, isolated in the silence of the forest, the two lines, both now footpaths, converge by the surviving platform. Beyond are the remains of derelict railway cottages, the only clue to the busy past of this delightful and secret place.

▼ *As the branch approaches the end of its life in the 1960s, a single-coach train drops down towards Killin from the junction, hauled by a former Caledonian tank locomotive, now in British Railways livery. This type of engine was in use on the branch for much of its life. The classic branch line scene could be anywhere in Britain but, ironically, since the closure of the Killin line, extensive conifer forestation has given the route a much more typically Scottish look.*

◀ *The Falls of Dochart, on the river Dochart just to the south of Killin and only a short walk from the town, is a famous feature of the region, and has been a popular draw for tourists since the Victorian era. The railway ran just behind the cottages on the left, and so the falls would have been visible, and audible, from the train.*

THE FALLS OF DOCHART, KILLIN

▼ *The Killin branch follows the river Dochart on its way to Loch Tay. Beyond Killin Junction, the line westwards to Crianlarich continues along Glen Dochart. This 1920s view gives a sense of the magnificent setting enjoyed by the railway.*

▼ *Killin Junction is now a clearing in the forest, where two footpaths meet. The path on the left, with the figure, was the Killin branch, at the start of its descent to Killin and Loch Tay. The path on the right was the main line south towards Callander and Dunblane. The photographer is standing on the surviving platform of Killin Junction station.*

GLEN DOCHART, KILLIN.

BALLINLUIG TO ABERFELDY

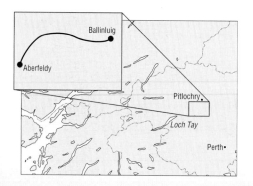

The branch line to Aberfeldy was planned in the early 1860s as part of an ambitious scheme by the Inverness & Perth Junction Railway to open up this part of Scotland. The branch was completed in July 1865, by which time its builders had merged with other companies to become the Highland Railway. The 10-mile line, from Ballinluig to Aberfeldy, closely followed the river Tay, and the major engineering features were two bridges near Ballinluig over the Tummel and the Tay. By this time, Aberfeldy was becoming known as a touring centre for this part of Perthshire, with attractions such as golf, fishing, a whisky distillery and Loch Tay itself, a few miles to the west. The line therefore soon became popular and continued to flourish until the early 1960s, when road competition took its toll. Closure came in May 1965, just short of the line's centenary.

Today the route is easily followed by road. Ballinluig station is long gone, but the overgrown remains of the bay platform for Aberfeldy trains is still there. The Tummel bridge is now a modern road bridge, but the original 1865 cast-iron Tay bridge now carries a minor road. The trackbed is largely visible across fields, through woods and by the side of the river until the outskirts of Aberfeldy. Some sections are walkable. The distillery, once a major user of the railway, has in its yard a preserved tank locomotive and a wagon loaded with whisky barrels. Aberfeldy has a Station Hotel but no trace of a station.

▼ *In the dying days of the branch, one carriage was usually sufficient for the few passengers still using the line. On a bright day in the early 1960s, the local train waits at Aberfeldy station, incongruously in the care of a large diesel locomotive. This was an unusual combination, for decaying branch lines were normally operated at this time by diesel railcars or elderly steam engines.*

(A. 436)
THE HIGHLAND RAILWAY.
LUGGAGE.
From ___
TO BALLINLUIG

► ▼ *This Edwardian postcard (right) shows the old Tummel rail and road bridges, with Ballinluig station in the background. Today both have gone, replaced by a modern road bridge. However, the railway bridge over the Tay, half a mile farther on, survives. Now carrying a minor road, it is also a cast-iron structure, similarly ornamented with fortified turrets. The picture below shows a train for Aberfeldy crossing the Tummel rail bridge in the 1950s.*

THE BRIDGES ON THE TUMMEL BALLINLUIG. 567

▼ *(Inset) After crossing the river Tummel and the river Tay, the Aberfeldy branch followed the Tay westwards. Parts of the trackbed survive, and short sections can be walked. Elsewhere, it has become a farm track. Here it runs away into the distance after crossing a minor stream on what was obviously once a railway bridge.*

DINGWALL TO STRATHPEFFER

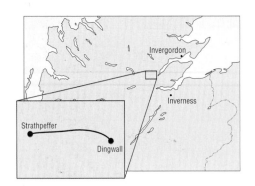

Established as a spa by the late eighteenth century, Strathpeffer had its first pump room in 1820. In the Victorian period its fame both in and beyond Scotland encouraged railway companies to include the town on their routes. First on the scene was the Dingwall & Skye Railway, which included a station called Strathpeffer on its heavily engineered line that ran westwards towards Kyle of Lochalsh. However, this station, later renamed Auchterneed, was over a mile to the north of the town. This route is, of course, still open and is widely regarded as one of the most exciting railway journeys in Scotland. In 1885 the Highland Railway did better, opening a short branch directly to Strathpeffer from a junction to the west of Dingwall.

The Highland took care to promote the line and the town's attractions, and soon there were through coaches from London, as well as the Strathpeffer Spa Express, which after 1910 ran regularly from Aviemore. The following year the Highland opened its own hotel, a grandiose structure that joined others already established in the town. The height of Strathpeffer's popularity was before World War I, and the appeal of taking the waters began to diminish in the 1920s. At a later date other attractions, notably tennis, golf and dancing, restored the town's popularity, but by then the branch was in terminal decline. Passenger carrying ceased in February 1946; freight services struggled on for a few more years, until 1951.

Today, the route of the branch, running westwards along the foot of an escarpment immediately to the south of the river Peffery, can be easily seen from a parallel road. Strathpeffer's station has survived, complete with its platform, its attractive glazed awning and delicate cast-iron supports, and is now living a new life housing a café, craft centre and museum of childhood.

(A. 474)
THE HIGHLAND RAILWAY.
LUGGAGE.
From
TO STRATHPEFFER

Strathpeffer.

◀ Set in its fold of hills, Strathpeffer is a small but elegant town, still looking much as it did in this Edwardian postcard. The large building set above the town is the Ben Wyvis hotel. The station is out of sight, below the church spire.

▶ A splendid building in timber and cast iron, in a style typical of the Highland Railway, Strathpeffer station is still doing sterling service as a café, craft centre and museum of childhood.

▶ (Inset) A local landowner forced the Dingwall & Skye Railway to build its main line well to the north of Strathpeffer, resulting in heavy and expensive engineering and a station a long way from the town it was supposed to serve. Raven's Rock, seen on this card, is a cutting on that line. The building of a branch direct to Strathpeffer made access easy.

RAVENS ROCK, STRATHPEFFER

RAILWAYANA

There have always been railway enthusiasts, but the collecting of railway artefacts is a relatively recent phenomenon. What had previously been an arcane activity was given a massive boost by the closure programmes of the 1960s and 1970s and the ending, at the same time, of steam on the British network. Vast quantities of railway relics of all kinds were disposed of, often in random and disorganized ways, and these formed the basis of the modern railwayana business. Today, there are collectors of every kind of object with railway associations, and their tastes are fed by specialist fairs, auctions, swapmeets and magazines. Most prized are bits of locomotives, such as name, number and maker's plates, many of which are now beyond the reach of the ordinary enthusiast's pocket. Next come station and trackside signs in enamel and cast iron, items that combine displayability with nostalgia. These are followed by posters, similarly appealing. After that the list is endless: clocks, lamps, seats and station equipment, uniforms and buttons, maps and timetables, books, signalling equipment, tickets and luggage labels, every other kind of paperwork, postcards and photographs. For every item of railwayana, there are keen collectors somewhere.

▲ Bureaucracy was all-consuming and labyrinthine, so paperwork was produced in prodigious quantities. Things that survive often tell interesting stories. What happened to the lady who lost her purse, and a large sum of money, in a first-class compartment on the Wirral Railway on 10 January 1896?

▲ Railway posters, especially the pictorial kind, have always been popular, and many feature designs by well-known artists. Posters were never intended to have a long life, and so those that by chance survive, such as this 1950s example, have both rarity value and period charm.

▼ Despite being printed in huge numbers and regularly revised, timetables are always of interest, particularly those issued for minor or long-closed lines, and for narrow gauge railways, such as this pre-war example from the Festiniog Company.

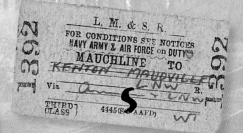

▲ Tickets have always been collected, and not just by the guard. All regions, companies and routes are open to the collector and there are many rarities, despite the many millions issued. This is an LMS forces ticket, used for a journey from south-west Scotland to Somerset.

▲ Luggage label collecting is one of the more obscure branches of railwayana. Every company issued its own labels for stations it served, and those that survive offer a fascinating insight into railway history. This example was issued by the London, Brighton & South Coast Railway, probably before World War I.

L. & S.W.R. BEWARE OF TRAINS

◀ In the Victorian era and well into the twentieth century, railway companies made many of their signs out of cast iron, particularly those that had to survive out of doors. An example popular with collectors today is this London & South Western 'Beware' notice. Many of these survived in lineside sites into the British Railways era.

JUNCTION ROAD

LNER PASSENGERS SHOULD PADLOCK REAR WHEELS OF BICYCLES

▲ Railway clocks have always been collected. Every station had one or more clocks, and they were often of good quality, simply because precise timekeeping was vital. The most popular have clear railway associations, such as the name or initials of the company on the face.

▲ Street names are often the only sign of a long-lost railway. This early example is on a wall in Leek, Staffordshire, whose railways closed in the 1960s.

▲ Each railway had its own style and look. After the Grouping of the 'Big Four' companies in 1923, a degree of standardization was established. This delightfully individual enamel sign is in the house style and house colour of the LNER.

CARBIS BAY

▲ Carbis Bay is a small station on the St Ives branch in Cornwall, and would have had only a few of these enamel name totems in Western Region brown on the single platform. This may be the only survivor. Such a totem would have great appeal and considerable value.

BRITISH RAILWAYS

▲ In the late 1940s, British Railways established a distinctive house style to be applied universally. Part of this process was the standardization of enamel station names and other signs, based on the totem. Regions, in this case the North East, were identified by the background colour.

▲ Lamps were used by guards and station staff, and were carried on rolling stock. This example of the latter has been repainted, which reduces its appeal.

RAC CROSSING NO GATES

BUNTINGFORD

▲ Railway station seats have always been popular. Thousands must have ended up in gardens all over Britain. Many railway companies produced their own distinctive designs and styles, and some included a recessed panel into which a cast-iron sign of the station name could be fitted. Similar cast-iron name panels were also made for signal boxes, and to mark junctions and tunnels.

▲ Road signs with railway connections are also popular with collectors, such as this pre-war enamel example, rescued from the Corfe Castle area in Dorset.

THE MOUND TO DORNOCH

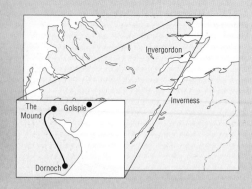

Dornoch has a long history, reflected in its thirteenth-century cathedral, which is said to contain the tombs of sixteen earls of Sutherland. Not too far away is a stone marking the spot where the last execution of a witch took place in Scotland, in 1722, after she had turned her daughter into a pony. However, the main claim to fame of this royal burgh is golf. Its course dates back to 1616, and some say the game was invented here. In any case, golf, the seaside and the expanding leisure market were the inspiration for the opening in 1902 of the Dornoch Light Railway, an independent operation until the LMS took over in 1923. Prior to that date the Highland Railway ran the trains, and in 1904 the company built its own 83-bedroom hotel. Aimed at golfers and their families, the hotel was promoted as 'overlooking the first green'. This handsome three-storey stone structure, now called the Dornoch Castle, still dominates the town.

The Dornoch railway was virtually the most northerly branch line in Britain, and for that reason always had a character of its own. The line started at The Mound, just north of the causeway at the head of Loch Fleet, on one of the loops and swirls that mark the extraordinarily circuitous route of the railway from Inverness to Wick and Thurso.

▼ *Against a backdrop of glorious Highland scenery, the old trackbed curves round the seashore of Loch Fleet. To the left is the road that used to share its route with the railway from The Mound, and in the distance are the ruins of Skelbo Castle, half hidden by trees.*

▼ *(Inset) From Embo to Dornoch the trackbed is a cycleway and footpath through the dunes, in sight of the sea. It ends near the old station at Dornoch, a typical Highland Railway building, now a café and souvenir shop.*

▲ *The 10.30am from Dornoch approaches the junction across The Mound causeway in 1956, a typical mixed train hauled by one of the famous Edwardian Highland Railway tank locomotives. The causeway was the creation of the great engineer Thomas Telford.*

◀ *Despite its remote location, Dornoch was a busy tourist town throughout the life of the railway. This 1950s postcard highlights some of the popular attractions, including the cathedral and castle, the loch and the coastline, the Castle Hotel and, above all, the golf, the* raison d'être *for both the railway and the hotel in the early 1900s.*

DORNOCH

DORNOCH

GOLF CLUB HOUSE & 1ST TEE

DORNOCH FIRTH FROM STRUIE

CATHEDRAL & CASTLE

SHIN FALLS

CASTLE & COUNTY BUILDINGS

THE SQUARE   D.3606

DORNOCH

1646

From here it curved round the shore of Loch Fleet to Skelbo, frequently sharing its route with the road, and then swung south to Embo and Dornoch, with vistas across sandy beaches to Dornoch Firth. Through the latter part of its life the line was famous for its mixed trains, with freight wagons attached to the carriages. It was also well known for its locomotives, and for a long time it was the last habitat of a type of Highland Railway tank engine otherwise extinct. At the very end of the 1950s these were replaced by something equally unexpected, former Great Western tank engines usually found on the branch lines of Cornwall and Devon. By then the end was in sight, and the line closed on 13 June 1960.

(A. 474)
THE HIGHLAND RAILWAY.
LUGGAGE.
From
TO EMBO

Following the route from loch to seaside

Despite the fact that the branch was built cheaply as a light railway, there is still plenty to see. The Mound station and the junction have vanished beneath a new bridge, and the improved A9 has similarly obliterated the line over the causeway across the head of Loch Fleet. However, the trackbed soon appears, running round the loch beside the minor road. A platelayers' hut houses sheep. From Skelbo Castle the trackbed can be seen in the adjacent fields, complete with bridges and the platform of Skelbo station. From Embo, where little survives apart from Station Road, the trackbed is a walkway and cycle path all the way to Dornoch, a fine route above the dunes with spectacular sea views. Dornoch station is much built over, but the actual station building is preserved as a café.

▼ *Shortly before the line was closed in the late 1950s, a typical mixed train stands ready to depart from Dornoch on the 8-mile journey to The Mound. At its head is one of the former GWR tank locomotives brought up to run the line in the last years, an unexpected sight so far from its home territory in either Wales or the West Country.*

HUMOROUS POSTCARDS

The humorous postcard, its image and text filled with innuendo, double entendre, misunderstanding, saucy repartee and classic vulgarity, has been part of the British holiday experience since the early 1900s. Lively, entertaining, outspoken and delightfully incorrect in today's climate, these cards are a vital reflection of so many aspects of British social life and changing cultural attitudes.

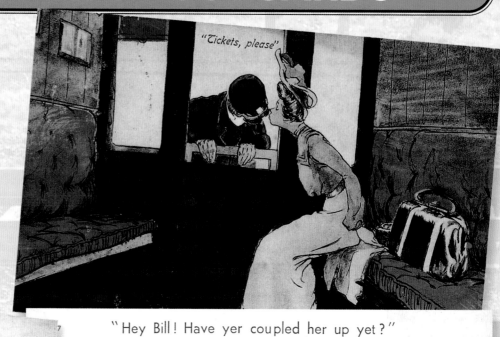

"Tickets, please"

"Hey Bill! Have yer coupled her up yet?"

"TICKET SLIPPED DOWN YER JUMPER, HAS IT? WELL, WHEREVER IT IS, I'VE GOT TO PUNCH IT!"

THE LAST TRAIN Home

These cards, dating from 1905 to the 1960s, are classic examples, featuring the problem of overcrowding on routes with limited services, double entendre and sexual innuendo – as in the drama of the lost ticket and the ticket collector's response. The perils of the single woman travelling alone was a popular theme in the Edwardian period, featuring in stories and films as well as postcards.

GET YER THINGS OFF, JANE – THEY'RE SHOUTING "ALL CHANGE!"
Imbécile! On nous dit de changer de train, mais pas l'arrière-train!

The railway provided a rich seam of humour for the postcard artist. The earliest cards date from Edwardian days, the most recent from the 1960s and 1970s. Many themes occur and re-occur regularly, including the lost ticket, the misunderstood railway announcement, the discomfort of travel and overcrowding. Equally common are themes of a more saucy nature, often involving suggestive exchanges between railway staff and female passengers – perhaps more comprehensible in the days when many trains had no corridors and separate compartments.

Guard–
"Have you a black Mackintosh there?"
Jovial Drover–
"Nae man, nae, we're a'
Red MacGreegors here."

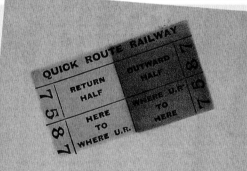

QUICK ROUTE RAILWAY
RETURN HALF   OUTWARD HALF
HERE TO WHERE U.R.   WHERE U.R. TO HERE
7587   7587

IN CASE YOU HAVE FORGOTTEN DEAR,
I SEND THIS ON TO SAY
THAT TICKETS LIKE THE PICTURE HERE
CAN BRING YOU ON THIS WAY.

YOU BUY ONE AT YOUR STATION,
AND YOU BOARD THE PROPER TRAIN,
AND THEN—HOW ABSOLUTELY GRAND—
YOU'RE WITH ME ONCE AGAIN!

1ST CLASS
Saturday to Monday
ENGAGED
D. Freeman.

Two of these cards, dating from around 1905 and the 1920s, illustrate the results of classic misunderstandings about train announcements. Many cards explore the 'All Change' theme, including the one at the top of this page, made in Britain for the French market. The other two postcards (above and left) reflect another popular theme in the Edwardian era, the role of the train as a vehicle for romance.

INDEX

Abbey Town 210, 212
Abbotsbury branch 31
ABC series 48
Aberfeldy 240–1
Aberystwyth 158, 165
Abingdon 4–5, 122
Adams, William 42
agriculture 39, 60–1
Aldeburgh 100–3
Allhallows-on-Sea 68, 69
Alne 202, 203, 204
Alston 6–7, 194, 195
Amlwch 174–7
Andrews, GT 214
Anglesey Central Railway 174
Angrave, Bruce 149
Annan 210
Anning, Mary 41
Ashbourne 140
Aspatria 210
Atlantic Coast Express 28
Auchterneed 242
Austen, Jane 41, 42
auto-trains 118, 224, 225
Axbridge station 61
Axminster & Lyme Regis Railway 40–3
Axminster station 43, 61

Bala 150
Ballachulish branch 111
Ballinluig 240–1
Bangor 174
Bank Holidays Act (1871) 120
Barclay, Andrew 216
Barmouth to Dolgellau railway 135
Barnstaple 20–1
Barry 168
Bass brewery 217
Bassett-Lowke 96, 97, 196
Bawden, Edward 154
Bawdrip Halt 120
Beeching Report 40, 76, 90
Bekonscot Model Village 97
Bell, W 49
Ben Nevis 156, 221, 222
Berkshire 78–9, 114–17
Betws-y-Coed 150, 153
Bickershaw Colliery 216
'Big Four' 18, 48, 132, 162, 245
Biggin Hill 67
Birkhill 226
Bishops Lydeard 24
Black Dog halt 74
Blackmore Gate station 21
Blaenau Ffestiniog 150–3
Blue Anchor 22, 24, 25
Blythe Bridge 124, 125
boat services 52–5, 183, 192, 238
Bodiam 58
Bodmin & Wadebridge Railway 32
Bo'ness & Kinneil Railway 226–7
Boot 196, 197
Borders Abbeys Way 234, 235
Boscarne Junction 32–3
Bowness 181, 183
Brasted 64–5, 66
    White Hart 67
Braughing 98, 99
brewing 217
Bridge of Dee station 232
bridges

bowstring (Uffculme) 37
brick (Yaxley) 108, 109
cast-iron (Tay) 240, 241
lifting (Sheppey) 56
Medina (Newport) 81
stone 133, 134, 165, 209, 232
swing (Caledonian Canal) 222
timber (Calne) 74
over Tummel 240, 241
Tyne valley 194
bridleways 132
Bridport 44–7
Bridport Railway 44, 132
Bristol and Bath railway path 132
Bristol & Exeter Company 22
British Railways
    1950s branch line look 190
    camping coaches 77
    central England 130, 136, 146
    Country Afternoon Tickets 65
    Eastern Region 87, 94, 95
    employees 72
    freight train re-creation 226–7
    Isle of Skye poster 218
    northern England 180, 181, 184, 192, 202
    numbering system 48
    railcars 110, 111, 128, 130, 212
    signs 56, 119, 245
    southern England 54, 58, 59, 70, 71, 80
    tank locomotives 13, 230, 232–3
    Wales 166
    walks guides 132
    West Country 24, 27, 40
Brockenhurst 52, 54, 134
Brontë family 190, 191
Brown, Gregory 134
Bruff, Peter 92
Brunel, Isambard Kingdom 12
Bruton, ED 49
Bull Bay 174, 175
Buntingford 98, 99, 245
Bures 92, 93
Burneside 182
Burrator Reservoir 34, 35
Bury St Edmunds 90, 91
Butlin's holiday camps 23, 24
Buxton 140

Caernarvon & Llanberis Railway 156
Caledonian Canal 222
Caledonian Railway 111, 220, 226, 228, 229, 238
Calne Railway 74–5
Camarthen 164, 165
Camarthen & Cardigan Railway 164, 170
Cambridge 90, 91
Camel Trail 32, 33
camping coaches 40, 76–7, 198, 236, 237
Carbis Bay 14, 15, 245
Cardigan 164, 165, 170–3
carriages 236–7
    see also camping coaches
Castle Douglas 230–3
Castle Hedingham station 92
Catterick Garrison 214
cattle 39, 55, 61, 108, 145, 202
Cauldon Low 140
Caverswall Road 124, 125
Chappel & Wakes Colne station 92
Chartwell 66
Chester & Holyhead Railway 174
Chetnole station 30

Chevening Halt 66
Chippenham 74
Cholsey & Wallingford Railway 122–3
Churnet Valley line 140
Cirencester 128, 130
clay industry 16, 32, 226
clocks 214, 245
coal & collieries 78, 124–5, 126, 168, 194, 200–1, 216, 226
Cockermouth, Keswick & Penrith Railway 133
Colchester 90, 91
Colchester, Stour Valley, Sudbury & Halstead Railway 90
Coldstream 234
Coleridge, Samuel Taylor 22
Coles, CRL 49
Colne Valley Railway 92
Colyton 28, 29
Combe Hay 154
Combpyne 40, 41, 43
Commondale station 185
Coniston 192
Constable, John 92
container services 88, 89
Conwy & Llanwrst company 150
Conwy Valley 150–3
Coombe junction 16, 17
Corfe Castle 26, 27, 245
Cornish Riviera Express 12, 14
Cornwall 10–17, 32–3, 61, 72
Corpach 221
Cowes 80, 81
Crianlarich 238, 239
Cromer 86, 94
Culkerton halt 128–9
Culm Valley Light Railway 36–7
Cumbria 30, 133, 180–3, 189, 192–3, 196–9, 210–13
cycle paths 32, 33, 34, 35, 74, 75, 132–5, 138, 139, 142, 146, 184, 246, 249

Dalegarth 196, 198
Darlington 214, 215
Dartmoor 34–5
David & Charles Ltd 49
Derbyshire 112, 113, 140
Devon 20–1, 28–9, 34–7, 73, 162
Didcot Railway Centre 127
Dingwall 242–3
Dingwall & Skye Railway 242
Dochart, Falls of 238, 239
Dolgoch 159, 160
Dornoch 2–3, 224, 246–9
Dorset 26–7, 40–7, 217, 237, 245
Drayton Green halt 30
drivers 73
Dudbridge 138, 139
Dumfries 230
Dungeness 62, 63, 236
Dunton Green 64, 66
Dyffryn Llynfi line 168
Dymchurch 62

Earley, MW 49
Easingwold Railway 202–5
East Anglian Railway Museum 92
East Coast main line 203, 204
East Suffolk Railway 100
Eastern & Midlands Railway 94
Eastern Belle Pullman 88
Eastern Counties Railway 98, 100
Eastern Union Railway 108

Ecton 143
Edinburgh 226, 228
Eil, Loch 222
eisteddfods 170
Elvanfoot 228
Embo 246, 249
Embsay 206
Embsay & Bolton Abbey Railway 208
enthusiasts 48–9
Esk Valley line 184–7
Eskdale *see* Ravenglass & Eskdale Railway
Eskdale Green station 197
Essex 77, 106–7, 132
evacuation 188
excursions 18, 49, 120–1, 192, 193, 194, 203, 206
    schoolchildren 188–9
Eye 108–9

Fawley branch 4
Felixstowe 88–9, 163
Felixstowe Railway & Pier Company 88
Ffestiniog Railway 150, 152, 244
films 154–5
fish 106, 220, 221, 230, 231
Fleet, Loch 246, 249
footpaths 132–5
    central England 141–3, 146, 147
    East Anglia 98
    northern England 184, 194
    Scotland 232, 234, 235, 238, 246, 249
    southern England 78, 79
    Wales 171, 173
    West Country 34, 35, 41, 46, 47
Fort William 220, 222, 223
Foxfield Railway 124–5
Framlingham 100
freight 216–17
    central England 116, 118, 124, 126, 127, 136, 137, 138, 139, 143, 144, 146
    East Anglia 88, 89, 90, 101, 102, 106, 108
    northern England 182, 190, 193, 202, 206, 207, 210, 214
    Scotland 220, 227, 230, 234, 242, 249
    southern England 55, 56, 57, 58, 59, 68, 69, 83
    Wales 150–3, 158, 160, 165, 166, 168, 173, 174
    West Country 20, 22, 26, 28, 32, 34, 36, 40
    see also clay industry; coal & collieries; fish; gravel; iron ore; livestock; milk; minerals; nuclear power industry; slate industry; stone
fruit 61
Furness Railway 192, 193
Furzebrook Railway 26, 217

Gaerwen 174, 176, 177
Gainsborough, Thomas 91
gardens 104–5, 114–15, 128, 233
gatepost with closing mechanism 232
gauge
    broad 12, 22, 44, 74, 122
    miniature 62, 196
    narrow 20, 140, 150, 152, 156, 158–61, 166–7, 194–5, 197, 217, 225, 228, 229
    standard 22, 44, 74, 114, 122, 190, 228
George, Duke of York (George VI) 63
GER *see* Great Eastern Railway
Glasgow 228, 230, 231
Glasgow & South Western Railway 111, 230
Glenfinnan 220–1, 222
Glogue halt 170, 173
Gloucestershire 105, 128–9, 136–9
GNER *see* Great North of England Railway
Goudhurst station 70
Grain 68, 69
Grassington 206–9
gravel 44, 45
Great Eastern Railway 88, 90, 98, 100, 106, 108, 163
Great North of England Railway 214
Great Northern Railway 144, 146
Great St Trinian's Train Robbery, The 155

Great Western Railway 12, 14, 22, 24, 34, 36, 44, 74, 78, 114, 126, 128
    auto-trains 225
    broad gauge 12, 44
    carriages 237
    gardens 104
    holiday brochures 18
    hotels 13, 162
    image and reputation 15
    and independent branch lines 122
    milk traffic 38
    railcars 79, 110, 116, 117, 121
    rivalry with London & South Western 14, 26
    South Wales poster 148
    station architecture 21, 30, 116, 118, 130
    station master 72
    tank locomotives 47, 73, 114–15, 124–5, 155, 249
    tickets 116
    in Wales 148, 150, 158, 165, 168, 170
Green, Benjamin 194
Greenly, Henry 62, 63
Grosmont 184, 186
guidebooks 132
GWR *see* Great Western Railway

Hadham 98
halts 30, 31, 39, 128, 170
Haltwhistle 6–7, 194
Hampshire 4, 52–5, 105, 155
Harris & Company 74, 75
Havenstreet 84
Hawkhurst 70–1
Haworth 190, 191
Haydn, Henry 158, 160
Headcorn 58, 59
Hellandbridge 33
Hemyock 36–7, 73
Henley-on-Thames 114–17, 122
Henllan 166, 167
Herbert, CCB 49
Hertfordshire 98–9
Highbridge 38
Highland Railway 1, 224, 226, 240, 242, 246, 247, 249
Holiday Runabout Tickets 181
holidays 18–19, 24, 25, 28
    East Anglia 88, 95, 100
    northern England 180–3, 190, 192–3, 196–9, 210
    promotions 18, 42, 77, 181
    Scotland 220, 238, 240, 246
    southern England 56–7, 82
    Wales 168–9, 170
    West Country 12–15, 16, 22, 40, 41
    see also camping coaches; excursions; hotels
Holyhead 174
Holt 94
Hoo 68
hop-pickers' specials 58, 60, 70
Hope Mill *see* Goudhurst
Hornby, Frank 96, 97
Horncastle Railway 144–7
Hornel, Edward 230
horse-drawn railways 34, 126, 210
horses, transport of 78, 79
Horsmonden station 70
hotels 13, 162–3, 168, 205, 242, 246
Howey, Jack 62
Hulme End 140, 142, 143
Hunslet Engine Company 216
Hythe 4, 62, 63

Ian Allan Publishing Ltd 48
industrial railways 216–17
    see also specific industries
Inverness & Perth Junction Railway 240
Ipswich 88, 237
iron ore 196, 197, 217
Island Line 84
Isle of Grain 68–9

Isle of Sheppey 56–7
Isle of Skye 218, 219
Isle of Wight 50, 80–5, 201, 224
    ferry links 52–5
Isle of Wight Steam Railway 84–5

Jackament's Bridge 128
'Jacobite' line 220
Jedburgh 234–5
Jedfoot station 234, 235

Keighley & Worth Valley Railway 155, 190–1
Kelvedon, Tiptree & Tollesbury Pier Light Railway 106–7
Kemble station 105, 128, 131
Kendal 180, 182
Kendal & Windermere Railway 180
Kent 56–9, 60, 61, 62–71
Kent & East Sussex Railway 58–9, 225
Kildale 186, 187
Kilgerran Castle 171
Killin 238–9
King Tor 34, 35
Kirkbank station 234
Kirkcudbright 133, 230–3
Kirkhaugh 194
Kirkstead *see* Woodhall Junction

'ladies only' compartments 121
Lake District 178, 180–3, 192–3
Lakes Express 180
Lakeside & Haverthwaite Railway 182, 192–3
Lambley 6–7, 194
Lambourn Valley Railway 78–9
lamps 28, 56, 64–5, 71, 102, 185, 245
Lancashire 181, 206, 216
Lancaster & Carlisle Railway 180
L&NWR *see* London & North Western Railway
L&SWR *see* London & South Western Railway
Lansdowne, Marquis of 74
Leadhills & Wanlockhead Light Railway 1, 228–9
Leek & Manifold Light Railway 140–3, 225, 245
Leiston 100, 102–3
Lelant 14, 15
level crossings 72, 90, 92, 102, 245
Leyburn station 38
Leysdown-on-Sea 56
Light Railways Act (1896) 40, 58, 106
Lincolnshire 61, 144–7
linesmen 73
Liskeard 16, 111
Liskeard & Caradon Railway 16
Liskeard & Looe Railway 16
Liverpool & Manchester Railway 154
Liverpool, Manchester & Newcastle Junction Railway 206
livestock 39, 55, 60, 61, 108, 145, 202
Llanberis 156, 157
Llandudno Junction 150
Llandyssul 164
Llanfriog 166
Llanglydwen 173
Lledr valley 150, 152
Llynfi & Ogmore Railway 168
Llynfi Valley Railway 168
LMS *see* London, Midland & Scottish Railway
LNER *see* London & North Eastern Railway
locomotives 224–5
    'Edward Thomas' 159
    'Emmet' 21
    'Enid' 157
    Foxfield industrial collection 124–5
    goods 78, 90–1, 194, 226–7
    'Home Guard' (Patriot) 193
    'JB Earle' 142
    K2 223
    'Lion' 154
    'Maude' 226–7
    'Naklo' (Polish) 195

numbering system 48
'River Mite' and sisters 196
'Ryde' 224
'Shannon' 126, 127
Stanier Black Five 220
Swedish 155
Swiss 156, 157
'Warrior' 216
  see also auto-trains; multiple units; push-pull
  units; railcars; tank locomotives
London & North Eastern Railway 88, 90, 94, 100,
  106, 108, 144, 184
  camping coaches 76, 77, 237
  enamel signs 245
  locomotives 194, 196
  milk train 38
  Ullswater poster 178
London & North Western Railway 110, 150, 153,
  156, 174, 175, 180, 181
London & South Western Railway 14, 26, 28, 32, 40,
  42, 52, 225, 245
London, Brighton & South Coast Railway 51, 236,
  244
London, Chatham & Dover Railway 56, 68, 70
London, Midland & Scottish Railway 140, 142, 174,
  175, 180, 192, 193, 230, 244, 246
Longmoor Military Railway 155
Looe 16–17, 111
Loyd Lindsay, Robert 126
luggage
  labels 244
  lost 19
Lyme Regis 40–3
Lyminge station 61
Lymington 52–5
Lynton & Barnstaple Railway 20–1, 163

McGill, Donald 19
Machynlleth 158
Maiden Newton 44–7
Mallaig 220–3
Manifold Valley 140–3
Manuel 226
Marks Tey 90, 91
Mawddach trail 135
meat 39, 74, 75
Mellis & Eye Railway 108–9
Melton Constable 94
Mid Hants line 105
Middlesbrough 184, 186
Midland & Great Northern Joint Railway 94
Midland Railway 112, 136, 138, 190, 206
Midlands, West 118–19
Mildenhall branch 31
milk 24–5, 36, 38–9, 143
Milk Marketing Board 38
Minehead 22, 23, 24
minerals 16, 32, 193, 196, 197, 206, 217, 228
  see also clay industry; coal & collieries; gravel; iron
ore; quarries; slate industry; stone
Ministry of Defence 78, 79
Minster-on-Sea 57
Miteside halt 30
model railways 96–7
Moel Dyrnogydd tunnel 152
Monifieth 226
Monmouth, Duke of 41
Moorswater 16
Morar 222
Morebath Junction 188
Moretonhampstead 162
Moulton station 214
Mound, The 246–9
mountain railways 156
multiple units 183, 186, 187, 195
Muncaster 198–9
Murthly 226
Nailsworth 136–9
Nant Gwernol 160

National Coal Board 124, 201
National Cycle Network 74, 75, 132–5
  see also cycle paths
Nene Valley Railway 155
New Forest 54, 134
Newbury 78
Newcastle & Carlisle Railway 194
Newcastle & Darlington Junction Railway 214
Newcastle Emlyn 164–7
Newlyn artists 12
Newport, IOW 80, 81
Nisbet station 234
Norden 26
Norfolk 86, 94–5, 237
North British Railway 210, 220, 226, 234
North Eastern Railway 104, 184, 202, 214
North Norfolk Railway 94–5
North Staffordshire Railway 140, 141
North Walsham 94
North Yorkshire Moors Railway 184, 186
Northumberland 194–5
Norton Fitzwarren 22
Norton Hill colliery 200
Norwich 94
Nottage Halt 169
nuclear power industry 63, 102, 150

Octopussy 155
Ogmore Valley Railway 168
Oxenholme 180, 182
Oxenhope 190
Oxfordshire 4–5, 122–3, 126–7

paddle steamers 29, 53
Paddock Wood 70
Padstow 32
Pencader 164, 165, 166
Pentre Berw station 176
Penzance 12
Pickering 184
Pilgrim's Way 64, 66
Pinder, M 49
platelayer's huts 46, 249
platforms, bay 91, 116, 118, 122, 182
Plymouth 34
Port Carlisle 210
Port Victoria 68
Porthcawl 168–9
Porthmadog 150, 152
Portishead station 110
Portsmouth 52
postcards
  central England 115, 119, 123, 127, 131, 139, 147
  East Anglia 89, 95, 99, 101, 109
  humorous 19, 250–1
  model railways 97
  northern England 181, 183, 185, 191, 193, 197,
    207, 211, 215
  rural scenes 39
  Scotland 221, 227, 229, 231, 235, 239, 241, 242,
    248
  southern England 55, 57, 60, 63, 65, 75, 80, 82, 84
  Wales 110, 152, 153, 156, 157, 158, 159, 166, 169,
    171, 172, 175, 177
  West Country 17, 21, 25, 27, 29, 30, 37, 41, 237
posters 244
  camping coaches 76
  The Cornish Coast 10–11
  Cromer 86
  hotels 162
  Isle of Wight 50
  Midland Railway 112
  St Ives 15
  South Wales 148
  The Titfield Thunderbolt 154
  Ullswater 179
Powerstock station 46
Prestatyn to Dyserth branch 110
Princetown 34–5

Purbeck, Isle of 26, 217
push-pull units 27, 64, 66, 71, 111, 117, 224
Pwllheli 158
Pyle 168, 169

quarries 16, 34, 140, 193, 208, 217
  slate 150–3, 158
Queenborough Pier 56, 68
Quelch, CS 201
Quinton, AR 26, 27

rail buses 94, 110, 111
rail motors 110, 111, 117, 118
railcars 110–11, 116, 118, 121
  diesel 6–7, 78, 79, 93, 94, 98, 110, 111, 116, 117,
    118, 128
  introduction of diesel 212, 213
railtours 49, 203, 206
  see also excursions
Railway Children, The 155, 190
railway clubs 49
railwayana 244–5
  see also posters
railwaymen 72–3
rambling 132, 133
  see also footpaths
Ravenglass 189, 198
Ravenglass & Eskdale Railway 30, 196–9
Raven's Rock 242–3
Red Wharf Bay 174, 175, 176, 177
Resolven station 121
Rhosgoch 176
Richard Garrett company 102–3
Richmond, N Yorkshire 214–15
Riley, Harry 11
road transport 40, 60, 126, 170
Robertsbridge 58, 59
Rodmarton halt 128
Rolt, Tom 160
Rolvenden 58, 225
Romney, Hythe & Dymchurch Light Railway 62–3,
  189
Ropley station 105
Rother Valley Light Railway 58
Roxburgh 234–5
Ryecroft station 136, 138
Rydal Water 193
Ryde
  Pierhead 80, 81, 84–5
  St John's Road 84, 201

St Boswells 234
St Erth 12, 14
St Ives 12–15, 162, 245
St Margarets 98
Sandplace 16
Sandy & Potton Railway 127
Santa Specials 123
Sawrey 183
Saxmundham 100
Scarborough 19, 186
Scarborough & Whitby Railway 184
school specials 6–7, 62, 188–9
Scorton station 214, 215
Scott, Walter 234
Scottish Railway Preservation Society 226
Seaton 28–9
Seaton & Beer Railway 28
Seaton Electric Tramway 28–9
Sesswick halt 31
Severn Beach branch 48
Shanklin 80, 81, 82
Sheerness 56–7
Sheppey Light Railway 56, 57
Sheringham 94, 95
Shiplake 114–15, 116
signal boxes 71, 79, 89, 114–15, 118, 226
signalmen 73
signals 69, 119, 176

signs 245
name plaques 56, 64, 71, 78, 102, 119, 164–5, 174, 176, 245
Silloth 210–13
single-line tokens 27, 84
Sittingbourne 56
Sizewell power stations 102, 103
Skelbo 224, 246, 249
Skipton 190, 206, 208
Skye, Isle of 218, 219
slate industry 150–3, 158, 160
Smallbrook Junction 84
Snape 100
Snowdon Mountain Railway 156–7
Snowdonia 150
Solway Firth 210, 212
Somerset 22–5, 38, 39, 61, 120, 200
Somerset & Dorset Joint Railway 104, 236
South Eastern Railway 64, 68, 70, 71
South Tynedale Railway 194–5
South West Trains 52
Southampton 136, 138
Southern Railway 14, 19, 20, 26, 27, 28, 56, 62, 70, 71
    auto-trains 225
    camping coaches 77
    and Isle of Wight 80
    signal box 71
    station architecture 30
    walks guides 133, 134
Southminster 77
Spa Trail 146, 147
sport 18
Staffordshire 124–5, 140–3, 217
Stanbridgeford 188–9
Standon station 99
Stanley Bridge halt 74
station masters 104
stations 30–1
    architecture 21, 30, 31, 64, 116, 118, 119, 128, 138, 139, 180, 192, 193, 194, 214, 215, 223, 226, 242
    cafés and restaurants 43, 47, 192, 242–3, 246
    conversions 20, 21, 46, 98, 102, 103, 139, 146, 147, 176, 182, 204, 212, 214, 215, 232
    name plaques 56, 64, 71, 78, 102, 119, 164–5, 174, 176, 245
    private 74
    restoration 21, 47, 92, 176, 194
    see also clocks; gardens; lamps; platforms, bay; water towers
Staveley 182
Steel, Kenneth 179
Stephens, Colonel 56, 58, 110, 225
Stephenson, George 174
stone 34, 140, 208, 216, 217
Stonehouse & Nailsworth Railway 136
Stonehouse cycle path 138
Stour, river 92
Stourbridge 118–19
Stranraer 230
Strathpeffer 162, 163, 242–3
street names 245
Stroud 136, 139
Sudbury 90–3
Suffolk 31, 88–93, 100–103, 108–9
Sussex, East 58–9
Sustrans 74, 75, 132, 133
Sutton Pool 34
Swallow Falls 153
Swanage Railway 26–7
Swinden quarry 208, 209

Switzerland 156
Symington, William 228

Talyllyn Railway 158–61
tank locomotives
    Aberfeldy distillery 240
    Adams radial 40, 42–3
    Beattie Well 32, 33
    British Railways Standare 207, 230
    Caledonian Railway 238
    Easingwold Railway 203
    GWR 13, 47, 73, 114–15, 124–5, 155, 249
    Highland Railway 224, 247
    industrial work 217
    Isle of Wight 81
    LMS 150, 232–3
    LNER 88, 98
    Manning Wardle 20
    North Eastern Railway 106
Tarff station 232
Taunton 22
Tay, Loch 238–9, 240
Teifi, river 165, 166, 170, 171, 173
Teifi Valley Railway 166–7
Telford, Thomas 247
Tennyson, Alfred, Lord 80
Tenterden 58, 59
Tetbury 128–31
Thorpeness 100, 102
Thurso 246
tickets 181, 244
timetables 244
Tiptree 106
Titfield Thunderbolt, The 154
Tiverton Junction 36–7
Toller 45, 46
Tollesbury 106–7
Tomline, Colonel 88
'Toy Railway' see Talyllyn Railway
toy trains 96–7
track
    maintenance 73
    rack-and-pinion 156
trainspotting 48–9
tramways 28–9, 57, 81, 84, 118, 126–7, 168
Trawsfynydd 150
Tregenna Castle hotel 13
Trouble House 128
Truman, Herbert 15
tube trains, retired 80, 84–5
Tummel, river 240, 241
Twyford 114, 116
Tyrwhitt Trail 34
Tyweli valley 166, 167
Tywyn 158, 159, 160

Uffculme 36, 37
Ullswater 178
Ulverston 192
Upper Don trail 135

Ventnor 80, 81, 82–3
viaducts 16, 27, 133, 152, 174, 194, 220
    Avon 226–7
    Cannington 42, 43
    Chappel 92–3
    Cheffham 20
    Glenfinnan 220–1, 222
    Lambley 194
    Larpool 184–5, 186
    Lledr (Cethyn's Bridge) 152

Slaggyford 195
Solway Firth 210
Teviot 234
Tongland 230, 231, 232
Victoria, Queen 80
Viking Way 146

Wadebridge 32
walks 132–5
    see also footpaths
Wallingford 122–3
Wallingford & Watlington Railway 122
Wanlockhead station 228
Wanstrow halt 39
Wantage 122, 126–7, 189
Ward, Dudley 23
Ware, Hadham & Buntingford Railway 98–9
Wareham 26
Wargrave 114, 116
Watchet 22, 23
water towers 78, 128, 129, 131
Waterhouses 140, 142, 143
Welford Park 78, 79
Wenfordbridge 32–3
Wesson, Edward 87
West Bay 44, 45, 46, 47
West Coast main line 180
West Somerset Railway 22–5, 225
Westerfield Junction 88–9
Westerham 64–7, 133
Weston, Clevedon & Portishead Light Railway 110
Wetton Mill 142
Weybourne 94
Whitby 184–7
Whitby & Pickering Railway 184
Whitby, Redcar & Middlesbrough Union 184
Whitehall Halt 37
Whitland 170, 173
Whitland & Cardigan Railway 170
Wick 246
Wilkinson's jam factory 106
Williamson, Henry 20
Wiltshire 38, 74–5
Windermere 180–3, 192
Woodchester 138
Woodhall Junction 144, 146, 147
Woodhall Spa 146, 147
Woody Bay station 21
Woolf, Virginia 12
Wootton 84
Wordsworth, William 22, 180, 192, 234
Worgret Junction 27
World War I 214
World War II 62, 188, 212
Wormit station 226
Worth Valley 190–1
Wortlington Golf Links 31
Wroxham 94

Yaxley 108, 109
Yelverton 34
York, Newcastle & Berwick Railway 214
Yorkshire, North 38, 184–7, 202–9, 214–15
Yorkshire, South 135
Yorkshire, West 190–1
Yorkshire Coast Railtour 203
Yorkshire Dales Railway 206–9
Yorkshire Moors 186

Zborowski, Count 62

RAILWAY WEBSITES

WEBSITES FOR PRESERVED RAILWAYS

Bo'ness & Kinneil Railway: www.srps.org.uk
Cholsey & Wallingford Railway: www.cholsey-wallingford-railway.com
Embsay & Bolton Abbey Railway: www.embsayboltonabbey railway.org.uk
Foxfield Railway: www.foxfieldrailway.co.uk
Keighley & Worth Valley Railway: www.kwvr.co.uk
Kent & East Sussex Railway: www.kesr.org.uk
Lakeside & Haverthwaite Railway: http://ukhrail.uel.ac.uk
Leadhills & Wanlockhead Railway: www.leadhillsrailway.co.uk
Lynton & Barnstaple Railway: www.lynton-rail.co.uk
North Norfolk Railway: www.nnrailway.co.uk
Ravenglass Railway: www.ravenglass-railway.co.uk
Romney, Hythe & Dymchurch Light Railway: www.rhdr.org.uk
Seaton Electric Tramway: www.tram.co.uk

Snowdon Mountain Railway: www.snowdonrailway.co.uk
South Tynedale Railway: www.strps.org.uk
Swanage Railway: www.swanagerailway.co.uk
Talyllyn Railway: www.talyllyn.co.uk
Teifi Valley Railway: www.teifivr.f9.co.uk
West Somerset Railway: www.west-somerset-railway.co.uk

WEBSITE FOR NATIONAL RAIL ENQUIRIES

National Railway Information for lines in the national rail network:
www.nationalrail.co.uk

WEBSITE FOR SUSTRANS

www.sustrans.org.uk

AUTHOR'S ACKNOWLEDGEMENTS

Photographs used in this book have come from many sources. Some have been supplied by the photographers and picture libraries credited below. Others have been bought on the open market, sometimes with no information about the original photographer. Wherever possible, photographers or collections have been acknowledged, but many images inevitably remain anonymous, despite attempts at tracing them or identifying them. If photographs have been used without due credit or acknowledgement where credit is due, through no fault of our own, apologies are offered.

For particular help with the tracking down of suitable images, thanks are due to Tim Bleasdale, Peter Cove, Brian Harding and Andrew Swift. Less personal but equally important thanks must also be given to ebay, the online auction site, and its many sellers around the world, the source of numerous images used in the book.

Branch Line Britain has been produced under considerable pressure by the hard-working team of Sue Gordon, the book's editor, and Julian Holland, its designer and picture researcher, supported and encouraged by Mic Cady of David & Charles. Without their dedication and enthusiasm not much would have happened.

Finally, I offer massive and special thanks to my wife Chrissie. Not only has she lived with the effects of her husband thinking about little else but branch lines for some months, she has also, without complaint, used her extraordinary computer skills to ease the passage of an otherwise impossible task.

PICTURE CREDITS

On behalf of David & Charles, Julian Holland would especially like to thank Dick Riley for his unstinted help with the picture research.

Unless otherwise specified, all archive photographs and ephemera are from the author's collection.

l = left; r = right; t = top; b = bottom; m = middle

Photographs by Paul Atterbury: title page; 29m; 30b; 33b; 35t; 37br; 41b; 42/43t; 46b; 47; 66/67; 69b; 71t; 75br; 79br; 99br; 102; 103; 107mr; 109br; 119b; 131t; 135tr; 135b; 139tr; 143br; 165tr; 166/167b; 167tr; 169bl; 169br; 171tr; 172/173b; 173tr; 177m; 176tl; 177br; 204tl; 205tl; 209; 210/211b; 211mr; 215br; 231br; 232tl; 233t; 235b; 237ml; 239ml; 239br; 241br; 243; 243br; 247br.

Other photographs are by:
JA Anderson: 238b.
Ben Ashworth: 137t; 138b.
Tim Bleasdale: 237b.
SV Blencowe Collection: 49tr.
Harold D Bowtell: 185tl.
FEG Burgiss: 126ml.
Ian Burgum/Burgum Boorman Ltd: 12/13b; 16b; 17b; 27b; 33tr; 63b; 85b; 92/93; 94tl; 140/141b; 151; 156ml; 157; 160tl; 160/161b; 186/187t; 198/199b; 223br.
WA Camwell: 31t; 176b.
HC Casserley 28/29b; 73tl; 78b; 107ml; 122b; 216ml.

RM Casserley: 129t.
Christie's Images: 10; 50; 86; 112; 148; 154b; 155t; 178; 218.
Peter Collins: 117.
Colour-Rail: 13m; 14/15b; 27tr; 32b; 33m; 44/45b; 52/53b; 54b; 59t; 68b; 81b; 83b; 98b; 104b; 106b; 108b; 114b; 116b; 130b; 139b; 144/145b; 150b; 168b; 171b; 174b; 182b; 184/185b; 187b; 193br; 194bl; 202b; 212/213b; 214b; 216b; 217tr; 223tl; 230b; 240/241b; 246b; 247t; 248/249.
Nick Cotton: 134/135t; 134b; 135br.
Peter Cove: 89m; 235m.
AG Ellis: 107tr.
Mike Esau: 24/25b; 55t; 57bl; 58b; 85t; 225mr; 226/227; 227t.
Tim Fediw: 123t.
PJ Fowler: 48bl.
John Spencer Gilks: 234b.
GF Gillham: 111t.
JG Glover: 119ml.
John Goss: 223mr.
GF Heiron: 121bl.
Dave Hewitt: 195t.
Julian Holland: 24tl; 105b; 244mr; 245mb.
Dr James Hollick/Adrian Vaughan Collection: 141tr; 143tr; 225tl.
RN Joanes: 56bl; 69ml; 170b; 173br.
Associated British/The Kobal Collection: 155mr.
Leadhills & Wanlockhead Railway: half-title; 228, 229t; 229b.
Locomotive & General Photographs: 152tl; 235tl.
Michael Mensing: 6/7b.
Brian Morrison: 153b.
Gavin Morrison: 89t; 90b; 93t; 183t; 190b;

191b; 192b; 193m; 199tr; 203t; 206/207b; 207t; 208/209; 220/221b; 232/233b; 241m.
Tony Nicholson: 21m.
RB Parr: 101t; 189b.
Ivo Peters Collection: 154tr.
Rail Archive Stephenson: 34b (RS Clark); 43b (DMC Hepburne-Scott); 66b; 79t (EC Griffith); 80b (OJ Morris Collection); 81t (OJ Morris Collection); 82/83t (KL Cook); 84bl; 142b (Colling Turner); 195b; 224tr (WJ Verden Anderson); 224b (OJ Morris); 225bl (FG Carrier); 247tr (WJ Verden Anderson).
RC Riley: 31b; 35br; 36b; 40b; 88/89b; 128/129b; 136/137b (W Potter); 164/165b; 203br (K Hartley); 217br; 236b; 245br.
Real Photographs: 20b.
Revd HDE Rokeby: 175t.
Brian Sharpe: 94/95; 124/125b; 125t; 146b; 147t; 155bl; 196b; 222b.
Neville Stead Collection: 18b; 38tr (BG Tweed); 59b; 100b; 118b; 159b. (RH Fullagar); 191m (PB Booth); 204/205b; 215t (LA Strudwick).
Andrew Swift: 20b; 21t; 23t; 30m; 31m; 38b; 39b; 61t; 61m; 62b; 69t; 103b; 105t; 107t; 107br; 110b; 111bl; 120b; 121t; 146t; 159m; 180b; 188/189t; 191tl; 191tr; 191ml; 197t; 201t.
Douglas Thompson: 74b; 145t.
Totem Exchange: 245ml.
RE Tustin: 96m.
Adrian Vaughan: 79m; 109tl.
Ian Wright/Sheffield Railwayana: 244br; 244bm; 245tl; 245ml; 245mr; 245bl; 245b.
T Wright: 30tr.